Entrepreneur's Marketing Guide

an
Entrepreneur Press
book

Entrepreneur's Marketing Guide

Roger F. Smith

Reston Publishing Company, Inc.
A Prentice-Hall Company
Reston, Virginia 22090

Library of Congress Cataloging in Publication Data

Smith, Roger F.
  Entrepreneur's marketing guide.

  Bibliography: p.
  Includes index.
  1. Marketing.   I. Title.
HF5415.S64   1984   658.8   84-3295
ISBN 0-8359-1743-6
ISBN 0-8359-1742-8 (pbk.)

Copyright © 1984 by Reston Publishing Company, Inc.
A Prentice-Hall Company
Reston, Virginia 22090

10   9   8   7   6   5   4   3   2   1

Printed in the United States of America

Chapter opening illustrations by Bruce Bolinger.

To my wife, Amelie

Contents

Foreword

There has long been a need for a book that deals with the basics of small business marketing. This new book, *Entrepreneur's Marketing Guide,* is refreshingly different from other texts. It is not based on theoretical strategies, but on practical systems for developing an effective marketing plan.

Owning and operating a business can be challenging, rewarding, and profitable. However, to be successful it is necessary to develop a systematic approach to identifying opportunities and problems, and then finding solutions. The essence of marketing is developing opportunities and finding solutions to problems.

The Oregon Small Business Development Center Network has worked with hundreds of small businesses, and we have found that marketing is one of the most misunderstood aspects of owning and operating a small business. Many small business operators are confused by conflicting marketing strategies and theories, or are overwhelmed by the seemingly unmanageable numbers of variables involved in developing a marketing plan. Yet developing an effective marketing plan is critical to the success of any business.

Entrepreneur's Marketing Guide is written in easy-to-read language that is readily understood. The information in this book is extremely valuable because it outlines the basics of marketing in a practical and logical approach. The author uses real-world examples, humor, and personal insights and observations to convey information to the reader. The real value of the book lies in the outlines and "menu" approach to developing a comprehensive marketing plan.

Most entrepreneurs don't devote much time to planning. They are just too busy trying to meet the day-to-day demands of their businesses. This book helps simplify the planning process. It outlines the key elements of planning, advertising, sales force development, and evaluation of a marketing plan.

I have found this book to be a valuable addition to the reference materials we use at the Small Business Development Center. It will be a useful guide and resource for people just starting a business and helpful to those who already have well-established companies.

Edward W. Cutler
Oregon Small Business
Development Center Network

Preface

"Build a better mousetrap and the world will beat a path to your door." Belief in this old adage has led many entrepreneurs close to bankruptcy. It's not true today and probably never was.

Marketing is the real key to success for an entrepreneur. But unfortunately most people don't understand marketing, or else think it's too complicated, too expensive, or both.

According to research by government agencies and independent consultants, entrepreneurs create more jobs and economic growth in North America than any other part of the private economic sector, and will continue to do so in the years ahead. "Entrepreneur" has become a glamorous buzzword, but it is one that is grossly misunderstood.

An entrepreneur is anyone with an idea for a product or service who creates a business based on that idea. In the last few years, computer technology and software have been the most visible examples of entrepreneurship. Fast-food outlets, small specialized stores, and service businesses are less obvious but more numerous examples.

Unfortunately, entrepreneurs often fail as business people. They create an idea and watch their business grow rapidly and profitably, only to see it mysteriously reverse itself just as rapidly. Most entrepreneurs experience some economic trauma before they recognize the necessity to adopt a systematic approach to management. The trauma may be brought about by a key employee leaving, a sales downturn, deteriorating economic conditions, or a new competitor, but the true reason for failure is nearly always a lack of systematic management.

If it's that simple, why do so many firms run into trouble? One reason is that the concepts of entrepreneurship and systematic management are diametrically opposed. It is those entrepreneurs who learn to adopt systems for marketing, finance, and production who survive.

This book devises some simple systems that any entrepreneur can use successfully for solving marketing problems. In fact, the primary emphasis is on defining the problems so that the solutions and systems reveal themselves. However, understanding theories and defining problems is not an end in itself. Implementing solutions is what really counts, so specific instructions are provided to implement solutions to marketing problems.

Simple-to-use planning techniques are the foundation of this book—not highly sophisticated, ivory-tower strategic planning, but simple ways to identify opportunities and schedule for results.

Understanding simple marketing concepts and ideas and developing your market position will enable you to focus your marketing efforts. Developing the strategy is actually quite simple, once you determine what your options are.

Since very little is written on any level that is easy and practical in the area of sales force development, we have devoted a large portion of the book to the subject. Organization, recruitment, and compensation are all essential to establishing a good sales force. Motivation and evaluation are also a critical part of the development process, so we've included some easy-to-use ideas that work.

Advertising shouldn't be the waste of money it so often is. We have set out ways to simplify your advertising development and focus on results. Also included is some information that will help you communicate with advertising professionals so they can help you be even more effective.

The book also covers some unique challenges that small manufacturers face. Marketing professional services is quite different from a conventional business selling goods and services. As a matter of fact, professional practices have a wider variety of marketing tools available to them, although they are seldom recognized.

Establishing workable and doable measurement devices is far less complicated than the financial specialists would have you believe. Measurement and evaluation are critical to recognizing success or disaster before it's too late. And it is important to involve your employees in the process so that they too will be committed to success.

Above all, being an entrepreneur should be fun! The whole focus of the book is to devise ways to implement systems for results and feedback, since it's results and feedback that provide the fun to compensate for the risks.

Now go build your better mousetrap, knowing that you can succeed!

Introduction

What is marketing? Why would anyone try to run a business in the current economic, political, and regulatory climate? What's in it for you?

Marketing is more than designing a package, developing an advertising campaign, and hiring salespeople. Marketing is planning to deliver what's needed by the marketplace. A marketsmith is the skilled person who puts together all the marketing plans and elements of the program, coordinates their execution, and evaluates the results. It is skilled labor, just as a goldsmith, blacksmith, or other craftsman.

Would you like to lead an orchestra? Or paint a work of art? Would you like to sit in the principal chair of a section of the orchestra? Or work in the studio of a renowned painter? You have the potential to succeed in small business if you like to be out front, directing the sections of the orchestra. If you prefer just to lead the violins, you can still realize the satisfaction of seeing a work of art executed successfully, although someone else wrote and directed the music. The satisfaction is in the execution. The rave reviews are incidental.

Small business is the exciting, fun, and fast-growing part of the private economic sector in North America, the United Kingdom, and Western Europe. There seem to be two principal reasons for this growth. First, big business does not seem able to respond as quickly to changing markets as small business. Second, because of the 1979–1983 recession-depression-adjustment (choose one), thousands of executives who thought that they knew what it would take to put a business together did just that. At the same time the general public was becoming more and more disenchanted with bigness, whether in business, labor, or government. Elections on both sides of the Atlantic confirmed that growing disillusionment.

In the late 1950s a college course in comparative economics introduced me to Joseph A. Schumpeter, the economist. The main lesson that I remember was that, according to Schumpeter, Marx was right—but for the wrong reason. Schumpeter felt that our free-enterprise, capitalist system would collapse—but not because of worker uprising. Rather the decline and fall would come because of its success, growing into a large, unresponsive, and unproductive mechanism, eventually to be destroyed by inflation.

In the spring of 1983 the management scientist Peter F. Drucker wrote a comparative article about the two great economists, John Maynard Keynes (1883–1946) and Joseph A. Schumpeter (1883–1950). Most *Forbes* readers, and many of their staffers as well, read about Schumpeter for the first time. As Keynes and the monetarists fall into disfavor in many circles, Schumpeter looks like he may be right.

Understanding the background of the phenomenon of small-business growth will go a long way to explain why this book is necessary. Little seems to be written from the perspective of experience in small business. Most of the writings with which I'm familiar are scholarly works on how to manage a small business, using the tools developed for big business. Even though you can't build the Alaska pipeline with hand tools, neither can you make quartz watches with crawler tractors.

More is demanded of the entrepreneur in the way of time and financial risk than of the executive in a large enterprise, but the rewards are greater. Not only can the material rewards be greater for more people in small business, but the personal satisfaction of directly seeing the results of your ideas increases the pleasure immensely.

In exchange for the fun and profit the small business manager needs to be a generalist with some in-depth expertise in a variety of disciplines. *Discipline* may be the key word. It is required to study and develop skills and knowledge when the area is not of special interest. Discipline is also required to apply the skills and knowledge on a consistent basis. Typically entrepreneurs are intuitive decision makers; but in order for those decisions to be correct, particularly in fields with which they have little experience, they must study the systems and understand how the systems work.

Most of our concern in this book is with the field of marketing. Marketing can mean different things in different contexts. Marketing is planning. Marketing is the process of delivering what's needed to the marketplace. Marketing is the interaction of the component parts of a marketing program.

Marketing isn't the mysterious pie in the sky that many people would have you believe. Marketing is a planned, systematic process of identifying needs in the marketplace, planning how to meet those needs, and then telling the marketplace how those needs will be met. The creative role, although extremely important, is a small portion of the marketing process. Once the proper planning is done, the creativity can be hired reasonably for the short time necessary to develop your theme and the vehicle to describe your theme.

Financial management is one field that most entrepreneurs don't understand or alternatively don't practice with any consistency. We'll discuss that in the chapter on evaluation and measurements. Suffice it to say that a simple, systematic record keeping and tracking of progress of the business and its individual projects not only will bring order out of chaos but also will help the employees understand what's happening and that they can get involved.

Because of the rapid expansion of the number of small businesses and the implicit need to be more competitive, managers of small business need to spend more effort in developing skills and information systems needed to operate a business in this environment. On a practical level the manager of a small business must spend more and more time in educational pursuits. But the factors that make this pursuit more important also put increasing time pressures on the manager; it becomes even more difficult to learn all that is necessary to survive and grow. Much of the writing that is intended for the use of small business unfortunately assumes that there isn't much time pressure,

3

or that the business is not in operation, and, therefore, you have the time to become prepared. However, in the vast majority of cases neither situation is accurate.

You need to *use your time effectively* and probably don't have the time or inclination, for that matter, to spend hours reading about a subject with detailed how-to instructions. The manager does not have time to read about what was developed for big business and then scaled down for small business.

The manager of a small business worries about the phone being answered promptly. The small business manager either must make sales calls personally or work in the shop on a workbench or supervise the production staff or see that the service department work quality is satisfactory. When the bookkeeper is sick or the service technician is on maternity leave and there is no backup staff, the small business manager usually must pick up the slack, perhaps at the expense of a golf game or dinner with the family.

Having spent 20 years in small business, I can relate to all those problems and worries about cash flow, meeting the payroll, and keeping an eye on accounts receivable. Time spent in learning about all the facets of business management was done catch-as-catch-can, in evenings, through seminars, tapes, and short spurts of reading—but mainly learning by doing and watching the results.

There are no right or wrong answers in marketing—only alternative solutions. Opportunities to be wrong exist if adequate planning is ignored. If the manager is properly prepared, it is difficult to go too far off track.

In all the various phases of the marketing program we will study how to put together a planned approach to the challenges. This planned approach will in all cases start with an objective. From the objective defined and solidified, we will then look at the total situation. That divides into two parts. One is to look at the resources available to do the job. The other is to look at the market forces, including the competition, that determine our probabilities for success.

It is only after these preparatory stages that planning leads to execution. Many people get the cart before the horse. They get an idea—a brainstorm. Then they figure out how to implement the idea. They don't study whether the idea will work, what forces work against it, and whether the basic idea even fits their objectives. Developing plans by starting with the solution and making the solution fit the situation usually leads to a hodgepodge of unrelated ideas, none of which helps meet any predetermined *objective.*

Few people, let alone managers, have any set objectives. They may have some vague, short-term objectives, like make a profit or get through school, but that's as far as it goes. To provide direction, an objective must be relatively simple but broad in scope and must be written and committed to in order to be attained. By writing down the objectives, and then returning to them later, you can begin to evaluate yourself as to whether your efforts are directed toward attainment.

We will use this same concept to examine, develop, and apply a plan of action for all aspects of the marketing program for small business, small man-

ufacturers, and professionals. But nothing works unless the objective is clearly
stated in advance.

Let us return to your time constraints. Because in small business you probably work more than 40 hours a week just to keep the doors open, the time that you spend on learning new systems is in short spurts, unless you study on vacations. With that in mind, the material here is organized and broken into short segments to fit your schedule.

In addition to breaking the material into chewable bites, the emphasis is on information that will lead you to sources for more detail, if needed, so that you can learn even the details quickly and easily. For example, there are several good books on advertising, some of which are listed in the bibliography. But the assumption is that if you had time and interest to read a book on advertising, you wouldn't bother with the chapter in this book. So the effort is spent on defining briefly the nature of the various elements of advertising and how you can develop advertising for your business. Also included are enough clues and hints that you can ask questions of the professionals, who will be glad to help you in exchange for your business. In order to ask questions that will produce usable answers, you need to understand the situation in terms that the professionals can relate to so that they can help. Telling the professionals that everybody is a customer won't help them develop your advertising for maximum effectiveness. Thus, the chapter on advertising is designed so that you understand the elements to be considered more completely. Then you can ask the right questions and understand the answers.

Sales force development, however, is a different matter. Little seems to have been written about sales force development, particularly for small business. Most of the writing, either books or periodicals, devotes an inordinate amount of time to motivational issues, such as goal setting and achievement. Practically all the writing operates on the assumption that the sales manager has nothing else to do but supervise the salespeople and that the sales force is defined in exact terms, including territory management questions and even, for that matter, the number of salespeople employed.

Sales compensation questions are usually dismissed by a "keep 'em hungry" statement or a suggestion to pay a combination of salary and commission. Again, there seems to be a lack of information presented from the point of view of the sales manager in a small business environment who may not only be sales manager but also general manager, production chief, or a salesperson. Simple, easy-to-administer systems to evaluate and guide the salesperson are included in this book so that in a minimum of time you can improve your sales force's effectiveness without sacrificing a significant amount of time from your other responsibilities.

All these considerations are based on the assumption that small business management must be involved in several aspects of the business simultaneously, even though they may be normally responsible for only one area of management. Another important element in the success of a small business is the opportunity to involve the employees. Not that those opportunities don't exist in big business, but outside Japan, employee involvement is still in the experimental stages on production lines. The relationship between management and labor has evolved into an adversary relationship, which is a loss for both labor and management.

On the scale of small business the employees can see directly and immediately the effect of their actions and can more easily develop pride in their work. This atmosphere needs to be "created" in big business, unfortunately. The employee involvement is one of the real pluses in small business, but small business managers have been slow to recognize this fringe benefit. Small business management has tended for too many years to try to compete for employees with big business on its terms. Recognize what is unique about the situation that you can offer a prospective employee. You may not be able to give four weeks' vacation with time off for ingrown toenails and birthdays, but you have far more to offer—job satisfaction.

Small business management too often overlooks one other benefit of employee involvement. Because the business is small and the employees can observe the effects of their action, they can more readily contribute to the solution of problems and help meet challenges. But management must provide the structure for this. It takes a little more time for management to provide background information for the employees. More importantly, management must be able to define clearly the objectives in terms that the employees can understand. To do that, management must have the objectives clearly in mind and well thought-out ahead of time.

Describing the challenge in terms that the employees can understand, starting with a statement of the objective, can be nearly as valuable as a training exercise for management, as well as a device to involve employees. Articulating the objective is a start. Defining the challenge and providing the background information require management to organize thoughts and present them in logical order. Following the objective comes the scenario, including the resources and hindrances to the attainment of the objective. By communicating this information to the employees, management can often see the information more clearly.

Employee involvement is not just a catchy concept that we have imported from Japan. Employee involvement doesn't mean merely telling the employees detailed information but rather sharing with them the challenges and opportunities. The real payoff comes when the employees together with management focus their attention on the challenge and develop an effective way to meet the challenge. The synergistic effect of more than one person focusing on challenges brings multiple results, not just double.

Time invested to prepare the information and clarify the objective to employees pays off handsomely so that in the final analysis your time can be spent doing those things for which you are particularly well suited. There is nothing wrong with admitting the areas of your weakness and seeking help in those areas from employees.

The thread through our efforts to define and develop marketing concepts for small business is planning. Planning and marketing are nearly synonymous. Start by setting the objective. Break the opportunities into component parts and analyze each part in terms relative to the marketplace. Breaking the components into technical subparts or into financial subparts is important for those exercises, but here we need to concern ourselves with the marketing concepts.

If we develop the plan, write it out, set schedules for completion of the component parts, and measure, test, and remeasure as we go, success will come more easily. The plan results in a coordination of the various pieces so that all phases come together at a predetermined time and point. Then the planning pays off.

The excitement of small business is the fact that through the planning, analysis, measuring, and testing processes we have the opportunity to modify our course of action in response to what happens in the marketplace. We are under no obligation to stick to the plan, no matter the results, just because those were the instructions from headquarters. And because we live with the results, rather than having to send reports off to corporate headquarters, we can have the satisfaction of seeing the job done well.

1

The Marketing Plan: How and Why

P lanning is nothing more than laying out in our minds or on paper the steps necessary to achieve our goals, although outside factors may affect performance. We will study in some depth the seven principal sections of a marketing plan. When we are finished, not only will you know how to achieve your objectives and meet goals that you set for yourself, but you may decide that you were too modest or conservative and may even revise upward.

In the process we will learn sales forecasting, situational analysis techniques, and definition of marketing objectives. The rest of the planning process is primarily establishment of the schedule and implementation mechanics. We will practice some of the concepts that we have learned, including market segmentation and positioning, as well as marketing and product mixes.

In other words, with the basics understood, we can actually start work on *your* planning process. I will try to provide descriptions and examples from retail, commercial, manufacturing, and industrial marketing. By describing situations from my clients' experiences, perhaps we can learn more easily.

Research

Much of what you will be doing to complete your marketing plan is normally called *research,* but don't let that scare you—this book is not a scholarly work devoting much time to the arcane world of marketing research. We'll keep our discussion simple.

Research has two major facets: primary and secondary. By *primary* we are referring to actual contact with users and potential users of your products or services to see what their market reaction is likely to be or to determine probable preferences.

This may take the form of questionnaires or interviews. Don't try this yourself unless you have done considerable study on the subject. The biggest pitfall is that you may not design the questions to provide the answers that you need, and then misinterpret the answers that you get. Not incidental is the danger that you may mess up your market by alienating your customers or inadvertently tipping off your competition prematurely as to your intent.

Secondary research is something that nearly anyone can do. Use of existing data, whether tabulated in the form that you need or not, is secondary research. During the course of developing your marketing plan, we will use secondary research extensively. For instance, looking at the population trends and the demographics of your service area is a form of secondary research. So is the informal study and evaluation of your competitors.

One of the best secondary sources available is personal conversation with key people in your industry or community. One caveat: Be sure that you have written ahead of time the information that you feel you need. Spell out the questions. Also it is helpful to write why you are going to ask your golf pro about population trends in the next county. Maybe he does know and can prove that he is a valid source. The point is that even though you may be conducting an informal survey using key people, be careful that your justification of whom you use is adequate.

Before you start in a new direction with your business, be sure to consult with people knowledgeable in the data that you are likely to need before making a firm decision. Sometimes this may require subterfuge, but every conversation aimed at the core subject is beneficial.

Above all select your resource people just as carefully as you select the population data. Some information is available from multiple sources, with multiple results. Consider the *source* before the data.

Elements of a Marketing Plan

To be a working document, serving as a guide to you, your employees, credit institutions, and suppliers, the plan should address past, present, and future. The plan starts with setting the objective, that is, deciding what you want to do. Then determine how you're going to do it, describing the tools necessary and the hindrances that may handicap you, including the economic environment and competition. Finally, determine your marketing strategy and the details of its implementation.

By going through the process of building your marketing plan together, we can learn more of what planning is all about. Much of what we discuss can apply to other areas of your business as well. Basically you learn by doing, but in this book we learn on paper rather than the more expensive trial and error use of your business.

Company Mission

This section of your plan is in turn broken into three parts.

Statement of Objectives

In written form describe what you want to accomplish in business. This should be something more than *make a living* or *build an equity*. For example, you may decide that you want to be the leading supplier of office equipment in town, operate a top men's clothing store, manufacture high-quality cabinets, or sell and service construction equipment. Keep the objective simple and basic at this point.

Probably your objective is determined by one of two considerations. You may have a particular affinity for a group of potential customers and may try to find a way to sell to them. Or you may have a talent for a type of product or its application.

If you are comfortable socially with office and administrative people, then selling office equipment will be an opportunity to develop that relationship into a living. The capabilities and application of office machines may hold a special interest. You may be frustrated because so few people seem to coordinate their clothing and furnishing purchases. You may like the simple, straightforward manner in which most people in construction talk and think. You may get satisfaction from seeing your products used and enjoyed. By the same token, you may be style conscious and interested in clothing material; then clothing is what you should do. A fascination with what construction equipment can accomplish could be furthered by knowing intimately which equipment is best suited for which jobs.

I am not emphasizing the need for technical expertise. If you are technically or design-oriented rather than function-oriented, chances are that you won't enjoy the necessity of relating your knowledge to customers or dealing with the ambiguities of people management. But you can either hire someone or bring in a partner with those talents and skills. Many small manufacturing and technically oriented firms contract for these services with outside firms. They can be learned to some extent, but management is a process of dealing with ideas and people more than things. Know yourself, and be honest with yourself.

Above all, make your decision and write your objective for your business for the honest, correct reasons. If your objective is simply to make money, you probably won't find that specific enough, although your frankness is to be commended.

Description of Business

Next describe in exact terms what you are in business to accomplish—specifically. Are you selling and servicing typewriters and adding machines or typewriters and word processors? or adding machines and bookkeeping machines?

Do you want to deal in outdoor clothes or suits? crawler tractors, cranes, back-hoes, or all three plus compactors and air compressors? Do you want to build and sell kitchen cabinets or furniture?

Nature of Customers

Last, for the mission section, is to describe your perception of the customer base that you want to serve. Is your market area experiencing a population boom? What effect will that have on your customers?

Is the area becoming a center for financial services? That would certainly indicate a growing opportunity for office equipment sales and services. Are local government services expanding or contracting?

How many potential customers are there? several big public and private entities or mainly smaller organizations?

Is your town a fashion center or a regional shopping center serving more than the immediate area? What is the basic industry? How many service and support employees are in the area? Is there a growing need for new roads and bridges and residential and commercial development within a practical service radius?

Let me offer some considerations, and maybe you can add some that apply in your particular case. A slow-growth, largely agricultural area would probably mean that the market for clothing, office equipment, and construction machinery would have limited growth opportunities. By the same token a booming resort area might mean that construction machinery and clothing sales would correspondingly increase. In an agricultural area that exports a cash crop that is becoming increasingly profitable, clothing and office equipment opportunities might be expanding, reflecting an increase in personal discretionary income and the need for offices to be more efficient and provide better and more timely information for management.

However, if you are a small manufacturer, what is happening to the market for your goods? That may be significantly different from the market in your immediate geographic area. If you are making furniture primarily for cabin or condominium use at the beach, your local community market would probably have little bearing on your actual market. Local conditions may affect your attitude but should be only incidental to decisions affecting your markets.

Whatever is going on in your community, geographic area, or customer group that you think will affect your business opportunity should be written in a brief statement.

We have now completed the company mission statement. You may notice that we didn't discuss positioning or segmentation factors. We will, but later in the plan. Try to write these sentences in the mission section without discussing detailed specifics, such as position or pricing or other strategic matters. (The reason will be obvious shortly.)

Situation Analysis

We are getting into the meat of the plan. Economic conditions that may affect your business, resources inventory, sales forecasts, and new opportunities require considerable study.

Economic Conditions

What is the general economic climate affecting your business *at this time?* If a recession is causing your repair and service facilities to be overtaxed because customers are keeping their old clothes, typewriters, and cranes, then

13

that fact should be noted in this paragraph. If so much customer equipment is idle and not even requiring maintenance, that is symptomatic of a severe downturn in activity. That type of condition also means that at some point, the rate of replacement will increase as well.

If you're in an agricultural area and crops have been bad for two or three years, and changing or diversifying crops is not a viable option for the farmers, the bright side is that a good crop must be coming. If the basic industry in the area is maturing and has seen better days, it is important for you to determine the impact of a changing economic base. In the late 1970s the timber industry reached advanced maturity as did the automotive industry. Careful planning will help you be one of the survivors when the others drop out due to decreasing demand for goods and services, if you are in an area heavily dependent on those industries.

The reverse, and more pleasant, example is the electronics industry. It has grown counter to the general economic conditions due to new products and broader application. If you were near Boston or San Jose during the early 1980s, you witnessed an unprecedented boom that was a complete opposite of the national and international economy. The clothing merchant, office equipment professions, and construction equipment people in those cities had growing markets to serve.

Incidentally population trends and demographics for your firm's service area should be considered. You know better than I how a change in the basic population will affect you. If your community is drawing more older people to the point of being a good retirement center, then some growth in financial and medical service outlets and professional services might help your office equipment business. But older people tend to be less style conscious, so your clothing store might not fare so well. Construction equipment might be needed for streets and utilities, but residential developments along the order of a typical suburban community may not be in the offing. The same sort of reverse trends, to younger families with children, could open up opportunities. In other words any significant change in the demographics *can* have a positive influence on your business if you understand and prepare for the trends as they develop.

Company Resources

This should be divided into three principal sections: physical facilities, human resources, and financial resources. In this section we will detail all the tools with which to achieve the objective of your business.

PHYSICAL FACILITIES. Your facilities should be addressed on two levels. Figure 1–1 shows some typical relationships. On the one hand list all the income-producing equipment. To continue our look at three businesses, the clothing store would consider income-producing such things as inventory and display equipment. The office equipment shop would have inventory and also repair equipment and demonstration equipment. The heavy-equipment

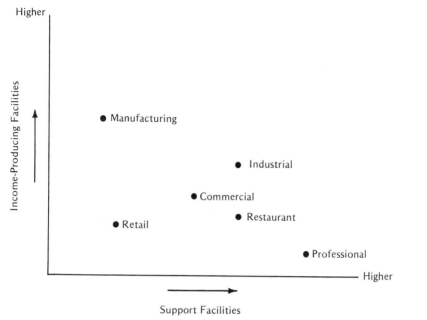

FIGURE 1-1. Relative Weight of Physical Facilities—Support vs.
Production

dealer would also have inventory, repair, and demonstration equipment. Professional services wouldn't be quite so dependent on physical facilities. Manufacturers, like the commercial firms, would have both revenue-producing equipment and support items.

All three would have similar support equipment, such as typewriters, file cabinets, and space where the business is located. In the case of the clothing store and professional office the space itself could substantially affect the ability to draw traffic and produce sales. In the commercial and industrial categories the physical location may not have as much impact on sales because most business is done off the premises, but perhaps even more importantly a small building, poorly maintained or located inconveniently for customers, has a considerable negative impact. Manufacturers' location and facilities probably have little effect on sales directly. The impact may be only on you and your employees' attitude toward the job, but what could be more negative? If you have a service department, it should be accessible to the customers even if most of the work is done on their premises.

Further, the firm that is organized, knows its field, and is stable, successful, and profitable *always* operates from a clean, suitable, neat facility. This trait extends to the company vehicles and personnel appearance. It demonstrates pride. You can't be proud of your job if you work in a pigsty and can't find last week's sales reports, much less last year's tax statements. By no means do the facilities need to be big, expensive, or fancy. I've seen successful

15

firms that had old but clean and well-maintained equipment, definitely not state-of-the-art, that were doing well and on a systematic program of upgrading. One of the immediate results of a disorganized mess is that collections fall behind, payables fall behind, and soon key employees begin worrying about your longevity. When that happens, you'd be better off trying to turn a battleship with a canoe paddle.

On the subject of physical facilities, a look at a service business, such as a restaurant, may be helpful. The income-producing facilities would include the kitchen equipment, of course, but also the tables and chairs and counter, items that in another business might be classified differently.

At any rate, your facilities inventory, for both income-producing and support items, should be listed. On the producing equipment, a tabulation as to gross revenue generated by line items may be helpful. As an adjunct to that study, you may want to consider each piece's profit contribution. A summary statement of changes that should be made would also be included in this section.

HUMAN RESOURCES. A simple list of your personnel will suffice, but the list should include major areas of responsibility, particular talents and education, and any other contribution that they make to the organization. In quick terms this is a reference list or inventory of your human resources.

Although we aren't spending much time discussing human resources, you no doubt recognize that they are the most important resource in business.

For example, in the clothing business your suiting specialist or furnishings specialist may be the best in town. Put that down. If your shoe department is staffed with inexperienced people, that should be listed. Assuming that your firm has relatively few employees, include on the list at least all the department heads and lead people but don't ignore the new hires or apprentices. If they don't have the potential to move upward in job category, they may be weak links.

If you have shortages on your staff—which is not unusual—try to define these shortages in specific brief terms. If you have overcapacity, this is as good a time as any to see what human resources can be moved to an area with shortages or at least define who is the most likely to contribute over the long haul.

The last consideration in your human resources inventory is whether the staff on hand is adequate in quantity and specific skills needed to meet the challenge of your company objectives. This may involve some intuitive evaluation if you think that it may be necessary to change your business emphasis, but continue to use the staff now on board. For example, if your clothing store should move into men's and women's business attire, you probably need an experienced salesperson with familiarity of styles and trends in your region and a good background in materials so your customers can be well advised for their particular needs. Just as obvious is the office equipment firm that wants to put more emphasis on word-processing equipment but has no staff with computer hardware or software background to match the customer application challenges with the appropriate equipment. In heavy construction equipment, if you need a line of paddle-wheel scrapers to round out your offerings, your salespeople should be familiar with various aspects of road construction, not just utility work. If you're a restaurant catering to meetings, your chef should know something more than 1,001 ways to cook hamburger.

FINANCIAL RESOURCES. This is not the place to list numbers meaningful only to the bean counters and number crunchers. Here you should describe whether you can get access to expanded lines of credit or you first need to finish paying your ex-partner or his widow. It may be helpful to make a comment based on your cash-flow projections when you expect to be finished with unusual and nonrecurring financial obligations. (If you don't have cash-flow projections, see Chapter 10.) If you have other nonessential, nonliquid assets that could be converted, list that fact. Some worn or slightly outdated equipment might fall into this category.

Sales Forecasts

A sentence or two describing all factors likely to affect your sales forecast should be sufficient.

ECONOMY. What economic conditions will affect your sales? In specific terms what economic conditions will affect your business in the next quarter? year? two years? We have talked about trends, but here we need to consider exact conditions.

NEW PRODUCTS. Although most of us in small business do not know what products may be two to five years away, our trade journals and contacts with principal suppliers and trade groups have probably provided some insight into developments anticipated within the next few months to two years. New products may affect how we market by changing the focus from one type of customer or application to another.

With the advent of less expensive word processors, many office equipment customers changed from a large firm to one much smaller and less sophisticated. New clothing styles render your inventory obsolete so it becomes necessary to get rid of your outmoded jackets with wide lapels or to make room for ultrasuede material. Articulated all-wheel-drive motor graders may be the latest trend that contractors want to use. The new products and their impact on your business should be dealt with here, but briefly.

MARKETING IMPROVEMENTS. As the label suggests, this deals with improved marketing methods on your part. This could take the form of improved advertising, either through the creative image process or plain better management and media selection with your advertising dollar. Or you might institute regular sales meetings or hire a competent sales manager. By the same token, perhaps the major manufacturer that you represent has developed a new marketing program, giving you the opportunity to get the jump on the local competition. As a small manufacturer, you switch to a representative firm that will do a better job for you.

All of these factors should be addressed when making your sales forecast. Incidentally in most cases it is helpful if you do the forecast by product or product group.

SALES HISTORY. A breakdown of sales history by product or customer group enables you to trace the historical trend of sales into the future. Probably the last five years is sufficient history, but you should go five years in the future no matter how much back data may be available. A simple line graph, such as Figure 1-2, will help spot trends.

PROFIT, EXPENSE, AND VOLUME. This calls for a sentence or two about the relative profitability or unusual expense load of a given product and perhaps some comment about volume trends in a nonspecific manner. For instance, typewriters have been profitable with little unusual expense, but the volume may drop off due to other products in effect replacing the typewriter in the "new-age" office.

A sentence or two addressing this category should be included for each product or product group or however *your* particular business can be *logically* divided. Customer groups can often be as helpful as product groups as a tool for analysis of trends.

NEW OPPORTUNITIES. This portion of the forecast addresses in specific terms the impact of outside influences on your customer that will help you. A new requirement for detailed calculations on monthly reports to the state for workers' compensation insurance might require more programmable calculators,

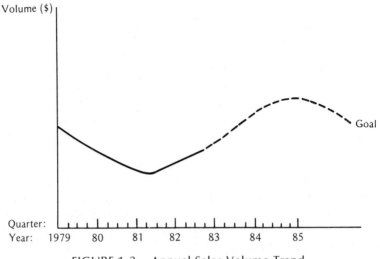

FIGURE 1-2.   Annual Sales Volume Trend

for example. Dress code tightening may result in more necktie sales. Road builders may need to dispose of trees and limbs offsite; portable chippers may be a device to meet the new regulations.

Complicated legislation affecting local businesses may require more legal work. A new condominium development at the nearby beach may open new markets for recreational furniture.

Because of these new regulations or conditions, perhaps a whole group of customers develops. Or by revising your marketing to new targets, the products can be used more extensively by another customer group than those you had been servicing. This should also be briefly addressed in your sales forecast.

Just to make sure that balance is represented, any of these factors that could have negative impact should be mentioned so your forecasted small increase is consistent with the information presented.

Competition

Here you may get some surprises. Who are your competitors? List them by name. What markets do they serve that you also serve? What percentage or share of those markets does each have? What specific products do they handle? What are the strengths and weaknesses of the firms? their products?

Your surprises will come from the information that this section will uncover. You think that you know your business and its competition. But when you list them by name, and try to write a sentence or even a word or two about them, you will suddenly discover how much you know and how much you don't know. The office equipment firm may not consider other local firms as competition but feel that most of the competition is from the large manufacturers or even the large retail outlets—until it tries to determine who is serving what group of customers, that is. Then you will uncover opportunities that you didn't know existed. A competitor that is not an aggressive marketer or has an unresponsive service department but is still in business and surviving, represents an opportunity. What is that firm doing now that's good enough to keep it open? Who is *the* customer? The clothing store that has poor displays, bad location, and dirty floors but is sound financially at the moment is doing something right—what?

If the construction equipment firm's used equipment is much higher priced than the rest of the market, why? If the firm has no rental or leasing program but still appears to be doing well placing machines for demonstration and delivery, what is it doing right? What are its specific weaknesses? the line of equipment that it handles or the salespeople? or physical facilities? Who's selling recreational furniture in your area? Where are people going for professional services?

List each positive and negative fact about each of your competitors and what markets or customer groups they're serving to stay alive, even though you know that you're doing a better job.

I've seen another phenomenon many times. You prepare a list as I've suggested. Ask your sales *and* service people *and* the department managers to prepare lists independently covering the same topics. You all will discover

19

things about your firm and competitors that you all thought that you all knew but didn't—and yet may be so critical as to alter completely your marketing strategy and operating tactics. Try it!

The next, extremely valuable step is to have someone—a consultant, your sister, your brother-in-law, someone *not* contributing to the process, and *not* an employee—assemble the information into a draft, synthesize, and summarize duplicate information. Then use the resulting draft document as a discussion point in a staff meeting, working through the draft item by item for several meetings. (Don't try to tackle it all at once. You'll lose interest.)

Another amazing phenomenon occurs. The discussion of the listed facts opens up conversation, and more new facts come rolling out, unsolicited. At the conclusion you'll know more about your market and competition than you or your staff could possibly have thought available. Even if you are small, with only two employees, just the process of organizing your thoughts and listening to the others will generate information always there but never before utilized.

Marketing Objectives

Now we can begin to develop the information into something to use as a working document.

Statement of Objectives

As the first step in this section, write a sentence or statement that describes in what direction you want your marketing efforts to be directed, in view of the information assembled in the previous sections. They may be somewhat different from the overall mission statement or company objective. Here we are talking just about the objective for the marketing effort to achieve.

Looking down the road, describe where the company should be in 5 and 10 years. Again, this is nonquantitative but takes advantages of opportunities that become obvious in the earlier sections of the plan. Finally, you can assign 1-, 2-, and 5-year sales goals (in current money terms).

Another stratagem is to ask your salespeople to write down and give to you confidentially two things: What do they think the company's sales goals should be for 1, 2, and 5 years? What do they think they can personally sell for those same periods?

The result of that exercise is twofold (if it is nurtured and developed with a sales program):

1. Their estimates of the company potential will be close but somewhat higher than yours.
2. Their individual sales goals will be higher than any that you could have reasonably expected.

Because the goals are theirs, not yours imposed on them, they will also make sure that they happen. Should the results fall short of their own expectations, you probably have some serious problems within the organization or some outside influences are strong negative forces. Many firms that set goals and forecasts with this technique experience substantially increased results over managements' own projections. The cliché may be worn but the forecast becomes a self-fulfilling prophecy, whether higher or lower than your projections.

Organization

Draw a diagram of how you think your marketing organization works. Anybody involved in your marketing should be included—your advertising agency account executive, your marketing consultant, your golf pro, or anyone else whom you regularly include in your marketing efforts. Show on the diagram their relationship to the other members of the marketing group and to you, as head of the firm.

Next list the individuals, describe their areas of responsibilities and particular qualifications. Your star salesperson and your last-place finisher should be mentioned as equals, but in both cases describe their successes and attributes. If anybody has an unusually high success ratio handling a specific product or a type of customer, that should be listed.

Strategies

Now comes the point of the whole exercise: What is our marketing going to do? Describe in nonquantitative terms whether you intend to rely on advertising or your hardworking sales force. Do this for each product or service that you offer. You have just described your marketing mix.

The tactics may be listed next, in terms of frequent sales promotions or regular advertising stressing our service department. In other words, these are not terribly specific but clearly define what tactics you will use, such as pricing, advertising, service.

Are there any programs available that you bought in the past, designed for you by your advertising agency? Do the manufacturers that you represent have any advertising cooperative plans available? Look for all possible resources. Don't fly by yourself if you don't have to. If co-op is available, what are the rules and guidelines? Will that help or hinder your overall effort?

What is the objective of your advertising? If retail, you will want to create store traffic but remain consistent with the broad objectives of your firm. You will not want to emphasize prices if you sell top-quality suits. Both the office equipment and construction equipment firms should target their advertising to customer groups but try to build name familiarity only for your company and possibly the manufacturers that you represent, if any. Your message should be consistent with your market position. Advertising for professional services can take two forms: regular media display advertising or publicity through news releases and articles.

Budget considerations are sticky. I have yet to hear an advertising professional who would be pinned down as to what amount may be appropriate. The amount varies according to seasonal considerations, whether a new product or service needs introduction, how much emphasis you are placing on advertising according to your marketing mix strategy. Usually less than 5 percent of your gross sales should be allocated to advertising and sales promotion activities as a steady plan. But concentrations for new products may be needed. Some advertising people say that as much as 10 percent of forecasted sales may be necessary to introduce a new retail item—short-term push, in other words.

The implementation and media selection should be spelled out exactly for the next 12 months, the next quarter, and finally the next month. Like everything else in the plan, be prepared to modify this but only after a reasonable time has elapsed to evaluate results. If you are to budget heavily for sales promotion activities, and that includes trade shows, golf tournaments, and anything else that isn't directly advertising- or sales-force-related, make sure that the portion set aside for a given trade show realistically represents a comparable proportion of the sales or potential sales derived from the attendees at the show. In other words just because your friends have a booth at the construction equipment show and a hospitality room in a local hotel, the same tactics might not be profitable for you. Is it cost effective to reach your market niche?

The sales force is the most expensive portion of the marketing program. What are the objectives expected of the sales force? What training is necessary and available to help them reach the objective and goals?

Describe the training that will be necessary and how much it will cost, both in terms of cash cost for the seminars and travel, etc., but also the production time lost while training. Overtraining is no less wasteful than undertraining. By listing the needs and what has been accomplished so far you will have a clearer picture of what's needed when the super-duper sales trainer comes to town for a $2,000 per person seminar, or technical training is available at one of your factories but you don't plan to sell much from that factory anyway.

Compensation details should be spelled out. We've spent considerable time determining an appropriate compensation package for your situation. When your decision is finalized—and it should remain in place for at *least* one year (see Chapter 5)—write it into the marketing plan. It represents your greatest single marketing expense but, like the others, should produce commensurate returns.

Schedule and Assignments

Spell out who is going to do what and when. The most effective way to accomplish this is to present the plan draft to your key employees as a group. Then solicit volunteers to draw up the implementation details and schedules for each section as appropriate. Make sure that specific dates are set for the completion of each section. Set the limits by indicating that the plan should be in place and become your working document by July 1, for example. Each section of the plan that requires action on the part of others needs to be completed before then. When you set the time frame, make sure that all affected personnel can meet the deadlines. Otherwise you lose their participation at the outset because they will perceive the plan as "the impossible dream" because the time deadline is not reasonable. Be careful how you decide.

Among the most effective devices is marking on a copy of the plan who is to take responsibility for each section, encouraging the staff to mark their copies as well. Write the scheduled completion dates, too. This is not supposed to be a pretty piece of paper to file away in the company safe but a working document.

A three-ring loose-leaf binder with divider tabs is helpful. If one section needs revision, it's not confining to prevent easy modification. You may also wish to have copies in each department. A three-ring binder is less likely to be lost, even in the service department.

Budget

Include appropriate budgets and pro forma profit-and-loss statements from your accountant and your financial analyst. These should include what-if projections using sales, advertising, modification of facilities, personnel, etc., as variables. The newer, less expensive computers along with some off-the-shelf software make these projections possible for *any* business, not just the larger firms with in-house mini- or mainframe computers and staff programmers. *All* businesses should at least have access to a microcomputer. There is no excuse for shooting in the dark.

Controls

Along with the budget and pro forma statements, you should depict graphically specific quantitative goals for all aspects of the marketing efforts, similar to Figure 1-3. Keep a "rolling" goal one, two, and five years in advance. Beside the graphics of the goals, graphically show achievements. Be sure to leave room for substantial overshooting of the targets, but each segment should be large enough to permit visual impact of shortages. The raw data may be collected in this section, but only distribute and show the graphic portrayal of your progress.

Summary Statement

You may wish to include a summary statement about the plan or the document. Spell out carefully the steps needed to modify the plan. Include provisions for discussion among key staff members. Use the same techniques that you used to prepare the first draft plan. No one, including you, should be able to modify any portion of the plan without carefully discussing considerations of the impact on all segments.

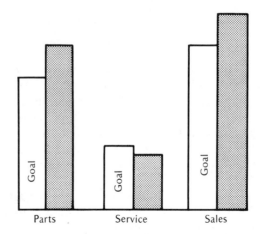

FIGURE 1–3. Departmental Goals vs. Performance

Require of yourself and your staff at least quarterly reviews and updating. If you don't think that you have the discipline to make regular reviews a reality, ask your accountant, lawyer, or someone else outside your staff to provide the discipline.

My biggest concern is that you and your staff will do an excellent job of writing a plan to suit your business, do your own high-quality data gathering, design your own plan format, only to put the book away and never check back. In several months or years you will be back where you started, with no direction, no well-defined goals for all to understand, using inappropriate tactics creating a chaotic strategy aimed at several objectives at once, missing all.

Require your accountant, attorney, or consultant to force you and your staff to review the data quarterly—not just the strategies or tactics described in the plan, but all the data. Is the competitive information still accurate, reflecting the current situation? Will new products cause you to change your marketing mix? Was the basic strategy based on incomplete or inaccurate data? Modify the data, then modify the strategy.

If your firm is small—less than 10 employees—the whole plan can be designed and the data gathered, assimilated, and finalized in 10 to 12 employee hours. You do not need to teach yourself about your industry and can probably write each section longhand in a few minutes.

Marketing Plan Outline

I. Company Mission
   A. Statement of objectives
   B. Description of business—what the company sells and services
   C. Nature of customers: who, how many, expanding area, other objective background

II. Situation Analysis
   A. Economic conditions
   B. Company resources
      1. Physical facilities: strengths/weaknesses
      2. Human resources: who? talents? responsibilities?
      3. Financial resources available (nonquantitative terms)
   C. Sales forecasts
      1. Economy
      2. New products
      3. Marketing improvements
      4. Sales history (3 to 5 years past)
         a. by product
         b. by customer group
      5. Profit and Expense/Volume
         a. by product
         b. by customer group
      6. New opportunities
         a. new customer groups
         b. additional marketing
   D. Competition
      1. Market served
      2. Market share
      3. Products
      4. Strengths
      5. Weaknesses

III. Marketing Objectives
   A. Statement of objectives
      1. Subjective, nonquantitative direction statement

      2. Results in 5 years, 10 years
      3. Sales goals for 1, 2, and 5 years
   B. Organization
      1. Structure
      2. People
      3. Responsibilities
   C. Strategies for each product
      1. Marketing mix
      2. Tactics to achieve objectives—specific courses of action
      3. Programs available
      4. Advertising and sales promotion
         a. objectives
         b. budget
         c. implementation, media
         d. co-op available
      5. Sales force
         a. objectives
         b. training
         c. compensation

IV. Schedule and assignments (to accomplish I to III)

V. Budget
   A. Financial analysis
   B. Forecast—cash and accrual
   C. Pro forma profit and loss by product line
   D. Pro forma profit and loss by customer group

VI. Controls
   A. Measurement tools for each section
   B. Review schedule

VII. Summary Statement—Provisions for modification and updating

2

Marketing Concepts

What is marketing? How can a small business like mine get involved in anything so expensive as marketing? Everyone is our market. You have probably had all these thoughts whenever you think about marketing for your business.

This chapter looks at some terms and perhaps we can begin to gain some insight into marketing for a small business. There is tremendous pressure on the small business to survive and make a profit. Not only is the economic environment seemingly in direct opposition to you; more and more small businesses are starting. Only the best will survive.

Let's start with some basics of marketing and see how they'll apply in your situation.

Elements of Planning

What may seem obvious is that to have a plan, we must first decide what we want to do. In simpler terms what is our objective? Are we to play football? basketball? sell widgets? repair office equipment? What do we *want* to do?

Let's consider definitions of some basic terms. These definitions are mine and may be different from some that you've seen, but at least we can understand what we're discussing.

OBJECTIVE. Objectives are open-ended, with no time limit or quantitative targets. For example, an objective is to maintain good sound growth and profitability while selling and servicing heavy equipment—or typewriters. Sometimes the stated objective can become the mission statement for your firm. What are you trying to accomplish?

GOAL. A goal expresses the objective with numbers and a time frame. If you want to maintain good sound growth, you probably want to grow 15 to 20 percent annually in sales. To grow from $250,000 your goal may be $300,000 by year end. An intermediate goal would be the steps between $250,000 and $300,000 expressed in sales volume at the end of each quarter or possibly by the month.

Your objective is to buy a new computer. Your goal is to have Brand Y hardware and Brand ZX software operational by the end of June.

Your objective is to make a profit. Your goal is to realize $25,000 net by year end.

MISSION STATEMENT. This is nearly synonymous with objective. However, here we mean the specific written objective describing why your business exists and what it intends to do to continue in existence.

STRATEGY. Strategy is the longer-term plan, a map of the route to the objective.

TACTICS. These are the immediate use of resources to achieve your objective as shown on your map, a selection of mode of travel.

With these terms in mind, we can go to a more thorough discussion of marketing and to the development of your marketing plan.

Marketing Components

Most managers and salespeople seem to think of marketing as something "out there" done by big business. The reason for that perception should become obvious as we continue.

Marketing is the combination of the components of the marketing mix. Marketing mix is the planned interaction of the components to achieve an objective. Figure 2-1 indicates some examples of relationships between sales and advertising for products over a range of price and/or complexity.

Marketing components are generally referred to by most textbooks as consisting of four elements:

1. Advertising (including packaging and product design; the "creative" processes)

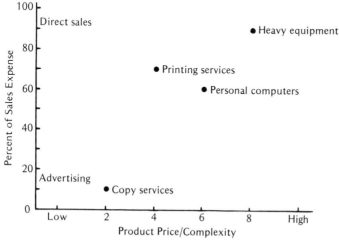

FIGURE 2-1. Marketing Mix Analysis

2. Sales: Direct personal selling; the customer-to-supplier contact point

3. Distribution channels: Wholesale, retail, direct; delivery and transportation functions

4. Pricing: A marketing tool to assign value

Advertising

Because we probably are most conscious of the advertising to sell products, create images, and focus on needs, we think that advertising and marketing are synonymous. This idea is perpetuated by many business and general periodicals. For example, the *Wall Street Journal* has a weekly column titled "Marketing." However, I don't recall ever seeing anything discussed other than advertising, packaging, or, at most, sophisticated market segments. Most people think that marketing is what happens to beer and detergents.

Sales

By the same token, *sales* and *marketing* are often used interchangeably—and incorrectly. Sales is strictly the personal interrelationship between customer and supplier as exemplified by the salesperson, whether a retail salesclerk or the account executive selling commercial airplanes and heading a multiple-person sales team.

Distribution

This usually brings to mind images of trucks, trains, and ships, but that is only part of distribution. In the marketing context, distribution refers to channels of sales from the manufacturer to the end user. For example, is your widget made for the consumer? Do you sell it through direct mail advertising? Do you deliver through UPS? Or do you sell heavy equipment, which you purchase from the factory direct? or from a distributor who purchases from the factory? Those all are descriptions of distribution channels.

Pricing

Despite the cost-accounting gyrations through which you go, pricing is a marketing function. Naturally your price is designed to recover your costs, but that doesn't go far enough. Pricing should also be part of your strategy. If Cadillacs were priced closer to Chevrolets, they probably wouldn't be quite so attractive. Pricing has a direct demonstrative effect on unit volume and ultimately on profit.

Therefore, the marketing mix is the synergistic effect of the components of the marketing strategy. *Mix* and *strategy* are closely related but not quite interchangeable terms. *Mix* refers to the interaction of the components whereas *strategy* defines the use of the components over a length of time.

Component Selection

Earlier we touched on some reasons for selection of certain tactics in the use of marketing components. The mix must be determined by:

1. Target customer group,
2. Product price,
3. Product application, and
4. Company objectives.

There are other considerations, but let's take a closer look at these first.

Customer Groups

To learn what we mean by the larger categories of customer groups, here are some more definitions.

- *Industrial* refers to customers who are purchasers of capital equipment and services to increase productivity, such as firms in manufacturing, logging, construction, and agriculture.
- *Commercial* customers are involved in business-to-business sales activity, such as wholesale groceries, office equipment, printing, real estate and business financial services.
- *Retail* firms are those that deal in sales to the off-the-street user of consumer goods such as clothing, jewelry, food, and household goods.

To see why it is important to define target groups, consider how the basic Chevrolet sedan might be sold to each group. It's one price (aside from a fleet quantity discount possibility) and does one thing (moves people), and yet the salesperson would need to make a slightly different presentation to each potential buyer based entirely on that individual's criteria used for decision making.

The industrial and commercial customer of Chevrolet sedans will be more interested in operating costs, the car's consistency with the perceived self- (company) image, and probable trade-in value or lease costs.

However, if the car dealer is selling Buicks, self-image of the customer probably is more important. The Buick may be sold as prestige executive transportation. Selling the Chevrolet on the basis of price will probably involve presenting the "stripped" model or volume discounts.

Selling on the basis of product application will involve a slightly different tactic. Is the sedan to be used as basic transportation for a field sales representative or multi-personnel conveyance, or serve as family or personal transportation? Those are all differences in product application. Consequently the sales presentation will be designed to answer the unique concerns for applying the same sedan to different situations.

All three of the previously mentioned factors affecting marketing com-

31

ponent selection are often closely interrelated. But the fourth, company objectives, often is independent of the other three. If the objective is to sell as many sedans as possible before going out of business, the sales and advertising tactics would be considerably different from the dealership that intended to be in business two generations from now. So intended longevity is one key.

Another key company objective could be the reason for selling sedans. If management felt that the reason for selling cars was to generate customers for the parts and service departments, the tactics would clearly be different from the dealership that wanted to sell new sedans to generate trade-ins because the used car department was extremely profitable, and those tactics would be different from the dealership that felt only new car profits were important. The overall marketing strategy naturally differs. You may have noticed in the advertising aimed at each group. Other examples might include personal computers or furniture.

Are your customers retail, commercial, or industrial? You need to decide if your target group is composed of Harry Homeowners or Connie Contractors. That's simple enough, but you'll probably want to take it at least one step further. If you're after Harry, are you looking for the urban condominium owner or the suburban affluent type? Perhaps you will want to construct a grid such as the one shown in Figure 2–2 to determine whom you sell to now and where you think the biggest growth potential lies. Your grass trimmer has little appeal to the condominium owner, and the suburban type doesn't consider room soundproofing important.

Pricing

Pricing affects how you sell. The high-priced item requires more personal selling. Not only does the higher price usually indicate complexity and therefore the salesperson's emphasis is more on education, but also higher-

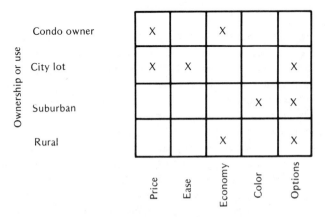

FIGURE 2-2.   Grid of Purchase Factors—Power Grass Trimmer

priced consumer goods need to be delivered on silver trays with much stroking of customer egos. There is nothing wrong with that. But be sure that you know why you do it and when.

Marketing in the industrial sector doesn't lend itself to mass advertising on national television, except possibly by the manufacturer. In some cases you may want to supplement your other marketing efforts with mass media but it won't represent a significant factor in your overall advertising expenditures— at least it shouldn't.

More emphasis in industrial and commercial marketing is placed on personal selling. Price and complexity of the products are part of the reason. The need for education is another. The customer is more interested in what specific benefits and return on investment will be realized by buying your product or service. Emotional appeal can't ever be totally ignored, but it should be less important in the industrial and commercial environments. The industrial and commercial customer is also interested in the probable longevity of the supplier. The customer doesn't want to buy a product or service, modify operation to take full benefit, and then find that replacement parts, backup service, or additional supplies are no longer available.

On the matter of the salesperson's educational role, industrial and commercial selling includes lots of tailoring of the product to fit the customer. Custom installation, modification of the premises, employee education, etc., are important roles for the salesperson.

Two familiar examples are the two-way radio and office telephone systems. The two-way radio system not only requires selection of components and customer installation to fit the particular needs of the customer; the sales agent also becomes involved in training the customer's employees in the use of the equipment and spends time making suggestions as to how best to incorporate mobile communications into the firm's daily activities in order to receive maximum benefit.

The new type of office phone systems, whether from one of the telephone companies or an independent supplier, also exhibits the need for the selling and installing organization to aid in the training in the use of the equipment to gain all the advantages. This is particularly true for the new computer-based multistation interoffice phone systems.

Computers have also had a dramatic affect on company operations, as is well-chronicled. The hardware and software people are involved in customer education to maximize benefits.

Larger manufacturers recognize this phenomenon and have developed excellent educational tools and informational pieces on the proper use of products and services. These educational tools become an integral part of the marketing program. A variant on this is the schools and seminars to teach the user's employees the maintenance and operation of the product.

What may not seem apparent is the basic philosophy of selling to the industrial and commercial accounts. The buyer needs to realize demonstrable specific financial benefits from the product. Therefore the seller is obligated to help the customer any way possible to get all the potential benefits. The net result is a satisfied customer, who will be an excellent reference, expressed or implied.

On the other side of the coin are the consumer-oriented widgets. Those items are of necessity dependent on advertising emphasis in their marketing mix to reach as many potential customers as possible. This advertising can take the form of mass media, such as newspaper or television or national magazines. Wouldn't the small business be more likely to use more focused media? in some cases, merely point-of-sale displays?

By the same token, if we comprehend what each component represents in functional terms, then it will be an easy step to perceive each component's selection and role in the overall marketing plan.

Before we leave marketing components, let's look at some strategy systems and the appropriate tactics that need to be considered when a manufacturer selects distribution methods. Sometimes marketing people talk about push versus pull strategy, and occasionally we hear of a firm that uses push-pull marketing. Figure 2–3 illustrates all three systems.

Push

Here we look at all four marketing components when the push strategy is employed. The personal selling becomes one of providing risk-reducing information, usually involving a complex product or application. The responsibility for advertising is placed on the retail outlet. High price and high margins are included to aid the higher unit sales costs and infrequent purchases by a customer. Men's suits or jewelry are examples.

Pull

As the name implies, the customer is supposed to pull the product through the distribution channels. There is a correspondingly low price, low margin, and high reliance on manufacturer's advertising, and the sales effort is merely to demonstrate superiority over competition, if any. The purchases are frequent and the risk is low for the consumer. Examples include home detergents or beer.

Push-Pull

Usually this combination of strategies isn't anything more than employment of both strategies, using the same sales and advertising and sometimes even pricing. But the emphasis on the distribution channels is changed. This strategy is most often employed for relatively expensive but low-margin items, where the channels can influence the sale as well as the consumer. A specific example is heavy trucks, where you can specify axles and engines; those manufacturers make their presentations to the truck assembler and the dealer as well as the buyer. Major home appliances would be another example. Mar-

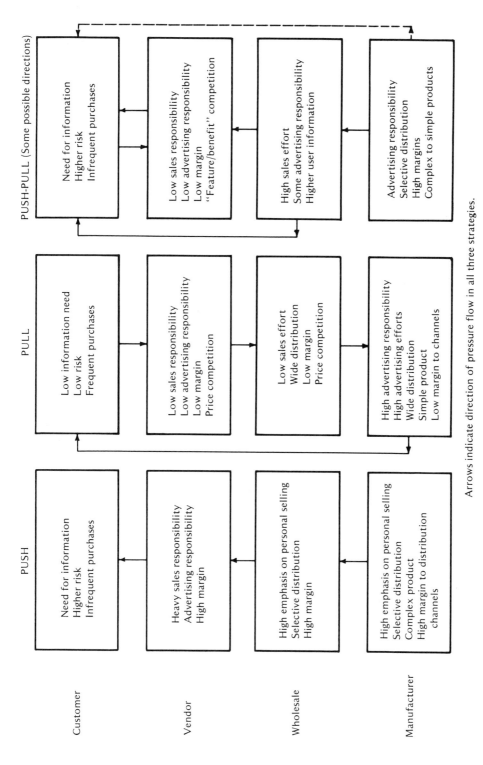

Arrows indicate direction of pressure flow in all three strategies.

FIGURE 2–3. Push, Pull, and Push-Pull Strategies

35

keting effort is spent to see that the wholesalers have inventory in warehouse, the architects and builders specify brands in homes built on speculation, and the consumer asks for specific brands when designing the house and purchasing after-market replacement units.

With a little thought you can probably find examples of all three strategies in your daily life. Normally the strategy is selected by the manufacturer, and in most cases small business is *in* the distribution channel, not selecting which one to use.

Product Mix

This is almost self-explanatory. By *product mix* we are referring to the composite of all the products and services that you offer. That's simple. However, it becomes complex when the products

1. Are in different stages of their product life cycle,
2. Overlap with each other as to function and application,
3. Serve different customers or groups of customers,
4. Vary from complicated to simple in terms of applications or operation, and
5. Vary significantly in price.

Other, less obvious factors may be important in your business.

We can't have a simple marketing plan when we're trying to do a complex job. Let me take an example from agricultural equipment. John Deere is the largest and most successful manufacturer of farm equipment. It makes a long list of equipment and many highly specialized items sold only in certain parts of the world. But isn't the job of the dealer's salesperson quite different selling large all-wheel-drive articulated tractors than selling plows?

In many other situations such complexity is even more obvious. In passenger cars, heavy trucks and equipment, and a host of other cases, the salesman selling service and replacement parts has a far different job than selling complete new units. If one salesman does both, chances are that one or the other of the areas of responsibility is slighted.

Office equipment has some parallels. IBM was a builder of bookkeeping machines and typewriters. It experienced great growth and profitability with the large high-capacity mainframe computers. Then it moved into minicomputers and personal or microcomputers. Simultaneously IBM's manual typewriters were replaced by electric, then replaced by "ball" type, then in turn by magnetic card memory machines, which gave way to word processors, which have become both more complex and simpler.

At each stage of IBM's development and the evolution of products, its salespeople became (1) more specialized and (2) spent more time on customer education as the customers became *less* sophisticated. The firm is in the retail business with salesclerks, stores, etc. Wouldn't it need to use salespeople with different talents and temperament for each product and application? We've all seen how advertising is varied according to the product and market. Wouldn't IBM's marketing mix vary widely according to the product or markets? Isn't its product mix fairly complex?

With automobiles, all models are designed to accommodate driver and passengers, move safely and comfortably from one point to another. But wouldn't the customer of the Cadillac expect and receive a more personalized sales presentation than the Ford Fiesta buyer? That is a function of price alone because both are equally complicated; do the same job; can't be driven legally over 55 mph; can have heat, air-conditioning, and stereo; and in all other respects perform the same job in the same manner.

At the other end of the spectrum the variety store item in the housewares section uses only a clerk to take your money, relying totally on advertising, including packaging and display and product design.

Product Life Cycle

When the product is new, heavy emphasis is placed on educating the customer as to potential use. The first buyers tend to be innovators and will probably develop even more uses. As the product matures, the next phase in the cycle requires more emphasis on the benefits of the product. During the later stages of the product most of the effort is spent communicating why a particular product is different from competitive ones. Before the product dies altogether, some marketing innovators may experience some sales increase by improved marketing or different applications. But eventually all products decline. Most business periodicals contend that the American automobile industry is in advanced stages of maturity.

The job of marketing is going to be quite a bit different for the same product depending on where it is in its life cycle (see Figure 2–4).

Summary

Now we have a clearer picture of the nature of the marketing components and some of the factors determining their selection. Let's see what happens when the incorrect components are chosen or emphasized. Have you experienced one of the following?

By use of excellent advertising a manufacturer has introduced a product that you recognize as filling a need in the operation of your business. You wait to be contacted by a salesperson, but nothing happens. Next you do some research and find the local dealer. You telephone. The salespeople are unavailable—no problem. Salespeople have other customers, sales meetings, etc. You leave your name and number for someone to return the call. You wait. Finally you call back. The net result is that you are now conscious of a product or concept to fill a need. In desperation, you find another source for a similar product. Their salesperson responds quickly. You buy.

Why did this happen? By not carefully planning marketing, the manu-

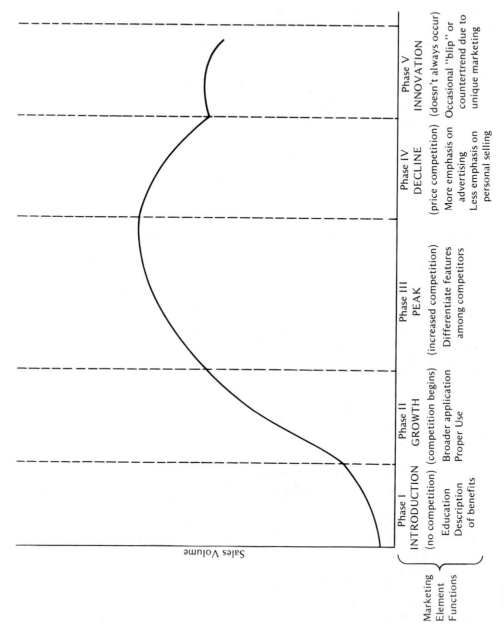

FIGURE 2–4.   Product Life Cycle Analysis

facturer created a need or solution to a need but didn't have the right number of effective salespeople or dealer inventory or whatever, causing you to go elsewhere. The irony is that the firm spending the time and effort on one phase of "marketing" merely cost itself sales and market share and, most importantly, damaged its reputation for response and sensitivity to customer needs.

We all see parallels in retail every day. You decide to buy a watch. From the advertising, you select a particular style, then brand, then store. But when you get to the store, you can't find a salesperson. When you finally succeed, the person is not knowledgeable about watches in general, knows nothing about recommending bands, and generally exhibits a lack of training or interest other than taking your money. For a watch under $50 you probably don't expect much more, but if you are prepared to spend $500 or more, you want to be sure of your purchase. The higher the price, more personal attention and information become important.

Keeping on the watch theme, let's look at another situation. A jewelry store has been located in the same place for many years, selling quality products and giving good service, and yet business is declining. Other similar businesses are doing well. What might be wrong? As times have changed, the retail service area has grown in population substantially, and more jewelry and discount stores are in business than a few years ago. However, the original store has not changed tactics. It still runs a small ad occasionally in the local paper, keeps good inventory and well-trained salespeople. It sells medium- to higher-priced items. But it failed to keep its name in front of the public and as the population changed, those who once had loyalty are shopping elsewhere and the new people in the area don't know that the store exists. The demise of the store would be blamed on the federal government or "the recession." As the store sinks, the salespeople will leave because the good ones want to be where they can practice their profession and contribute to success. Their commission is almost incidental. Sadly the store doesn't have much traffic and what does come in is not handled properly. By the time the real problem is discovered, the financial reserves are nearing exhaustion, and little can be done—all because the marketing components were not selected or reviewed carefully. The store's only alternative to failure is an aggressive, well-executed marketing plan and may include a complete change in strategy and market position.

Even in situations where it would appear that the marketing mix is correct on the surface, poorly conceived advertising or poorly-trained salespeople destroy the plan. Excellent location, displays, and merchandise selection are only part of the marketing plan for a retailer. In commercial and industrial markets, it takes more than a good product and good service department. With a carefully drawn plan, the deficiencies are more apparent and can be corrected in a logical, well-thought-out manner.

Because small business doesn't normally have much latitude in pricing or distribution channels, we'll concentrate on advertising and sales force management. The manufacturers of your product have established the pricing upper and lower limits, making it difficult to move out of that range. Service pricing is set with a careful eye on price competition. Occasionally you have opportunities to deviate from the market norm but usually only by being highly specialized in a large population market.

The same thinking applies to distribution. Most small businesses, whether commercial and industrial or retail are selling their products or services to the end user, whether Harry Homeowner or Connie Contractor.

There is one exception to the rule. Wholesalers supplying the retail establishments aren't selling to the ultimate user. By definition they *are* the distribution channel, rather than having a choice of distribution.

In this chapter we have defined *marketing, marketing mix, product life cycle, product mix, goals, objectives, mission statements, strategy, tactics,* and *marketing components.* During this discussion we have looked at some cases of good and poor marketing for small business. In later chapters we explore in more detail the how and why of component selection and spend considerable time discussing the proper use of the two marketing components most likely to be controlled by the entrepreneur: advertising and sales.

We never attempt to say that there is any black-and-white or right-and-wrong relationship between any set of alternatives. The purpose is to help you understand how and why components are selected, developed, and used successfully. With a better understanding of why you're succeeding, you are in a better position to improve even more.

The theme of planning is constant. By having clearly defined objectives, specific goals, and a plan for their achievement, you will attain success in marketing or anything else that you attempt.

3

Position for Results

Segmentation and positioning are two separate but closely related steps that shape your total marketing activities. The techniques of segmentation and positioning are usually thought of as tools of large mass merchandisers to capture a small percentage of market share, which translates into millions of dollars in annual volume.

What we discuss here, then, is how to use these techniques in the small business environment. In some cases you may accidentally be doing the right things, but by understanding the process and its proper application you can improve your market effectiveness. We not only deal with the application of the techniques but also look at why they are important tools for success of any business or even professional practice.

Segmentation

Segmenting, as defined in the dictionary, is the division of a whole into its natural parts. For example, a railroad train would be segmented by individual cars. In marketing, the working definition isn't that much different. For clarification we suggest the inclusion of a phrase that suggests *division into the smallest homogeneous groupings possible.* By understanding the market segment that you are serving, you can deliver your message more effectively by aiming at the right group.

Earlier I referred to large firms that segment their markets in order to capture a small percentage—with extremely high dollar volume results. As a practical matter how does this apply to a small firm dealing in one market?

Market Size

The first consideration is the size of your market. Are you operating a retail store selling clothing in a city of 100,000? Or are you selling construction supplies statewide? The question really is, How do you know when to divide the market?

It's simple. Segmentation is a factor of the market size and the number of competitors. To illustrate, if your business is a retail clothing store in a city of 100,000, you may have 10 competing stores serving the market. On the other hand, your construction supply firm may have only 1 or 2 competitors, and you all operate statewide. From these examples we can see the obvious.

Your *market size,* whether it is defined by geography or customer group, is the first step in segmentation. You've segmented the world into the smallest logical group with which you can deal profitably.

How many customers do you need to be profitable? To be meaningful, you need to translate the quantity of customers into dollar volume. Each of a relatively small number of customers could represent a large enough dollar volume.

Geographic Area

No matter what type of business—retail, commercial, industrial, or professional—the next step in segmentation is to define the *geographic area* from which the customers come. The area could be defined as a neighborhood or state. To determine the area can be accomplished by a simple procedure.

On a map with your location as center, mark spots representing the location of your customers. For a retail store this map may be your city map such as shown in Figure 3–1, while the commercial firm may need a city or state map. Once you have located most of the customers physically, use the same technique again, but try this time to assign the dollar volume represented. This process should be simple, using data on hand for commercial, industrial, and professional firms. Retail may take more research, assuming that you don't have the names, addresses, and dollar volume represented for each customer for the previous year or calendar quarter as a minimum.

Research can be easy. For a smaller store where nearly all customers come in contact with only one employee per visit, that employee, whether it's you or a retail salesperson, can discreetly inquire as to the customer's residence by a simple "Are you from this area?" A great percentage of the customers will gladly tell you if they live in the neighborhood or are from "Mt. Pleasant, which, you know, is three miles away." Those who don't let you know where they live need not cause you any concern as long as a substantial percentage of the customers respond, so you can mark your map, both for location and dollar volume.

Logical sampling techniques suggest that this process be done for a short period of time periodically, such as one week a year. More frequent surveys would need to be made only if the store volume changes dramatically, up or down, in a short time. Use your monthly and weekly sales figures to spot volume trends, comparing with comparable periods earlier, such as previous year.

Perhaps the process may be impossible in a supermarket where there is a large volume flow through multiple check stands. In that case hire temporary help to ask customers as they leave, "How far did you come to shop here?" The responses can and should be categorized by time of day to cross-check with residence. A supermarket can then compare distance with hour of the day and with purchase volume by looking at the cash register tape and deter-

44

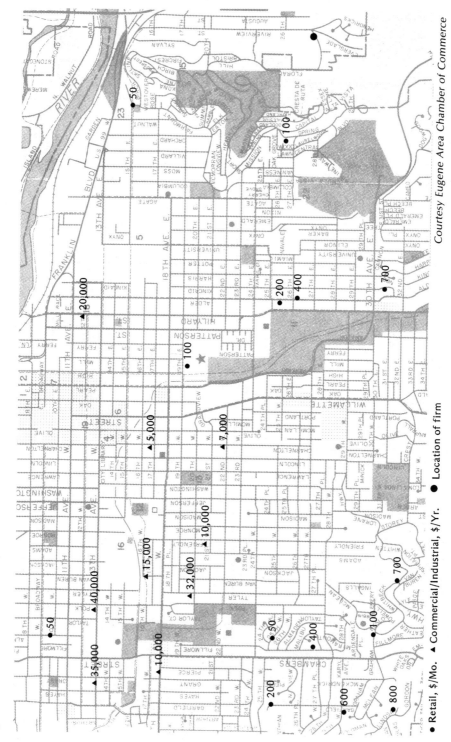

FIGURE 3-1. Customer Location and Revenue Analysis

Courtesy Eugene Area Chamber of Commerce

● Retail, $/Mo.   ▲ Commercial/Industrial, $/Yr.   ● Location of firm

mining not only who the customer is but also that the customer will change according to the hour. Assuming that the store is a one-location business, you need to know whether you are competing with the convenience stores or the large chains.

Demographic Grouping

For retail and professional firms, *demographics* can be as important as defining the geographic market area. Demographics is grouping by age, sex, and family status. A sporting goods store specializing in active sports gear, such as football, hockey, and soccer, would need a substantial population of younger age brackets. A location in a retirement community wouldn't work well; neither would it for a restaurant and lounge featuring rock music. In the case of the professional firm the type of personal accounting or medical practice would be a factor of the age group of the clients.

Socioeconomic Grouping

Socioeconomic groupings are also extremely important. By socioeconomic we are defining occupation, income level, and education of the customers. Short of an in-depth, professional survey, the best-guess method of informal questions and location of residential neighborhoods as a determinate would normally be adequate for small businesses.

The commercial, industrial, and, in some cases, professional clients need to be defined in comparable terms. For example, are you serving the construction industry? If so, what phase of construction? residential? Are your customers putting in the utilities, doing the cement work, framing, installing the plumbing, or all these?

In the office equipment business, where are the products you handle in relation to competitors for price and quality? Or are your customers primarily professional offices or retail stores? Whether you are selling typewriters for small offices or sophisticated word processors with multiple work stations, you need to know who your customers are and their intended use of the equipment.

A truck dealership certainly needs to understand who the customers are to call on the right accounts. If your customers are primarily long-haul highway users, your service shop hours and policies as well as your truck inventory must reflect your customers.

Market Share

Let's take the process one step further. Referring to the planning guide in Chapter 1, we also need to examine our competitors relative to the same questions. Who are their customers? Are they serving the same segment that you are by geography? demographics? socioeconomic groups? special interests? Or in the case of commercial and industrial equipment firms, are you selling typewriters or tractors to the same users as your competition? in the same price and quality range? Make a simple chart, such as that shown in Figure 3–2, to consider where on various relevant continua you and the competition are. Look for gaps.

Let's see to what minimum level we need to segment our markets. The decision is a quantitative one. Simply, how many customers do you need?

Specifically, assume that you can sell 10 percent of the customers in the category that you choose. The category should be chosen by customer group. In our clothing store example, can your store sell 10 percent of the clothing bought by people within a six-block or six-mile radius of the store? The most appropriate radius is a function of the size and type of community. A clothing store in Manhattan would be fortunate to sell 10 percent within three blocks, but by the same token Manhattan is considered a fashion center. That store would draw from contiguous areas, such as New Jersey and Connecticut, as well as distant customers who go to New York to shop.

That introduces the other factor. What price and quality segment of the market are you sharing? Isn't it logical that higher-priced goods require more population? The reason hardly needs repeating here. Upper-income brackets with higher levels of discretionary spending represent a small fraction of the total population. Therefore, the socioeconomic groupings of the contiguous areas become important for retail stores. That would be the case whether located in primarily business or residential neighborhoods.

RELATIVE PRICE
(important to any business)

Low		Mid		High		
Brands or stores #1—2—4—7	#3—6—9	Vacant	#10	Vacant	#11	Vacant	#12

AGE GROUPS OF CUSTOMERS
(important to most retail and many professional practices)

Young		Adult		Senior
Competitor #1	Vacant	#2, 3, 4	Vacant	#5

PRODUCT APPLICATION
(such as construction equipment size, capacity, and horsepower ratings)

Home use		Utility		Heavy
Brands #1—2—5	Brand #3	Vacant	Brand #3	Brands #4, 5, 6

FIGURE 3-2.   Market Segment Analysis

It's possible to make a case for retail stores creating their own traffic by their unique mix of merchandise and mode of operation and location. However, those situations are so unusual as to cause them to be case studies in business periodicals. L. L. Bean's retail store in Maine is certainly unique. So are the specialty stores on Fifth Avenue in New York. But don't overlook the lessons that they can teach. They have segmented the market to such an extent that they serve a tiny fraction of the general population. They get the glamour and attention, but the volume and profit potential more readily available are in serving larger segments of the population with businesses or residences contiguous to the store.

For the commercial and industrial equipment firms, essentially the same principles would apply. In the office equipment example, if you are selling typewriters and word processors and using the conservative 10 percent rule that you can sell replacement equipment to 10 percent of current users, how much geography must you serve to generate enough volume to cover your overhead? Certainly your overhead can be controlled, but there is a point where you won't project the image of a firm that will be around to service after the sale or provide replacement parts. Start with the absolute minimum overhead needed to project stability.

The commercial and industrial equivalent of demographics and socio-economic groupings is not that much different from the retail situation. Only now we look at the customer as a firm, at the type of business, and at the management style.

Construction equipment is segmented according to size, among other things. Larger equipment requires far more potential customers strictly due to the lower number of units sold in a given time period. Larger equipment also requires significantly different service and parts support from small equipment, at least due to size and dollar impact, if nothing else. How large an area must you cover to provide the sales volume necessary to supply the service and overhead requirements?

With commercial and industrial equipment it may be more logical to segment along customer-industry lines. For the construction equipment there is a great deal of difference in selling to a large construction firm that is building freeways and dams and in selling the same equipment to an independent logging operation using the equipment to build forest access roads. If you are dealing in equipment or services that have a variety of uses with little change in the hardware that's delivered, you should understand how it's being used so you can have a better perception of who your customer really is and be more responsive.

Use these same techniques to analyze your competition. What segment of the market are they serving? Segment the market to such an extent that you have a clear perception of the competitors' customers. During the planning process we looked at the competition to try to understand what they were doing. This is the time to look closer. Now we probably have a good idea of what customers we have and who they are. We also understand to whom our competitors are selling.

Positioning

The next step in determining the marketing strategy with the most profitable growth potential is to establish position. The dictionary definition, "the location or place at a given moment," doesn't go far enough to help our understanding of the marketing technique. For one thing the position in marketing is relatively constant, requiring some time to change significantly. In addition the *perceived* attitude or relative location within a group is as important as the actual position.

Image

Let me explain what I mean by perceived versus actual position. Retail examples abound. Have you ever been in a store that had merchandise stacked to the ceiling in cartons, sloppy displays, garish signs, and posters everywhere? Don't you perceive that type of operation as a low-price or discount store? In the case of a service establishment would you expect the work quality to be less than great but volume the important consideration? With that type of image, no matter how high the quality of merchandise or service, or even the price, for that matter, the image conveyed would be one of lower price and quality, no matter how hard the salesperson talked. You may have seen the other extreme, although it's somewhat unusual: fancy fixtures and subdued lighting, displays well arranged with space between items, roomy aisles, neat and tasteful signs, deep carpeting, yet low-priced goods and services. There is nothing wrong outright with either approach. But the inconsistency between the perceived position and the actual will confuse the customers to the point that neither category will be attracted in sufficient quantity. Not only should the image be consistent with the goods and services, but also make sure that it's consistent with the environment. Is the store location appropriate for a discount operation? The other extreme is more critical. Is the luxury store located in a neighborhood of similar stores or residences?

Location

For commercial, industrial, and professional firms the business location is every bit as important as for retail. The dealer selling high-quality crawler tractors and motor grades should avoid the area where the used equipment and salvage operations gather. The attorney or accountant specializing in corporate legal and tax matters needs to have the office in a location that transmits that message. A plastic surgeon specializing in elective cosmetic procedures won't do well in a run-down office neighborhood.

There are many successful matches between location and price: discount operations near a major shopping center; high-priced fashion on Rodeo Drive in Beverly Hills or Fifth Avenue in New York. In many cities industrial equipment dealers, supply warehouses, and other groups locate near each other. Even though their salespeople generally conduct business on the cus- tomer's premises, location is still important.

Use of Product or Service

But there is much more to position than an image. In a medium-sized city three or four office equipment dealers are all profitable. Why? Each has segmented the market and developed a position unique to it. One may sell nothing but electronic typewriters and word processors. Another may concentrate on calculators, programmable calculators, or point-of-sale equipment. But none of them has concentrated on selling its service department. If one decided to focus attention on service through advertising repair and mainte- nance, wouldn't it succeed in establishing a position as leader in taking care of equipment? Customers who have had trying experiences with equipment re- pair and maintenance would be most receptive to the suggestion that service is important, rather than secondary. The firm that put its advertising em- phasis on the service end of the business would carve a niche from the other categories and the more conventional segments. Instead of capturing a signifi- cant portion of a customer group, such as legal offices or retail firms, the firm pushing service could take a significant share from all categories.

Most towns have several dry cleaners and laundries. But how many have clothing restoration services? Aren't they really the same? Perception is the difference. The message must be transmitted with creditability, of course.

Another example is the magnet. Look in the housewares section of your local discount or variety store. How many magnets are there? But how many are sold as magnets? Most are sold as towel holders, household tools, retriev- ers, etc. Until I had a client who was selling magnets, I hadn't noticed. But my client's magnet was packaged and positioned to perform a specific function. Sales were in the many thousands of units.

Continuing the example, what's wrong with calling a jewelry store a shop dealing in expressions of love? A lesson that I learned from a jeweler friend years ago is that nearly all such purchases are to express love. Few cus- tomers make purchases for their own use, using their own funds. This seems to be particularly true for stores in smaller cities.

Perhaps it is becoming more apparent why assessing not only our own position but those of the competitors is important. The opportunities for growth may come from segments other than demographics, socioeconomic groups, etc., or even from others in the same price and quality niche. The promising segment may be a result of the perceived use or dependence on your product or service.

Competition

When you are examining your customers to learn what segment of the total you are serving best, don't overlook the segments that you think you should be serving. If your competition is serving them, what are they doing that you're not? What can you do differently? (When we discuss advertising and sales force management in other chapters, we'll talk also about how to communicate your position.)

Segmenting to break the market into parts, followed by positioning yourself in the vacant slots, is the purpose of the exercise. But don't be too structured by "normal" segment boundaries. There is nothing wrong with creating segments to divide your competitors' customers into groups that you can address.

The only consideration is to segment the market into the smallest parts possible to generate sufficient dollar volume for you to be profitable. If you are operating a jewelry store in a large city you will segment into small pieces. But a jewelry store in a small town with only one or two competitors means that the segments will be relatively good-sized in order to generate a sufficient number of customers.

Resources

In order to use the techniques of segmenting and establishing position effectively, one other consideration is extremely important. Not only should you segment into groups as small as possible to generate a profitable level of business, but also you need to be certain that you have all the resources needed to serve the targeted segment or segments.

With the clothing store model, if it is necessary to carry a wide variety of items, then make sure that you have adequate inventory in each category. A clothing store in a small town may decide that to generate adequate revenue, it is necessary to handle both men's suits and casual clothes, maybe even recreational clothing in addition to furnishings and shoes. But don't have such a small selection in each category that the customers go to another store or a larger city to satisfy their need for choice. They may buy an item identical to what you carry, but they'll feel cheated if they don't have a variety from which to choose.

Successful retail operations in small towns can teach us many lessons that apply in retail, commercial, industrial, or professional situations. Let's assume that the store has good inventory control, salespeople, location, appearance, advertising, etc. Let's focus on the merchandise. The store concentrates on the segment chosen to serve. Specifically it carries goods that are consistent in price range. Suppose that the particular community is middle income. In order to generate adequate dollar volume, the store carries general-purpose clothing but within a well-defined price range for comparable goods. Suits, sports clothes, work clothes, recreational clothes, and shoes are in the medium price range. If the store tried to handle seconds or price merchandise, the image of the store would be of lower-quality merchandise so that the justifiable medium-priced suits would be perceived as overpriced.

I've also seen small stores that were successful handling a wide price range. However, they handled only suits or business clothes. Even there, they can't successfully handle extremely high-price or low-price clothing without changing the perception of the broad middle range.

If it is easy to see several right options, the wrong option is somewhat obtuse. A store cannot successfully handle both a wide price range and a wide variety of clothing. In other words, suits in all price ranges as well as casual, recreational, furnishings, and sports clothes in all price ranges will only confuse the audience. As a practical matter, in order to have any selection of size or color in each price and use category would require a huge inventory. A large inventory and the necessary store and display space would be financially impossible. Even large stores in large cities don't make any serious attempt to cover all price and use categories. Big-city department stores tend to handle moderate to upper-priced goods generally. In some cases they may have a bargain basement. But there's the clue. They physically segment their customers. In women's clothing this tactic is most apparent. Different departments are not only physically separated but also usually have distinctly different furniture and fixtures.

Commercial and industrial equipment and service firms don't have as wide a variety of optional tactics as retail stores, but there are parallels. An office equipment store, no matter how small the town, cannot handle everything from cheap calculators to sophisticated programmable calculators in addition to everything from cheap portable typewriters to word processors, copying machines, furniture, and supplies. In the first place businesses buying from businesses rightfully expect knowledgeable assistance with purchase decisions, and it would be nearly impossible for a small staff to be expert in all products. In addition, even assuming that the store had adequate space and could "afford" the inventory, turnover would be extremely poor, to say nothing of the dollar volume to space ratio. Therefore, profit would be virtually impossible. The net result would be that purchases would be made from competitive outlets. Office equipment can even be ordered through mail order. In most areas transportation to larger cities is easy. The competition could be a catalog or the highway.

Industrial equipment, such as machine tools, construction and agricultural machinery, presents even fewer choices, but they should be obvious. Due to the infrequent purchases and high dollar volume per sale, the competition could easily be hundreds of miles away. Therefore, doesn't it make sense to concentrate on the segment that you can best serve?

Take electric motors. You'll probably be much more successful handling the horsepower range most commonly used in your area than trying to supply all sizes. But within the power range you may decide to offer a range of quality, including used and rebuilt. Your plan should have told you where the best opporunities are.

Professional practices may not have the luxury of specializing in a small town. But, like the other examples, there is nothing to say that you can't draw from a larger area to specialize. Logic must be applied. Practicing admiralty law in the mountains of New Mexico would obviously be exceeding the limits of credibility.

Your strategy can be to serve a unique and different segment target, or you can position yourself to aim at the same target but with a different message creating a segment. In some cases, particularly in retail, including cars and residential real estate, the object may be to segment by attitudes and life styles within the more traditional demographic or socioeconomic groupings: tennis versus golf, opera versus theater, apartments versus single-family homes.

But why is this of so much concern? You need to focus the sales and advertising efforts to support the price and distribution strategy aiming at the segment that you want to serve. All elements of the marketing mix must be coordinated to convey the message. We'll talk about this more in Chapter 7; for now it suffices to say that dealing in high quality but being located in the low-rent district won't work well.

Trying to be all things to all customers is as futile as shooting a moose at 200 yards with a shotgun; what pellets do hit won't make much impression.

Segment your market into the smallest logical and homogeneous group that you can serve profitably. Keep all your resources utilized adequately, but don't overstrain by trying to do too many things. At the same time make sure that you're doing enough.

4

The Marketing Strategy

When all is said and done, the marketing strategy is the system used to increase sales revenue. We will spend some time looking at the principal components of the strategy and specific examples from different facets of small business. In the process perhaps you will begin to develop your thinking about increasing sales revenue.

The key word is *system*. By system in this context we are referring to the interaction of the various marketing elements engaged in a strategy to achieve predetermined objectives. A lack of a systemic approach to marketing results in a disjointed set of inconsistent strategies, which confuse both the customer and your employees. Chances are that such confusion is only symptomatic of the fact that *you* are confused. From time to time in this discussion, we return to the system approach, but much of the discussion is on individual elements. However, whether in marketing or overall business management, no one factor is most important. We all know that it takes good financial management and good production management along with good marketing to succeed, no matter what the business or profession. What many of us don't do often enough is consider the interaction of the principal disciplines of business management. By the same token those of us who concentrate on marketing sometimes overlook the extremely important interaction of various elements of the marketing program, and we pay the price in mediocre results. Marketing strategy is really a system of strategies, and we need to keep the systemic approach in mind.

Although we continue to talk about the concepts, this section is more relevant to you if you completely understand the ideas presented in Chapter 3. The key theme, which repeats several times, is to know your customer. We build on that phrase and learn different aspects of the customer, which affects how we present our advertising and sales message. There are really only three ways to affect sales: price, market share, and market demand.

Price

Changing price is a complicated process with far-reaching effects on the business. Price is the quantitative label for value and therefore is tied directly to the perception of quality. Price setting interacts with the other elements of the marketing program and can't be changed independently without disastrous results.

Let's look at some examples of price changes. Consider upward changes in price, independent of any other changes in the marketing program. The first and obvious result is that revenue per unit will increase—to a point. That point at which revenues will start decreasing is the price-sensitive point. Quite literally it is the point of no return.

Although it's an example from big business, we have seen such a case in the 1970s, and we all have paid dearly in one form or another: energy prices. When gasoline in the United States was priced at less than 35¢ a gallon, no one was much concerned with fuel economy or conservation methods. Only the largest and most cost-conscious consumers, typically large corporations, devoted much attention to energy conservation. We have seen how we've come to accept gasoline prices four times what they were 10 years earlier. But hasn't it been interesting that with every seasonal or cyclical temporary decrease in energy prices, sales of big American cars increased?

This process has also demonstrated what happens when acceptance of price levels occurs. Any change from the accepted level, up or down, produces corresponding changes in consumption patterns. In other words, in the 1980s several price points have been crossed from both directions.

Applying this concept to our small business arena, let's look at specifics. For the jewelry store, price is very much a function of perceived value because in jewelry, perhaps more than in most other goods, the customer knows virtually nothing about gem stones, metals, or watch mechanisms.

Changing the price upward, therefore, may not have much of an immediate effect on unit sales, other than the reduction in prospective customers with adequate discretionary income. But with jewelry the other elements of the marketing program are an all-important means to convey the desired message of value to the customer. The artful display of merchandise, store furnishings and interior design, advertising, and the actual packaging of the merchandise are part of delivering the intended price message. We can easily see, then, the interaction of the elements to reinforce our price strategy.

Clothing offers a slightly different circumstance. Information is more readily available to the consumer about styles, material quality and characteristics, and finishing details. To some extent price can be more isolated, and various quality levels and manufacturers' price-targeted merchandise can be bought at traditional retail stores. But the same items can also be available at off-price and discount houses if distribution through those channels is permitted by the brand. The higher-price, targeted goods are generally not permitted access to those channels in order to maintain price integrity. As with the jewelry store the other elements reinforce the price strategy but do remain somewhat more independent from the process of determining value by price.

Concentrating on one item for sale, let's see what happens with price changes. As an office equipment dealer, you are selling a line of typewriters. Most of the newer electronic typewriters require special ribbons available through the machine dealer. As an independent dealer, you have the latitude to set the price for ribbons. The first consideration is the cost to you, not just the invoice cost plus freight, but the storage space required, amount of necessary inventory due to availability of replacements from sources, and other similar considerations. After you consider all these factors, what price is appropriate?

One of the pieces of relevant information is the price of comparable ribbons for competitive machines. If the other machine in the same price class requires captive supplies, how much are those ribbons? Is the ribbon quality comparable? What seems to be the competitor's ribbon pricing strategy: to milk maximum profit or to build unit volume? With answers to those questions, we can then ask the same of our own product. How high can we take our price without undermining our overall reputation for fairness? Because the product is captive, the temptation to "sock it to 'em" must be avoided. If the ribbons are much higher than comparable products, not only will we lose ribbon sales, but the next loss will be typewriter sales closely followed by losing market share in all areas of the business—simply because we have undermined our reputation for fair treatment of the customer.

Household gadgets are even trickier. What is the value to the customer? Household gadgets tend to be price sensitive. In other words, if a product is unique as to design or function and improves the way things are done in the home—but productivity is not usually equated with monetary considerations as in business—household gadgets' unit volume is inversely proportional to unit price: lower price, higher quantity.

Perceived Value

Commercial and industrial merchandise price strategy requires careful consideration of perceived value. Usually value is equated with productivity efficiencies, safety, or some other demonstrable return on investment. Therefore, price increases not only might increase the sales revenue but also may be perceived as a statement of quality and therefore longer service life cycles.

Lowering prices does not necessarily mean that your quality is lower, but that could be the message. Lower prices may increase unit sales but perhaps not enough to offset the revenue per unit change.

Jewelry items are one example that may actually lose unit volume by lowering the price. If you could buy a Rolex, Baume & Mercier, or Piaget watch for $100, wouldn't you worry? Gem stones probably would be even more adversely affected by a price decrease that didn't seem to match the product. Again, the customer's understanding of value is closely linked to price, and most consumers know little about jewelry.

The same thing could apply to clothing, but the perceived value may be a function more of snob appeal. Designer jeans are an excellent example. One brand of prewashed jeans carries a retail price twice that of high-quality, heavier, new denim jeans at the same store. To duplicate the appearance, but admittedly not the label, take the less expensive ones and wash them a few times. But price and labeling are integral to the marketing strategy.

In the case of the typewriter ribbons, however, lowering the price may not only increase ribbon sales by discouraging use of "will-fit" brands but also actually increase machine sales and other merchandise in the store.

Quite often new products that are directly competitive with existing brands use the introductory price strategy. By gaining wider acceptance through that price strategy, it may be easier to raise prices later. The initial lower price is part of the direct cost of advertising. That same money could be spent on more media buying, for example, but that would naturally depend on what the competitive strategy indicates.

Market Share

The next major strategy concept used to raise sales revenue is to increase market share. We hear a lot about market share in the business press. Most of the time these are slivers of a multimillion unit market. Cars, cigarettes, and beer are the most obvious examples. In all three cases a market share change of less than one-tenth of 1 percent represents sales revenue of many millions of dollars. For those of us in small business, it's hard to relate to those kinds of numbers. Let's be realistic and see what this concept can mean for us.

Market share means nothing more than the share or fraction of the market. The share may be expressed in fractions or percentage points. The choice is usually a factor of how many are in the market. Perhaps some more basic definitions are in order.

Market is the total of all the potential customers for our product or service. All home builders, whether a large general contractor with several developments under construction or a single pickup with magnetic sign, and everything in between, comprise the home builders' market for such things as tools, supplies, and new-installation major appliances. All recreation-minded adults may be the market for golf equipment. It is just as valid to describe all golfers as the market.

Another way is to say that the market is the opposite of *segment*. Segment is the smallest homogeneous fraction. Market is the largest target group.

Share does not mean the Sunday school concept of dividing equally. Share is whatever portion of the market we can sell. In other words, if four golfers buy clubs and two buy Walter Haig, one buys Spaulding, and one buys Wilson, then market share for Haig is half, with one-quarter each for Spaulding and Wilson.

You would probably be in violation of the U.S. antitrust laws if you and a competitor even talked about how to divide the market. If you talked about which kind of customer you wanted and agreed to a mutual pricing policy, no matter how small your business, you can and likely would be prosecuted. Just like football, you must understand your own strengths and resources and use them to achieve your objectives. Opposing coaches don't decide together what their game strategies will be.

In small business it is more likely that you are competing with a relatively small number of others for market share. The grocery store may seem to have much competition, but not necessarily. If it is a convenience store located in or near a residential neighborhood, carrying small packages of supplies, staples, and quick food and maintaining long hours, it isn't directly competing with the supermarket. The supermarket carries a wider variety of merchandise and package sizes, focuses on price, and keeps the overhead as low as possible by fewer open hours and higher inventory turnover per square foot of store. Geographic segmentation also reduces the total market.

In a city with six heavy-truck dealerships, most of the competition is between two or three. They are the only ones that cater to the dominant form of trucking in the area, whether logging, construction, or highway hauling. Trucks are a good example for another reason. The truck manufacturers talk about market share by truck weight and horsepower class. But in fact the manufacturers build the truck with a particular mission in mind, and the dealer sells the truck to users whose application is suitable. They each have small fractions of the others' dominant market segment.

In the case of the grocery stores and the truck dealers each has a percentage of the total market but a larger share of the market segment that they're serving. In another hypothetical example, assume that 12 families are buying cars. There are three car brands to choose from. One retails at $5,000, one at $10,000, and one at $15,000. Four families buy the $5,000 car, four buy the $10,000 model, and four buy the $15,000 car. Each car, therefore, has a one-third market share. But each has total market segment for the price classes. None of the cars directly competes with one another, because each appeals to a different market segment. Yet each can claim only one-third market share.

Why is this definition clarification of so much concern? Like everything else in the book, it is to help focus the marketing efforts on the things that can be done best. If you are a small convenience store in one of the major North American cities, your market share for that city is miniscule. But if you define market segment shares as the convenience store customers in your neighborhood, you can more effectively spend your advertising dollar. That's why you need to define your market: simply for efficient use of your resources.

Increased Market Share

To increase market share brings into action many of the concepts that we've discussed. One simple way to increase market share is to try to add another market segment to our customer base. Let's see how that would work.

The office equipment dealer sells primarily typewriters for business use, light- to moderate-duty applications. An insurance company establishes a local underwriting office. The typing and clerical staff will exceed 50 people, most needing typewriters of some variety. In a city of 100,000 an office of that size has considerable impact on the local economy. Many small and medium city office equipment dealers don't sell that many typewriters in a year. The total market for typewriters has expanded considerably. But our office equipment dealer friend still won't be able to realize any gain in market share; in fact, because the market is now larger, his share potentially is smaller.

What is the obvious strategy? (How many cases do you know where people missed the obvious?) Expand into another market segment. In this case add a line or models that are developed for the heavy typing requirements of an insurance office. By being the first local firm moving into that segment, our friend stands an excellent chance of capturing the new segment in its entirety.

Many small office equipment firms missed out altogether when word processors came along, expanding the market by creating a new segment, although at the expense of some conventional machines. By allowing the new segment to be dominated by the larger, direct-sales organizations or large dealers, they missed significant growth opportunities, and we all know what the opposite of growth is.

Truck sales provide another example. During the late 1970s fuel prices began to climb. Many pickup and delivery fleet owners began to realize that diesel engines were much more efficient and although more expensive, they would pay for themselves in fuel savings even though mileage covered wasn't high. What was high was operating time, which obviously consumed fuel. When the discovery was made by those fleets that other operating costs were lower with diesel due to less frequent maintenance requirements, the growth of diesels for the medium trucks began in earnest. Most of the American truck manufacturers building for the medium-range category, such as used by parcel delivery and food and beverage distributors, weren't prepared. The European builders had proven trucks all ready to go, because they were used in Europe for many years. When medium trucks were segmented into gasoline and diesel power, not everyone was ready.

By expanding into newly created segments or adjacent segments to the existing position, do not overlook the negative considerations. That is, don't expand into segments that don't fit well for position or geography or other customer groupings and won't be complementary to and compatible with your current customer base. Some of the potential dangers of that strategy are discussed in Chapter 3.

Although we are on the one hand saying not to be overly concerned with market share and on the other hand giving examples of how to expand market share by adding segments, perhaps we should see why this seemingly contradictory discussion is important.

Importance of Market Share

The simple, straightforward reason to expand market share is to expand one measurement of dominance by any given firm. We talk about and measure market share as much as we do because it's the measurement that most people understand. But, consistent with the discussion earlier, doesn't it make more sense to concentrate on a smaller number of segments and dominate those segments? That way, your resources can be focused more effectively. To illustrate, let's look at a totally imaginary situation to understand why segment share may be more important than market share.

There are 100 types of chairs selling well in your area. Each type represents a different quality and price level or different use application. Some are for dining room use, some for vacation residence use, some for offices, some for pool side; the price varies from less than $10 for a deck chair to more than $250 for a high-quality dining room chair. First, let's consider some physical requirements. Think of the space required to have only one sample of each in stock and the inventory control problem maintaining that level. Second, consider the impact on management time dealing with many different wholesalers and manufacturers' representatives and handling that many shipment arrivals. But I'm not terribly concerned with those considerations at the moment, despite their impact on operations.

Carefully consider the impact alone on your advertising and sales efforts. How can you possibly advertise all 100 chairs adequately? Use microscopic ads in the appropriate sections of the local newspaper? No one will notice. Advertise all simultaneously? Those looking for dining room chairs will be confused with the deck chairs and the office chairs and not see what they want.

Take this ridiculous example one step further. To keep the arithmetic simple, suppose that there are 9 competitive stores, for a total of 10. Each sells the same dollar volume of chairs, meaning that each has a mix in price ranges and application. Each store has $100,000 in annual sales. Nine of the stores concentrate on one segment each by functional use, with a range of price segments within the use segment. The remaining store handles all 100 chairs.

The market is $1 million in annual sales of chairs. Each store has a 10 percent market share. Nine have control of their segments. One has a little bit from each segment. The nine stores focus their advertising in media that reach the segments that they're serving, and their salespeople work with the most likely prospects. The remaining store has spread its resources so thin, covering advertising and sales efforts in all segments, that practically no impact is made. But each store has equal market shares.

It doesn't take a genius to see that this scenario will remain static for only a short time. The first likely victim will be the store with 100 chairs. The remaining battle will be among survivors trying to get segments and shares from the others.

The lesson here is not only understanding the significance of market share and segment domination but is admittedly another variation of the theme developed in Chapter 3. By focusing on the segment most likely to offer growth and concentrating resources on that segment, you establish a clear position. Simultaneously market share growth has been profitably enhanced.

Like all of marketing, it is difficult to look at any one element, technique, strategy, or other portion without seeing something of the interrelating and correlating parts. In other words, truly independent study of the parts is impossible.

Whether we want to increase our market share by adding market segments or increasing our penetration in our current segments, we need to look at some specific tactics that can be used to increase sales revenue, which is the real objective.

Methods of Increasing Share

There are *five* principal ways to increase market share. It is impossible to consider any of these options without considering their impact on the overall position strategy, but let's try to isolate these options as much as possible.

Changing product quality can increase market share. Whether it is improved or degraded, product quality can have significant effect on share. Product quality includes perceived or strictly aesthetic changes. One school of thought suggests that any change will get attention. Right or wrong, that thinking is merely an extension of studies in a manufacturing production facility and often cited, whereby lighting changes, both increases and decreases, caused production to increase. The researchers felt that just paying attention to the labor force caused the improvement. But because this isn't a work on industrial labor relations and productivity, I'll avoid the argument. Even if valid as applied to the marketing sector, it is unlikely that small businesses have enough unit volume to isolate and measure the effects of product change on unit sales increase or decrease and any direct or indirect correlation.

But we need to discuss in specific terms both positive and negative results in product quality improvements or degradations. Start with the more obvious product improvements that bring about positive effects on unit volume, thus market share, again assuming *no* other changes. If outdoor chairs are painted a more attractive color and the webbing is color-coordinated, it's safe to assume that unit volume will increase immediately. If driver seating is improved, truck sales will increase. Better seams will increase the sale of clothing. There are many examples of cases where product improvement resulted in increased sales volume.

Should the product quality increase too much, particularly in products about which the average customer knows little, such as jewelry or computers, and most of the changes are merely aesthetic, it's possible to have a negative effect. The reasons are not always clear, but the probable cause is an undermining of customer confidence. If the customers perceive the aesthetics to be substantially better than the other elements of marketing, such as price, they may actually distrust the inner workings because there is no practical way to be sure. In other words, it may be possible to make the product so attractive that its appearance is not in keeping with the rest of the position strategy, and the customers will think that the important mechanism or circuitry, or whatever, has been correspondingly cheapened.

The corollary is the degradation of product quality that results in increased unit volume. This can work well, particularly for items of infrequent purchase by customers with little knowledge of the product. Such a case might be restaurant meals. Haven't you seen "bistro dinners" or "businessman's steak sandwich"? Both cases are describing meals that would seem inexpensive and contain less food volume. And yet, at least from my experience, the prices don't indicate cheap meals. So actually degrading the product but retaining the price results in increased sales by appealing to the person's sense of economy, diet, or both.

Briefcases may be a more obvious example. By removing the internal dividers, locks, or button from the briefcase, it would be assumed that the price would be lower because the product would be perceived to be simpler. To restate the ground rules, pricing has not been changed; because the briefcase in question appears to be simple, the natural assumption is that the price is lower than for comparable quality at another store. If the customer wanted a simple briefcase to carry the paper, lunch, or whatever, the simple but good-looking unit would probably sell better than the one with dividers at the same price level. Perception is the key.

In the area of service, if the dry cleaner offered both a valet service by using hangers and garment bags and featuring automatic free repairs versus a quick service, but in fact did no differentiation other than naming and packaging, *in fact* performing the *same* services at the same price, most customers would opt for the quick service for older clothes and valet service for newer or more expensive garments. There are similar cases where lowering perceived product quality will increase sales.

We probably don't need to spend as much time on the obvious cases where product quality is lessened and the result is lower unit volume. Adding more sawdust to the hamburger isn't likely to increase unit volume. Clothes returning from the cleaners unrepaired or pressed wrong won't increase unit volume, unless you count the resultant re-do. And that's not profitable volume.

Customer Support Services

The next major area to affect unit volume is the customer support services. Customer support services include all the things done to keep the customer happy, including use training and after-sale repair and maintenance.

Two personal computers have practically identical features. They both have 64K RAM, 8K Buss, letter-quality printer, and software that's interchangeable. But two differences exist. One selling agent does not have any facilities for repair or maintenance of the equipment. When a machine malfunctions, the customer must go to an outside firm for service, which removes the selling agent from responsibility and accountability, whether the actual repair is covered by warranty or not. If in addition the problem were found not to be hardware-related but caused either by software problems or lack of adequate operator training, the independent agent would be at an even worse disadvantage. Buying an automobile through a broker would have some of the same risks to the customer. However, most drivers know more about care, operation, and maintenance, or at least where to go, than personal computer customers.

In these examples we're assuming that the pricing strategies are identical. In real life they probably would be significantly different due to the alternative distribution channels.

Clothing probably would not require significant customer support facilities, nor would groceries. Jewelry could, assuming watch sales were included, but support service would not be as crucial to sales.

Deciding whether customer support services should be added or improved is a function of studying the niches in the market for your product or service. If the nature of the business not only requires but also places a high degree of emphasis on customer support services, you should coordinate your advertising and sales efforts and also the "presentation" of your service to maximize the benefits to the customer. Briefly, do this with a neat and clean service department and well-designed materials for customer education and provide adequate training for the employees who work with the customers.

Sales Effort

Another major area to be addressed is *sales effort*. We will spend considerable time elsewhere discussing the management of the sales force. Here let us look just at the likely effects of increasing by adding both more salespeople and making the salespeople on staff more effective. Consider the generic description to include both quantity and effectiveness.

Usually it is assumed that increasing the sales effort will more or less automatically increase sales. To a point, that's true. By increasing the number of customers that the salespeople contact and make presentations, sales will likely increase. If the salespeople are talking to more people about typewriters, successfully closing more sales should follow fairly predictably.

But there are cases where an individual business or even an industry will increase the sales effort so much that sales will actually decrease for a time. It essentially is a result of not segmenting the market adequately and overloading some niches. Poor planning results in too many salespeople chasing too few sales.

Two phenomena occur to decrease sales. First, some customers are repelled by the pressure, bow their necks, and refuse to buy anything. That's a common but strictly emotional reaction. Second, too many salespeople may present too many different messages and confuse the customer so that the decision-making process is completely muddled, the input circuits overloaded, and the customer can't come to a decision.

This can happen to either industry, as occurs periodically in office duplicating products or life and accident insurance, or to an individual firm. The latter seldom happens other than automobile sales, audio reproduction equipment, or major appliances.

The symptom is too many salespeople physically approaching the customer. There is obviously some awkward shuffling about while they try to decide the pecking order. Finally one takes over the presentation. The perception by the customer is that too much pressure is being applied, and the customer will usually turn and run. Some firms use this technique to sort out lazy salespeople or use this tactic to increase sales short-term by keeping pressure on vulnerable customers.

In commercial and industrial environments this overkill tactic almost always has negative repercussions for the company or industry. Good planning and segmentation should avoid this problem.

Advertising and Promotion

Advertising and promotion can also result in sales revenue increases. Returning to planning, the only time that advertising and promotion will work against you is if you generate more interest than you can fill. Disappointed customers quickly become disgruntled customers, and word of mouth will more than offset the positive exposure of the advertising.

Increasing the amount of advertising alone won't suffice. We'll talk elsewhere about effective advertising, but consider here that if you don't provide so many options as to confuse the customer, and the advertising is aimed correctly for your audience using the correct media, it's hard to make much of a mistake on our level. We're not spending millions to achieve a small fractional percentage of market share. We need to get the message out only to a relatively small number of customers.

New Products or Services

New products or services are another way to increase sales revenue. Studying the marketing plan may help identify possible products or services that are not as available to customers as they should be. Before you seriously pursue the addition of products, take into consideration how good the fit is.

Consider all implications when adding a new product. Inventory costs, additional customer support facilities, more advertising requirements, display space, and similar logistic issues need to be addressed. If, after considering all those things, it appears that you will attain sufficient volume to be profitable in an acceptable period, and you decide to proceed, stop and look at one most important consideration: the customer.

I am assuming that you have identified the prospective customer for your new product. You have determined that you can get sufficient segment penetration to achieve a level of sales to be profitable. But have you carefully considered who that customer is? Is that customer considerably different from your existing customer? Will the new product increase your business with existing customers or will you be doing business with a whole new group of customers?

The temptation to move into a new market niche or to serve a new customer group sometimes overpowers common sense. Doesn't it seem logical to stay with your present customers? Changing or adding customers is risky for two reasons. First, you divide your advertising and sales resources among more markets. Second, you and your employees know the current customers, their expectations, and personal idiosyncrasies and how to make them happy. When considering new products or services to increase your sales revenue, make sure that the customers for the new product are the same customers as for the existing line or at least are from the same segment of the market.

If you decide to add a line that brings a substantially different customer, you may erode your existing customer base. If that is likely, make sure that the new customer potential is worth the risk. During transition you may lose the old customer but not quickly add the new while the business is changing the position that it occupies in the mind of the audience. The only answer to that dilemma is a complete understanding of the arithmetic of the old and new customer bases and the effect of an interruption in your cash flow while the transition period works itself out.

Market Demand

Market demand is, for all practical purposes, beyond the control of the small business. But it is necessary to look at the factors that would alter market demand so that they are recognized and appropriate tactics devised should they occur.

Market growth or shrinkage falls into the uncontrollable category. Population changes affect the grocery store, both for total volume and types of merchandise sold. More households where all adults are employed increased the sale of convenience foods. Lower birth rates affected baby food. Those types of examples are well known and written about frequently in the business and general press.

Less well known at this point is the growth of numbers of small businesses. How does this growth affect marketing? For one thing, more businesses require more office equipment, particularly accounting and computer equipment. Store fixtures and furnishings also are required. All types of professional services have increased opportunities with small businesses.

Government policies also affect sales. The change in agriculture and timber harvests are to a large extent controlled by government policies, either directly or indirectly. An increase in the wheat harvest requires more diesel fuel, machinery, labor, transportation, etc. Increased timber harvesting on publicly owned lands requires more supplies and equipment; but the harvest rate is certainly not controlled by small business, and not even by big business, other than the home mortgage market. War, rumors of war, pestilence, and natural disasters can cause increases and decreases in business opportunities.

But other than natural disasters, most market size changes can be predicted fairly closely if the planning process is part of your management program. Reading the business and general press along with a continual monitoring of your customer base should provide clues to market size changes that may affect you.

We don't need to dwell on what to do to adjust to changes. Everyone knows (but few practice) that sales and advertising expenditures should not be cut during market shrinkage if the shrinkage is not believed permanent. Many firms in a position to collect and study before-and-after data found that they increased market share by advertising during an economic downturn. True, the market shrank and their sales may have actually gone down, but when the recovery came, their increased share remained; the increased market meant substantially increased sales because both market and share growth were realized. We've all read about those studies, but how many of us have the courage to take advantage of that situation?

Other uncontrollable factors that would affect sales revenue are *competitors' entrance and exit* from the market place. Perhaps they didn't maintain advertising during the economic slump and became a victim or didn't lower their variable overhead sufficiently. At any rate their departure means an increase in your market share, which in turn should mean an increase in sales revenue.

Looking first at the effects of competitor exit from the market, when would such an event actually have a negative influence on your sales? The answer, like all answers, lies with the customer's perception. If the customer thinks that the competitor was well established and profitable and still quit the arena, customers may decide to cut back on their own spending to conserve cash for an overall downturn in business. Even if that dire circumstance isn't perceived by the customer, your business may still suffer because the competitors' marketing efforts aren't interacting with yours to raise the customers' awareness of your product, and the "out of sight, out of mind" syndrome sets in.

Perhaps, particularly in commercial and industrial markets, the competitors' salespeople, or the service department for that matter, came in contact with many customers frequently. But due to their poor sales or service practices, such as late deliveries, overpricing, poor quality—perhaps the very factors that caused their exit—they alienated many customers. But without them in the market getting customers mad at them, the customers no longer spend the mental resources looking for a good alternative supplier—you—and in fact scale down their purchases altogether. But if everything is equal, which it seldom is, a competitor's exit should leave a gap in the market, which you should be able to fill and increase your market share *and* your sales revenue.

The situations whereby the exit from the market of a competitor causes a decrease in your sales normally are short-term, a few weeks or months. We talk about wishing that we didn't have much competition, but in fact some weak competition is better than no competition. At any rate after the adjustment period a competitor's exit from the market should work to our advantage, so long as we still have some competition. But don't overlook the possibility that the exit may be a harbinger of an eventual disappearance of the market. Try to learn exactly the reasons, not the stated excuses or the "street" explanation, for the loss of a competitor.

When the competitor enters your market, that entrance, if done even partially right, will stir up interest in the product and you should get some residual effect. If the grand opening of a competitive firm doesn't result in an increase in your business fairly quickly, after the initial shock waves you may be in serious trouble. If stirring up the market by your competitors doesn't help you to some extent by temporarily effectively expanding the market (even though your share may be down), your customers were probably looking for and welcoming an alternative to your firm.

The best factor that you can't control but is a big help to your business, is the competitor with a weak sales force. If the competitive sales force works hard, talks to a lot of customers, has an organized lead generation program, but *doesn't close* sales, you will be the beneficiary. By the same token make sure that your salespeople aren't the ones helping your competitor by not aggressively closing sales. Weak competition is the best competition. Pray that weak competition survives and is not replaced by a well-operated firm.

Don't blame your shrinking sales and declining market share on the competitors. They are succeeding because you are failing to deliver what the customers want and need, even if only in perception. Your knowing what is best for them may salve your conscience, but it won't help your cash flow.

In one sense the entrance of a competitor to the market may be indirectly controllable by you. Make sure that you know why you are getting additional competition. Is it because the market is growing? Or is your penetration shrinking so much as to allow an opening that encourages a new competitor? Misreading the signs can be disastrous.

Probably the best and most practical way for a small business to gather more information on market demand is to do customer research. You no doubt have read that large multinational corporations do market research to learn why they lose customers. But there is no good reason for you not to do research also.

As discussed in Chapter 3, simple, easy-to-conduct, informal surveys that you can do may be sufficient. Strenuously avoid using customer survey research to confirm your predispositions. If you think that you are losing customers due to price alone, your research will confirm that. By the same token, if your eroding customer base is being caused by large out-of-town firms, I suspect that your research will confirm that also. But if you honestly approach the problem without any preconceived ideas as to why business is slipping, you stand a better chance of finding what's wrong.

Monitor your customer activity carefully at all times. In Chapter 10 we'll look at how to do this simply but adequately for your needs. But if a customer or group of customers is missing for any length of time, or the patterns of activity with you are changing, find out how much is changing and why, quickly. Find out by asking the customers. Write down their responses, not your interpretation of their responses. See if a pattern develops. Validate their responses by checking the consistency with their actions, individually or as a group. Learn why you have new competition.

Too many firms try to keep competition out at all costs. Should you have new competition, don't panic. One strategy that may be profitable is to scale back on market share goals, increase penetration of fewer segments, and maintain profitability by that means.

Trying to "buy" market share by discounting is attempted disturbingly frequently. Customers who can be bought on the basis of price are normally not a good base on which to build. Some will always go with price, but if that is your only significant advantage over the competition, you are vulnerable. Anyone else can decide to operate with lower overhead, lower margin, or higher inventory turnover and beat you on price; you may not have those options.

Summary

Understand clearly all the factors that can affect your sales revenue. Make sure that you understand the result of changing prices, both the positive and negative results of lowering and raising your prices. In other words your pricing strategy must be carefully considered so that it meshes with your other marketing element strategies.

Study market share information. This information for small businesses is best obtained by informal interviews by you and employees and by comparing results in staff discussions. Some cases, such as car dealerships, have registration data from the state to study. Any industry that is regulated requires some type of data. That's a help.

Study total market demand. Is the market growing due to intramarket causes or external causes? Is the change in market size due to competitor entrances or exits? Why are competitors arriving or leaving? To understand that requires complete understanding of the customer base.

All through this discussion, and those in most of the other chapters, the recurring theme is planning and customer knowledge. If you get nothing else from this but an appreciation for a total understanding of the customer and how to do quality planning, your time and money will be well spent. In a small business we have the wonderful flexibility that big business does not. When big business learns about significant changes in the customer or the market, it can't react or anticipate as well as we can. That's our chief advantage. But we can use big business's techniques, developed at huge expense, to understand our market and our customers. Don't reinvent the wheel. Learn from big business, but don't try to copy it.

5

Sales Force Development: Organization, Recruitment, and Compensation

Most business managers, no matter what their area of primary responsibility, tend to blame poor sales performance on lazy or, at least, ineffective salespeople. Either or both responses may be correct. But is the ineffective salesperson created by poor sales management, or did management inherit the salesperson's bad traits?

Firing the salesperson may not cure anything. Adding more salespeople may not improve anything. Paying straight commission may not solve anything. In order to be an effective sales manager, all these issues and more need to be addressed.

Sales management is the science *and* art of managing the sales force. We will not go into actual sales techniques to any great extent for the simple reason that so many books, pamphlets, cassette tapes, and seminars are available on the subject of sales techniques. But there seems to be a shortage of literature on sales management, or sales force development, written particularly for small business applications. What little I've read seems aimed at the larger corporation field sales manager who has several layers of management over him or her and the sales management job itself is only one step up the ladder from senior sales or account management.

The Sales Manager

Sales management or sales force development usually falls to the senior salesperson in the small firm. In ranking of pecking order, the sales manager typically is equal to the office manager or service manager or if those positions are not filled, the position is below the owner or principal.

There are no magic solutions as to who makes a good sales manager or who in your company is the best for you or any other consideration of that nature. What we can do is reiterate that the sales manager is the orchestra leader and should at least be able to read music. The duties also include administrative functions, particularly in the preparation and reporting of sales efforts and performances, graph preparations, counseling, and similar duties. Therefore, the best salesperson may or may not be the best sales manager.

You may not need a separate position. The best guide to use is whether you have four full-time salespeople or more. If so, a separate position is probably indicated, but two people in full-time sales may require a part-time sales-sales manager position. Somehow all the various sales development techniques discussed here need to be implemented but shouldn't require a great deal of time per salesperson. The reason that four is suggested as the point when a full-time sales manager is indicated stems from the personnel management concept that no one should try to directly supervise more than five or six people, and certainly full-time supervision shouldn't be needed for less than four.

In a small firm profitability for each employee is necessary. We can't afford to carry dead weight. So a sales manager with four salespeople probably needs to manage some territory or accounts to help pay the overhead, but those direct sales duties should not detract from the sales management job.

Sales management compensation appears an even bigger mystery than sales compensation. Other duties not connected with normal sales management duties take time and probably should be accounted for with a straight salary. Sales management usually gets an override payment of approximately 10 percent of the commission of each salesperson. Four equally successful salespeople provide the sales manager with an income of only 40 percent of what could be made as a salesperson. These considerations and the careful consideration of the time impact of other duties, such as handling the advertising, participating in general management, etc., should all be considered when penciling out a sales manager's compensation package. The sales manager normally also requires a larger expense account and time to participate in trade, service, professional, and educational groups.

The one last parting thought on sales management compensation is to develop and test on paper various combinations of packages. But the sales manager should be rewarded for maintaining a stable, productive sales force, although the straight salary is probably not the best way to reinforce and reward. Try various override percentages on for size. Consider what is normal for your industry and geographic area. Direct compensation and perks are more important for management than for salespeople because salespeople theoretically have a chance to improve their income via performance.

If your firm can't justify a separate sales management position and the owner and general manager also serves as sales manager, then the assumption is that the sales force is small, say, one or two people. But that doesn't lessen the importance of any sales force development techniques. Firms of that size have less room for error and need as much performance from each employee as possible, so taking care of all aspects of the business is extremely important for survival and profitability.

Another quite common situation is the senior salesperson holding the title of sales manager and yet in fact barely having the name, much less the duties and responsibilities. In the process of describing what a sales manager can do to affect sales performance, we will try to place the position where it should correctly be in small business.

A sales manager, strictly speaking, does not manage sales. It may be the job of top management to plan and execute delivery of products sold. Usually the operating plan in a small business is controlled by the principal. The operating plan deals with management of sales.

The sales manager manages the salespeople. The job may hold some secondary responsibilities in the other areas of marketing, but the primary responsibility is the hiring, training, motivating, and evaluating of salespeople. The sales manager may also have some impact on the design of the sales compensation program, advertising, sales forecasting, and other related areas. But the primary, extremely important responsibility is the management of the sales force.

A common misconception is that a good salesperson does not make a good sales manager. This may or may not be true, like all oversimplified generalizations. By completely understanding the job of the sales manager, we can determine when and under what circumstances the star salesperson will be a good sales manager. Too often the senior salesperson or the top performing salesperson is given the title and responsibility of sales manager without understanding what the job is or should be. Usually when that happens, two negative results occur. First, that salesperson's performance goes down to the point that the person may no longer be the top producing salesperson; second, interaction with the other salespeople takes on a nonconstructive slant so that in fact their performance also suffers.

The person who is given the title of sales manager and the responsibilities of the job without understanding what is involved will experience downturn in personal sales production while trying to learn the job. During the learning process in the new job, time and energy are spent apart from direct sales efforts developing the new relationship with management. As different questions arise about the new job duties and responsibilities, time must be spent learning the methods of dealing with those questions. Among other things time will be spent getting definitions of limits of responsibility. Should your sales manager make the decisions about advertising? approve expense accounts? handle all sales leads no matter what geographic area or product line? Should the new sales manager have primary contact with suppliers?

These questions and more arise whenever you install a new sales manager. The problem is particularly difficult if it is a new position and the firm is growing fairly rapidly. If the position existed previously, you at least have some precedence to guide you, whether you want to honor or deliberately overturn precedence. By discussing the issues facing sales management, you can make some decisions as to how you want to structure the job and how to make it as profitable as possible.

Your particular firm may not have a separate sales manager. Or the sales manager may have other duties aside from direct sales responsibility. More typical is the situation where the sales manager for the small firm also is a part-time salesperson.

The general rule for supervisors is that not more than six people should be directly supervised by one person. For sales, that suggestion is equally valid. So the upper limits of the sales force of six people and the lower limits of one full-time salesperson require someone serving in the sales manager function. Should you have more than six salespeople, split the groups by geography or product line or some other logical division so that each salesperson receives adequate supervision and assistance.

In short, the sales manager is responsible for hiring, evaluating, training, and sales forecasting. All other duties are tangential to those primary functions. Therefore, we need to spend some time looking at the nature of the sales job from management's perspective in order to understand what the sales manager is supervising.

Forecasting

Whether you have enough salespeople or need to add or subtract is strictly a numerical decision. From the evidence that you gathered in the marketing plan process, is there enough sales potential to support the salespeople whom you have or think you have?

Sales forecasting is the name of this process. For a small firm, adequate sales forecasting probably consists of graphically depicting sales volume for five years ago, last year, and this year and projecting your reasonable and conservative estimate for the trend line next year after considering the feedback of the salespeople. When drawing the line as done on Figure 5–1, consider carefully all elements involved in the marketing plan. If trade association, chamber of commerce, or any and all other outside projections and guesses are available, include those in your considerations. Don't accept any as gospel but don't ignore any.

When you finish projecting your growth curve and folding in the information from outside sources, you will probably want to revise your final figure downward. Despite your best efforts, your advertising may not produce as many leads, a member of your sales force may quit or move away, you or some other key employee may get ill, there may be deaths in the family or the death of an employee. Those factors usually are ignored when small firms make forecasts. When actual results are less than anticipated, budget shortfalls and poor cash flow result. The best way to avoid that problem is to plan for fewer sales than logic suggests would be reasonable. But make sure that your marketing and operating plans can be adjusted to reflect actual results.

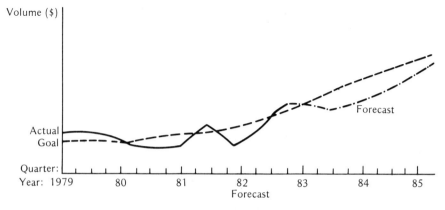

FIGURE 5–1. Forecast of Sales Volume

The Salesperson

The salesperson's job in simple terms consists of representing the company to the customer and, equally important, representing the customer to the company. In other words all the salesperson's duties consist of acting as an intermediary between the customer and the company. The sales manager's job is to control this customer-salesperson-company interaction for the good of the company.

Because of the importance of the customer-company interaction, recent research has found that the most successful salespeople have equal parts of ego drive and customer empathy. In other words the successful salesperson is equally driven by the need to succeed and by an empathetic relation with the customer. Either trait in excess results in a lack of goal-oriented activity or a lack of customer concern. Without the need to succeed, a salesperson won't. At the same time, without concern for the customer's problems, sales success will be temporary. Understanding these personality traits for sales career success will help the sales manager guide the sales force. Figure 5–2 illustrates a way to think about how much empathy or ego drive controls a salesperson's behavior, and the results.

The salesperson has more effect on your company than any other single factor. The personal contact between your customer and the company is more important than physical facilities, advertising, or product pricing and packaging. People still do business with people. There is no way to automate personal interaction.

The sales profession requires an interesting set of skills and attitudes. At this point we won't go into any detail as to what skill and attitude mix you may need for your situation, but it is sufficient to say that the emphasis is on

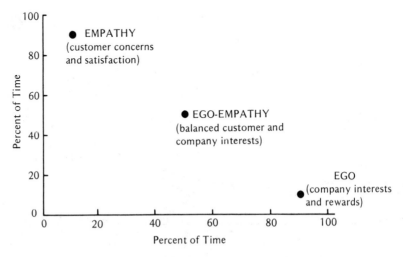

FIGURE 5–2. Salesperson Behavior Pattern

relating to people. That implies that weaknesses may exist in areas requiring much structure, such as paperwork and administration.

A salesperson has a lonely job, although potentially rewarding. When salespeople are communicating with the customer, they are alone. No one else can do what they are doing at that particular moment. No one can determine how any given salesperson can be most effective. No one can tell how they should handle objections to the sales presentation or how best to handle complaints after the sale. Those and many other decisions must be made on the basis of judgment and intuition.

Emotion plays a key role in the life of the salesperson. To have the courage to ask for the order requires a great deal of self-confidence. Many otherwise excellent salespeople do presentations and proposals, handle objections and customer complaints, organize their time to result in a high number of contacts with qualified prospects, but can't close a significant percentage of sales due to lack of self-confidence. When I say emotion, how else would you describe self-confidence? There is no logical explanation as to why one person knows and understands the limits of ability and the next person doesn't, even though both have identical education, job experience, and ability.

Physiological studies found that salespeople actually experienced more rapid pulse rates and high body temperatures when closing a sale. That point in the customer-salesperson relationship is the pressure point. The salesperson is forcing the customer to make a decision. The customer is forcing the salesperson to practice something difficult: discipline.

The salesperson is responsible for developing sales leads, qualifying the prospect as to financial ability to pay and whether the product will benefit the prospect, make the presentation of the benefits, close the sale and follow up any postsale requirements. That is the sales job in a capsule. If you understand that, you can do a better job of guiding the sales manager, who in turn guides the salespeople.

For most small businesses the expense of a salesperson is larger than almost any other single expense paid on a monthly basis. Almost any other resource that a firm uses that costs upward of $3,000 a month or more would get far more attention than the salespeople do in most firms. But like any other expense, you should get something in return. The key may be with the sales manager. But to understand what the sales manager can do, we need to understand the salesperson's environment.

The Sales Program

The *sales program* is the term used to describe the overall operation of the sales force. The sales program includes the description of the exact duties of the salespeople, the compensation plan, the goal-setting and activity-planning process of the sales department, and the evaluation process of both the department and the individual salespeople.

Sales is but one of the elements of the marketing program. Advertising, distribution, and pricing are the other elements. Sales is frequently, but incorrectly, used as a synonym for marketing, as in *sales and marketing*. They are closely related but separate fields of endeavor. Although it may be impossible to examine the sales force completely independent of the other marketing elements, we will try to do so in order to understand better how all the pieces fit together. We will look at the sales program to see if it is consistent with several factors in the marketing strategy.

Consistency with Market Position

Is the sales program consistent with the market position established? Because the sales force has personal contact with the customer, it is critical that the sales force project the position in the market established by the firm. To illustrate, it will be easier to look at extreme cases. Should you be established at an upper price position, providing quality products and services, your salespeople must also communicate that message. In clothing the salespeople must be tastefully dressed, whether conservatively or in high fashion, with colors and accessories coordinated such as you would like your customers to look. The salespeople should not be dressed in high-fashion, trendy clothes if you are selling primarily tailored clothes for the professional and businessman or woman. Equally inappropriate would be the conservatively dressed salesperson selling high-fashion merchandise to the younger age brackets or entertainment clientele.

It may be even easier to see the relationship in an auto dealership. Mercedes or Cadillacs are built and sold for upper-income customers. Generally those customers are fairly conservative. Salespeople casually dressed in high-fashion styles will not put the customers at ease. That mode of dress may be more correct for the sports car dealership, or even dealers located in entertainment centers, but not for most car dealerships.

Also, even though most salespeople tend to above-average intelligence and education, considerable emphasis should be placed on making sure that the educational level of the salespeople is similar to most of the customers, not very far below but certainly not too high above the level of the customers.

Should your position in the market be that of leadership, and you present the image of innovation and advanced products or services or market dominance by virtue of customer quantity higher than your competition, it will also be important that your salespeople project that image as well. They should be an extension of the leadership position of the firm by their expertise in the product and their leadership in community or trade groups.

Basically make sure that the customers can identify with and relate to the salespeople. The customers and the salespeople should match in life styles, as well as socioeconomic and demographic groupings. A mismatch will mean that the customer will not be at ease. One of the principal concerns that we must have in business is to be easy to buy from, which could include everything from credit terms to salespeople who are compatible with the customers.

Consistency with Company Objectives

Company objective is another significant consideration for consistency. A group of hyperactive salespeople whose inclination is high sales volume for short periods of time would not be consistent with the market position of a stable conservative leadership role by the firm. The firm that projects the image of rock-solid, long-term conservative customer relations would not be able to gain the most from salespeople who were more inclined to the quick close. There is nothing wrong with either strategy, but mixing the two won't work for any length of time. The two types of strategies are at opposite ends of the spectrum and will normally succeed best with two different types of customers, assuming that all else is equal. The result of improper mixing is that neither group of customers will be penetrated in sufficient quantity to maximize the market segment.

Consistency with Product Objectives

Another way to determine if the salespeople are consistent with the company objective is to ascertain consistency not only with market position but also with product objectives. When the product mix allows the salespeople some latitude, but certain products clearly represent entrance into a different market segment from the mainstream of the business, the company objectives need to be clearly understood. The product mix may not suggest the company objective. If some or all of the salespeople don't emphasize the company objective with the products that they sell, again the customers will be confused. In addition, the products that were supposed to be complementary to the objective will instead dilute the main effort. The product that was to be the main objective was chosen for that role due to growth or profit potential. Other products will detract from that important purpose.

Perhaps salespeople sell products or services that you prefer not to emphasize because they either don't have adequate information, at least from their point of view, or find the intended focus product difficult to sell. Telling salespeople what to sell isn't sufficient. They must understand and believe in the products before they can successfully be sold for more than short periods of time. Even preferential or loaded commissions won't work by themselves.

Consistency with Services and Applications

Services and applications are another set of variables that must be consistent between the salespeople and the customer groups. The salespeople need to be attuned to the customer and product. If the product requires considerable customer application or operator education, then "hyper" personalities will not do well. For that matter, the methodical lawyer-engineer types won't relate to the customers who want simple and quick solutions to problems.

Selling office equipment in the 1980s requires just such a mix of talent and education. Whether selling electronic typewriters, microcomputers, or programmable calculators, the salesperson also needs to understand thoroughly the benefits to the customer of the various products, as well as superiority over competitive equipment. In addition, the salesperson will need to spend a considerable part of the presentation and postdelivery time in operator and application education.

With the understanding of the job to be done in mind, it is easier to match the salesperson to the product and customer to maintain the all-important consistency of the overall position. In the case of sophisticated office equipment, the hyper, frequent-closer salesperson may succeed for a time, especially in the larger population market. But eventually, and perhaps quickly in the small to medium markets, that tactic will undermine the reputation and sales for the simple reason that too many customers will have purchased the product but may not have the correct model or may not understand its proper use because the salesperson was too interested in getting to the next prospect.

A clear understanding of your company objective is important. Should your objective be boosting sales to prepare to sell the business, then the sales tactic just described may be appropriate. But longer-term sales and profit is the most common objective in office equipment and the quick closer would be counter to that.

The company objective, product service, and application are intertwined along with market position as factors to be considered when attempting to make the sales force consistent with the overall sales program. And it goes without saying that the overall sales program must be a mirror of the target audience.

The most obvious and perhaps easiest way to determine consistency is to concentrate on matching the salesperson with the customer in terms of demographics and socioeconomic groups. If you pay careful attention to that factor and at the same time get honest assurances that the salesperson does *enjoy* the customer group, you can't go too far wrong in that aspect of developing the sales force.

Recruiting Salespeople

Now that we have discussed the objective of the sales program and the importance of consistency between the sales program and the company objective, let's try to understand how we can recruit and hire salespeople who fit those objectives.

Earlier we talked about the nature of sales work, the reliance on emotion and self-confidence, and some specific personality characteristics that spell long-term success. That may seem somewhat esoteric or at best a series of considerations that must be determined by extensive psychological testing, brilliant intuition, or blind luck. Actually none of that may be necessary. There

are logical and simple ways to recruit and hire salespeople who fit your needs
and will perform. We'll walk through the process step by step by recruiting, hiring, training, compensating, motivating, and evaluating salespeople for maximum success.

Recruiting is the base of the sales program. It is also a "chicken or the egg" situation. Many managers don't know where to look for good salespeople. Their recruiting process is hit and miss or nonexistent.

The best recruiting program is a successful sales program. If you have a successful sales program, recruiting will be almost automatic. Good salespeople will be attracted to your firm. Building this perpetual success machine is not impossible.

The Written Plan

The first step in drawing the circle of successful sales that attracts successful salespeople that leads to successful sales program, etc., is the simplest step of all. Following the type of outline used in the chapter on planning, write what you want to achieve with the sales program.

The written plan is as valuable in the development of the sales program as it is in the development of the marketing plan and serves the same type of function. With a written plan you can focus your resources on the achievement of your program development. A written plan also helps you examine the component parts of the plan in isolation and requires you to define specifically what you want to achieve and how.

A good *written plan* defining your objectives and the means to attain those objectives in the development of your sales program should not require more than an hour of your time if you already know what you want to do. If you don't know, more time in the plan writing is required, but how can you accomplish anything without knowing what it is you want to accomplish? That one hour may be the most valuable hour spent in terms of profit impact for the firm. Due to the high cost of salespeople in relation to other expenses, the one hour of planning will reap great rewards if that $3,000 a month expense can be profitable.

The *first* step in writing the plan is to address the *specific objectives* of the salespeople. This should not be just an extension of the objective expressed in your marketing plan but an expression of the specific accomplishments expected of the salespeople. What kind of image do you want them to project? Earlier we spent some time describing the importance of the salespeople projecting an image consistent with your market position and customers. This is the place in the plan to spell out your expectations in that regard.

In describing what you want the salespeople to accomplish, include the *specifics of their duties*. Do you expect them to spend a considerable amount of time in public and community service on behalf of the company, or do you want them to spend time on customer education after the sale? Do you feel that their time should be devoted entirely to generating sales leads or generating the leads and closing the sale? How much staff support is available for handling leads, preparing proposals, and other necessary paperwork? Are the salespeople expected to do their own application evaluation or engineering work or is staff assigned to that function? Is the salesperson expected to generate the leads, make the presentation, close the sale, deliver, and collect, or are part of those duties assigned to other staff? An exact description of all of these considerations is necessary to describe adequately the sales position.

Do not overlook describing *your expectations* of the *salespeople's specific sales performance.* Spell out in exact money or unit volume terms what you feel needs to be accomplished within specific time frames. You need to establish ahead of time what will be required to be profitable for you and the salesperson. Neither of you can work exclusively for the love of the business. Money must be made to continue. Both you and the salesperson need money to survive or you both will be looking for other opportunities. If neither of you is making adequate profit, changes need to be made. It should be a partnership, not an adversary relationship.

In writing the sales program plan, borrow from your marketing plan the *descriptions of the products and services* that you offer. Include not only a brief paraphrase of the mission statement, but also describe the particular market segments on which you want to focus. Don't just name the markets or segments but also describe the traits of those segments. Pay particular attention to describing the customers. A word or two is sufficient, but write it down.

By now you should have two or three pages of valuable information describing the sales position, its challenges, and opportunities. Make the plan realistic. See that it accurately describes the nature of the sales job that you need done and how the sales program fits into the overall marketing plan.

Besides the normal benefits of any written plan, the written sales plan can serve one other important function. It can be the *focus point of the interview* with prospective salespeople. By using the written plan at interview time, at least two things occur. One, if you use the plan honestly, you will describe the job accurately to prospective salespeople so they know ahead of time your expectations and they will have a complete understanding of the job to be done. They can then assess whether they will contribute and probably will be in a better position to make that determination than you are at that point. Second, the prospective salesperson will be properly impressed that you know what you're doing and understand what the salesperson's job is. A really good and experienced salesperson wants to know what is expected, and what the opportunities are before accepting the job. So the plan itself contributes to your attracting salespeople that are better suited for the job.

The Hiring Process

Here is a step-by-step hiring process to select the proper salesperson. Using the sales program plan as a guide, you can decide what you want in a salesperson. Also, using the plan you will know how many salespeople are needed.

Sources of Recruits

The recruiting process can involve several elements. One route is to look at salespeople working for the competitors to see if any are qualified and successful. Competitive salespeople know the product application and the customers, even if they are concentrating in a slightly different market segment from you. They have a basic understanding. The chief disadvantage of looking at the competitor is that you may tip off your competition as to your needs and strategy. The competitive salesperson may have some habits and product information that need to be reversed before being effective for you. Perceived disloyalty may be a problem also. Weigh carefully the advantages and disadvantages before approaching any competitive salesperson and don't approach any but the best and most professional, who haven't grown to full potential. Those already at their peak won't develop further with your firm, and the opposite of development isn't attractive.

Another route is to look at supplier salespeople. These may include suppliers to your business as well as suppliers to your household. If you have done business with them for any length of time, you certainly know their habits, their concern with performance and obligations. Their integrity and personal habits are probably also known. If they pass all those tests to your satisfaction, then you have to decide only whether they seem to have the particular talents and educational background required by the sales job that you are trying to fill. Are they dealing with products or services for a similar customer group or market segment? Visualize them working for you. Do they fit? If you have any significant reservations, don't approach them; the reason for not approaching them is the same as not approaching the competitive salespeople prematurely. You don't want any supplier or competitor to know your strategy before it is implemented.

If you have a truly attractive sales program and good segment penetration, you probably will be approached by both competitive and supplier salespeople whether any openings exist or not. (That is the ideal condition, which should be your objective.) At trade conventions you may also learn of "eligibles" who may be coming on the market soon. All these leads should be treated as if you had initiated the approach. Don't discuss the job or even whether you intend to create a job until you are certain that they meet all your criteria as determined by your informal inquiries, preferably under subterfuge. Look at all the cards on the table and analyze the possibilities before showing your hole cards.

If none of those informal channels turns up any good leads, move to the next level, putting out word to your peers, both in your industry and your community. Don't be more specific than you're thinking of expanding your sales force or filling a vacancy. If after a few weeks no substantial leads develop, then, and only then, move to the next level. But before we do that, let's

remember to treat any leads the same as if you had initiated the contact with
competitive salespeople, learning as much about them as possible, visualizing
them in your organization before making any statement, implicit or explicit,
about the job that may be opening.

The next level to try is an employment agency or a sales recruitment
firm. Which one is appropriate for you depends on the sales job available and
your industry. Generally speaking, the salespeople available through a conventional employment agency tend to be less skilled or less educated. Normally you won't find college graduates with established sales records through
such an agency. But when I was in active management, I did on one occasion
find a truly good salesperson that way when the other steps had produced no
results in the time frame I needed. However, the reason I was lucky should be
understood so you can take advantage of my good fortune if your situation is
similar.

At the time I was in charge of marketing for a rapidly growing firm, and
we had developed enough business for one product to spin it off from our regular sales force and establish a separate program. Therefore, it was difficult to
put too much word on the street lest the competition be tipped off prematurely. The new sales effort would not require the technical or customer experience as our traditional line, so much discussion would have shown that we
weren't expanding in our normal manner.

Additionally we have the good fortune to be in a medium-sized city that
is attractive to people in other regions of the country, particularly in the late
1970s. As a result we had an influx of highly educated and qualified people
who moved without jobs already arranged. Because the economy was growing, that situation didn't present more than a temporary minor inconvenience
to the new arrivals. All these factors meant that good people were becoming
available through regular employment agencies. I had considerable good fortune hiring staff through agencies but had never hired salespeople that way.
Reputable employment agencies provide confidential reference checks and
verify background information, which saves the employer considerable time.
But in a normal situation a salesperson who relies on an agency to find a job
probably isn't aggressive or self-confident enough to succeed. Even though
logic would suggest that you not use an agency or some other channel that
doesn't usually work, don't overlook the possibility. It's a gamble that may be
stacked against you, but failures in hiring through the preferred first or second
level also occur.

Sales employment agencies can work in larger cities or unstable population centers where an influx of talent makes getting access to them all difficult.
By the same token executive recruiting firms may work if you need to go outside your industry and are willing to look on the regional or national market.
All these decisions are a factor of the relative sophistication of the product or
service that you sell and the level of sophistication of your customers versus
the quantity of likely talent available through normal channels. In other
words most small businesses will not likely benefit from using executive or
sales recruiting firms, but understand when and why they may work should

you be in a situation that can take advantage of those agencies and channels. If all these attempts still haven't produced likely leads for qualified people, then the last step is advertising. Which advertising medium is strictly a function of the job and how many people regionally are probably qualified. Only in larger cities should you need to advertise in the local paper. Again, the reason is simple. If you have a good program, your success will attract good people automatically.

Whether the particulars of your situation suggest local, regional, national, or industrywide advertising, most experts agree that you will generally attract a higher quality and higher quantity response by *including your company name.* There are several reasons for this, not the least of which is that salespeople may not respond to blind boxes because that may tip the wrong people that they want to change jobs. If you are proud of your firm and its opportunities and are growing, the competition knows that you need more people. But your ad shouldn't reveal the details of the job duties or product responsibilities.

Advertisements that describe in correct but general terms are sufficient. Stating whether the job involves travel, car, salary, or straight commission will sort out many who wouldn't qualify. Specify the method of response, whether to phone for appointment, to mail resume, or to contact your firm in person. Those decisions are a function of the likely quantity of applicants and level of sophistication. Make a notation of the ability to follow directions.

Screening Applicants

Before the interview have applicants complete an *employment application form.* Use a standard form available from your local stationery store. The reason for this exercise is to judge neatness, attention to directions, and ability to handle paperwork. You then have a standardized form to compare side by side for all applicants. If they use a resume as well, check that the application completed on the spot agrees with the resume. That may seem silly, but inconsistencies occur and may be masking any number of problems, the least serious being vagueness.

After the deadline for applications or you have enough applicants, begin the process of verifying the information on the application. Check with your attorney regarding how much information and the methods that you can use to check their background. Usually checking their driving record, if your insurance agent can arrange that, and checking their credit rating will be all that a small business can reasonably attempt. In most states even those perfunctory checks require the applicant's permission, so be sure to start with clarification from your attorney before checking.

Previous employment, if the applicant permits you to check, turns up only inconsistencies in the application. Practically no one divulges any confidential or controversial information. Some large firms respond only by saying that the person was an employee. If you can verify dates of employment, duties, pay at leaving, and eligibility for rehire, you will be extremely fortunate.

83

I learned the hard way that checking former employers and personal references was not valid unless I had the good fortune to be a personal acquaintance of the one whom I was contacting for information. Due to the legal climate, few will provide any substantive responses. Verifying the dates usually suffices to determine authenticity. In the final analysis the decision is a judgment call by you anyway. You cannot be 100 percent successful.

Going through these quick steps, which any small business can do, will eliminate several applicants that might appear qualified otherwise. But be sure to stick to your plan and don't allow deviations because someone impressed you personally. That's in the person's favor only if all the criteria are met.

The Interviews

The *first interview* (I believe in at least three before finalizing the employment) is only for the purpose of your telling applicants about the job arrangements, following your written plan. That way they can decide whether they want to pursue your opening. Also, by sticking to your plan description, you reduce the possibilities of being convinced by applicants that they are the persons for the job regardless of ability. Describe the company and its opportunities honestly. If at all possible, take them on a tour of the facilities and introduce them to as many of the staff and other management as possible. Conclude the interview with a definite agreement as to when you will contact them again and who is to initiate the contact. The tour and introductions may seem meaningless, but several things happen. Applicants see the company as more than the front office, and if they don't mesh with your staff immediately, don't hire the applicants without further consideration. If there is discord immediately, it's unlikely to go away with time, and more than likely will worsen. Your staff's assistance is invaluable. (Make sure that they know ahead of time that you're looking.)

The *next interview* should be devoted to learning about the applicant. Prepare a list of questions about the person. Use that same list for all applicants. If minor discrepancies or legitimate questions require answers, this is the time. I am assuming that any significant discrepancies on applications have already been canned or filed in your personnel files if required. (Again, check with your attorney as to the disposition of applications that were rejected.) I don't pretend to keep up with legal requirements. It is extremely important to make sure that you are following federal and local labor laws in handling of all phases; get guidelines from your attorney, who will defend you if you are wrong.

The *third interview* includes the job offer. Perhaps you may have a third interview without making a job offer, but certainly don't make one before the third. The decision is extremely important to the life of another person, so caution and certainty must be practiced diligently.

Additional interviews may be indicated if you can't make an offer due to either the applicant's or your own uncertainty. My personal preference is to make the offer but request that a fourth meeting deal with acceptance or additional questions by the applicant. The last thing that you need is an employee with nagging doubts, muddled understandings, or an unhappy spouse or family. Of course, more interviews may be necessary for protracted negotiations. Don't rush. Too much of your company and the life of another individual is at stake. But be decisive on your course of action and your preference for the priority list of candidates. Balance selling the company and being realistic about the challenges.

Alterations in the Process

Before we leave the hiring process, consider circumstances when you would not follow this guide with its long, involved scenario. Perhaps understanding why it may not be necessary to follow the script may help explain why the script is important.

There are times when compressing the process is valid. Consider the exact nature of the particular sales job. If it requires little education or expertise, dealing with customers who are making frequent purchases, and the job itself is projected to be relatively short-term, then some of the cautious steps can be ignored. The first change that you may want to make is first to use advertising and simultaneously to seek employment agency help. I would be reluctant to see the investigative steps be eliminated, but the job presentation process could be shortened.

Some of the situations that suggest shortening the process include retail sales of relatively inexpensive items involving frequent purchases by customers as well a short-term sales jobs. Such short-term jobs at home shows and fairs require little in the way of long-term relations with either your other employees or the customers. Short-term canvassing jobs are another likely possibility. But in all those cases, to describe them as true sales jobs might be stretching the definition at bit. By and large there would be little need for the traditional sales steps of generating the leads, qualifying the prospect, making the presentation, closing the sale, and doing any follow-up work. Generally such short-term or low-expertise jobs by definition are involved only in the presentation or possibly the lead generation process.

Nearly all other true sales jobs ranging in complexity from the retail sales clerk to sophisticated computer or heavy equipment and financing should follow the steps of hiring spelled out carefully, following the prepared plan for the sales program. Only in big business is it possible to try techniques of going through the multitude of applicants or a multitude of employees to attain the desired results. In small business we don't normally have that margin of error.

My own experience, and those of my clients, has served to reinforce the idea that only by sticking to the plan and being careful in the recruitment and selection process will you operate a successful and profitable sales force. For example, one client, against my advice, hired a salesman who was experienced in the field, personable, known by the customers, and had been working for a competitor in serious financial trouble. My client did not even take the time to talk to existing customers of the salesman, which could have been done easily under subterfuge. The attitude was that "we take a chance when we hire any employee." That's true, but why not get as much information as possible before making a decision that impacts so heavily on both immediate cash flow and on the relationships with valued customers? The sequel to the story is that the new salesman didn't work out well, as he was not calling on customers, not taking care of details, not closing many orders, and generally not being profitable. The client, due to that and admittedly some other errors, ran into cash-flow problems. The ex-client is slipping quickly, on C.O.D. with suppliers, behind on other payments. The underlying reason is the whole attitude about personnel decisions, particularly sales positions, which was a reflection of lack of planning or following a plan.

The Compensation Program

Now that we have hired the salesperson, let's look at sales compensation programs. In practice this should have been done before hiring. However, sales compensation is a unique, specialized field. It requires a great deal of involvement on the part of the financial manager as well as the sales manager, both working under the direct supervision of the general manager or principal of the firm.

Step one is for the management principals to define the long-term objective of the company and also the short-term product objective if more than one product or service is sold. Without the objectives clearly defined, it will be virtually impossible to design a compensation program that will meet the objectives. The financial officer must be involved. The objectives should be chosen on the basis of profitability. Most small businesses are not capitalized sufficiently to mortgage the future for market share. It's no secret that most small businesses are undercapitalized by conventional standards. They are not in a position to gamble heavily on the future. This should be reflected in their objectives.

Risk vs. Responsibility

Sales compensation theories abound, but the essence of determining the type of compensation, or, if mixed, how much dependence on salary and how much on commissions, boils down to a simple concept: *who is going to assume the most risk,* in contradistinction to *who is going to assume the most responsibility,* as illustrated in Figure 5–3. All other discussions of sales compensation must start and end with that premise.

Risk assumption is one concept that few salespeople and fewer sales managers seem to grasp. The opposite of risk is security. Commissions are risky. Salaries imply security. Salespeople who are willing to accept higher levels of risk are the frequent closers who prefer to sell items that allow them

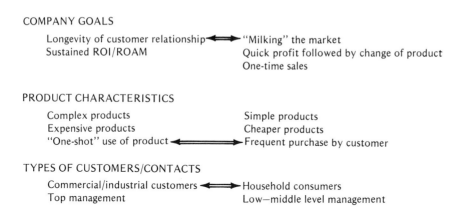

FIGURE 5–3. Sales Compensation Determinants

to practice their specialty often. Closing is so important to them because they have high needs to prove themselves, usually to themselves and frequently.

Salespeople who work best on a *commission-only* plan are those who *tend to be less concerned with details* and customer education or use training. In other words, selling in the purest form is their prime concern. They want to make as many presentations and closes in a given period of time as possible.

Real estate and insurance salespeople, who traditionally work on a straight commission basis, fit in this category on the basis of risk assumption. The only difference between them and the salesperson who sells lower-ticket items and makes frequent closes is that higher per-sale commissions result from successful presentations and closes. The main point here is that the salespersons are assuming great financial risk and thereby proving to the world and themselves that they can succeed. Everyone knows that the commission-only salesperson is on straight commission, and therefore making a good living in that environment provides the feedback so desperately needed. You may have noticed that commission-only salespeople tend to display their material success in some not too subtle ways. They have to prove to the world, really to themselves, that they can make it.

Security-minded persons on the other hand need to have a salary for comfort in order to function effectively. They perform only from a comfortable base. They tend to have fewer requirements to prove themselves. But they still want to close sales and solve customer problems. They just don't need the direct financial feedback system to keep them motivated. If they were put on straight commission, they probably wouldn't function well because their foundation would be slippery. They need stability and security.

But to understand better when to use the salary-oriented, security-

87

minded individuals, let's understand how they work and their strengths. The people who are less willing to take the financial risks of straight commission are willing to take responsibility for their actions, although somewhat indirectly. Although they are less willing to take direct financial responsibility, they are willing to take moral and legal responsibility for performing specifically required duties. They are willing to work in the areas of customer education and training, product application and analysis, with reports and documentation as an integral part of the selling process.

The security-minded persons are much more willing to perform detailed clerical work so long as they understand its relevance to the selling process. They will make follow-up calls on existing customers and do public relations work willingly. They think much more in terms of longer period customer relations and not immediate impact.

The trade-off is that for less emphasis on closing sales, you pay a salary but receive in turn the ability to provide more specific direction of their activities. They are selling their higher risk but potentially higher return straight commissions for security. Management is trading high sales performance for control of the salesperson's activities. Consider the salesperson traits' relationship to types of compensation shown in Figure 5–4.

But let's not overlook the other trade-offs. The higher sales performance of the straight commission salesperson also means that *management* needs to assume direct *responsibility* for long-term customer relations. In other words, the higher sales performance will be made at the expense of higher sales returns due to credit and proper product education or application.

With straight commissions, management must assume greater direct responsibility for the actions of the salespeople. With straight salaries, manage-

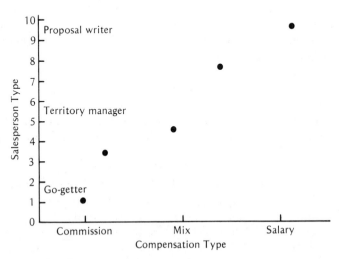

FIGURE 5–4. Salesperson Trait/Compensation Plan

ment is passing the responsibility to salespeople in exchange for security. Security-minded people need and want more direction and gladly concern themselves with long-term customer relations.

Do not overlook the fact that even the lawyer-engineer type who wants straight salary and will assume a great deal of responsibility still needs feedback. The feedback must be direct and in some form of remuneration, although not necessarily in monthly commission. Salespeople by definition need to close sales and also need something to show for their efforts and discipline. They need to prove their ability just as much as the straight-commission type. The difference is that perquisites and spiffs are more meaningful, such as expense accounts, cars, and club memberships. The trappings of success are just as important, only in a different form. Banks and law firms reward the good salesperson by conferring titles.

Product Life Cycle

Another factor that must be considered is the stage of the product life cycle you are in. Take a look at Figure 5–5. In the various stages of the product life cycle, different functions need to be performed by the salesperson. Early in the product history, introduction to the 10 percent innovators is the objective. In that phase the specific task of the salesperson is to get the product into the distribution channels and the hands of the customers. During that early phase more emphasis may be placed on salary because the salesperson needs to begin to build the base for the future.

Later in the cycle the emphasis shifts from introduction to education. The customers probably know the product exists but need to know the bene-

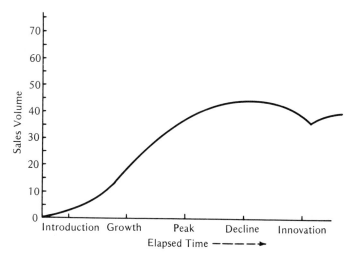

FIGURE 5–5.   Product Life Cycle

fit to them. During the latter stages of this phase there is increasing emphasis on looking for other applications of the product. Ideally and theoretically, but admittedly not practically, the compensation should start heavily loaded toward straight salary, but as the product moves into subsequent phase of the life cycle, the compensation emphasis should shift toward commission. Broader acceptance in the marketplace also brings increasing competition and the need to spend less time on education and application and more on differentiating between your product and the competitors. There is a point when little real difference exists between you and the competition so the salespeople are under pressure to qualify prospects and close sales.

Soon after this phenomenon of identical competitors, the pricing structure begins to soften. When that process starts, then the salesperson is strictly the qualifier, presenter, and closer. As prices slip and more and more price competition becomes evident, the salesperson is strictly playing the numbers game, that is, seeing, presenting, and closing as many sales in a period of time as possible. Little concern is paid to education, application, long-term relations, etc. At that point the salesperson should be commission only.

By following the sales function through the product life cycle and understanding the traits of salespeople attracted by different compensation plans, it is relatively easy to make a determination of the appropriate strategy.

In the case of multiple products, the problem becomes complex, but by studying the growth and profitability potential of all your products during the marketing plan, the choice of product emphasis should be fairly easy. In the case of multiple products in various phases of the product life cycle you must make some arbitrary decisions as to which product or products govern your strategy.

Product Complexity

The question of product complexity and price is even more subjective when considering those factors as determinants of the compensation plan, and therefore the type of salesperson to hire. Consider the examples in Figure 5–6. Ironically, because it is more complex, we'll spend little time pursuing this subject but give the key criteria for determining where your product falls.

Complexity in this context is strictly the variety of application options available. In other words, if the product needs to be especially put together for the customer's application, such as with mini- and mainframe computers or office communications systems, then more time is spent by the salesperson for each sale. To encourage good application design or at least have the salesperson take adequate time determining the customer's needs, a salary is necessary.

Simple products that don't require application differentials can be sold by straight commission people. This class of product includes established products like cars or insurance, where the products are prepared and only need selection by the customer, rather than design and application for semi-custom sales.

Price

Pricing as a consideration can take two forms. First, consider your price in relation to the competition. When we looked at position and market strategy, we discussed why higher-priced items do better with a sophisticated salesperson who relates well to customers and establishes a peer relationship. On the other hand, lower-price strategy means that the sales presentation is based on price alone, with little concern for the customer's education in the product's use. Closing the sale is essentially all that matters.

The second type of price consideration has little to do with relative price to the competition but *absolute price*. The higher-priced items mean fewer total sales. It follows that some form of support of the salespeople is necessary to keep salespeople interested in long-term projects. Salary is the most logical alternative. A draw against future commissions doesn't work well for infrequent sales, though a quarterly or annual bonus based on a predetermined formula works. The draw against commissions makes the salesperson commission-only, with all the positive and negative factors of that mode of operation.

Product life cycle, relative and absolute price, and product application complexity are easily expressed as continuums, as shown. But also understand that all marks on the continuums are shades of gray. There is no black and white. As a practical matter, if you place your product or products on the continuum where you think most logical, additionally considering your longer-term objectives, the answers as to what type of salespeople and how to compensate them are relatively easy. But be sure to include all these factors. Remember tradition within your industry, but don't necessarily let tradition for its own sake govern your decisions.

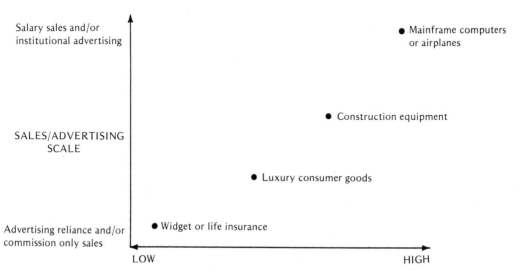

FIGURE 5–6. Marketing Mix Analysis for Sales Strategy/Compensation

Program Examples

Perhaps with an example, I can make the point more clearly. The principal of the firm feels that there is a substantial market for high-quality cabinets and counters for offices. His reasons for feeling good about the potential are substantiated by an increase in new office space that will be coming on the market in the next two to three years. According to his market plan, analyzing the local production facilities of the likely competitors, no one else is in a position to develop the market without being at a price disadvantage, due to their inefficient and poorly located shops. Further, he doesn't feel that they will fully develop the market even for their share due to lack of attention to marketing. Even though our manager has the advantage of price and distribution and can mount an effective advertising program, he rightly feels that personal sales will actually spell the difference between modest sales and overwhelming success. Because the product, cabinets and counters, is purchased infrequently by any customer, and because the product is complex in terms of price and application options, personal sales efforts will be required to close the orders. That all seems simple enough. But there is a catch.

To keep the facilities in profitable operation and to keep the key staff people employed, our manager needs to find an interim opportunity. This interim opportunity should not require any significant modification of facilities nor any substantial change in staffing. The sales force should be able to sell the interim product as a stopgap while working on the longer-term products. The cabinets and counters will require working with the leasing agents, the architects and interior designers, and the prospective tenants, as well as the general contractors doing the actual work. So the sales development time will be substantial. The interim product must therefore be easily sold and may even be something that will continue selling well after the office cabinet and counter sales have peaked in two or three years.

To keep the facilities in operation and maintain positive cash flow, the manager has decided to sell home kitchen cabinets and counters. Due to heavy competition and the availability of catalog and unfinished units, our manager has chosen to produce and sell cabinets and counters that can also be used as furniture supplements for recreational homes. The concept will fit well because that market is not as price-sensitive as the market for home cabinets in development tracts, and recreational home construction is seasonal. But due to the nature of recreational home construction, the cabinets can be premanufactured rather than custom-built, again enabling the production facilities to be utilized on a more even work flow basis. The purchasers, and in fact the whole distribution channel, are similar in structure but different in composition from the market for office units. But the objective of the sales force is more getting the brochures and pricing information into the hands of the decision makers and closing the sales. Considerably less emphasis is placed on working with various levels of the market developing custom designs and pricing.

The product is functionally different, and there isn't the requirement for

mechanical quality—although appearance remains important—due to the
lighter duty of the drawers, doors, and counters in recreational homes used for
weekend and vacations, as opposed to heavy office cabinet use. Margins are
not as attractive either for the manager.

Importance of Sales Compensation Plan

In this marketing scenario, why is the sales compensation plan so important? The main objective for higher profitability is custom-made cabinets
for offices. The interim "volume" product to utilize facilities is the cabinets for
recreational residences. Therefore, the sales compensation structure should be
designed to achieve these two separate objectives, although they are not mu-
tually exclusive.

Because the custom-made office cabinets take more time to sell and require more presentations, no matter how formal or informal, to an audience of
relatively diverse and sophisticated decision makers, the salesperson needs to
be relatively sophisticated and patient. The product is purchased infrequently
by the customer and is relatively expensive. The firm's objective is longevity,
rather than a "milk and run" strategy. Based on these assumptions and the
product objective, a logical compensation package would include a fairly high
percentage of salary with substantial rewards for closing orders for the custom
office cabinet work. But the salary should not be so high as to preclude the
necessity of selling the easier and less expensive recreational home units. Nor
should the salary be automatic but should be in exchange for developing the
longer-term, more profitable market. A call-reporting system, which we'll discuss in detail later, will generate the information as to whether the company's
longer term objectives are being met.

Staying with our case, let's plug in some specific numbers. To attract the
type of salesperson who is less emotional and more methodical, traits required
to succeed with sophisticated decision makers, a compensation floor equal to
an amount near that of skilled labor is necessary. In 1983 dollars in some regions, this would be around $2,000 a month. But logic says that this will not
require performance. Additionally a good salesperson requires ego feedback
and wants to have a larger incentive. The straight salary portion of the compensation package could be $1,000 per month. The next $1,000 could be
made up with commission for the recreational home cabinets. Picking a ran-
dom number, let's suppose that the typical set of the most popular model in
the most popular finish sells for $3,000 delivered. Please bear with the as-
sumption that the gross margin, before selling expenses and overhead contributions, is 20 percent. So the company generates about $600 from each set. If
the salesperson were paid on the basis of gross margin, allowing room for other
sales expenses, a reasonable commission would be $200. But our salesperson is
already receiving a salary. In order to have an income of $2,000, five sets of
cabinets need to be sold each month, in addition to the salary.

Whether the quantity and margin assumption are correct, or close,
varies by individual circumstances. We don't know here what the overhead

93

costs are, nor the volume potential, nor the volume required for profitability. Consequently all we can reasonably do is talk philosophically. But even getting a clear concept in general terms should help design a profitable sales compensation program that will accomplish the primary and secondary objectives.

One option to consider, using the numbers shown here, is pay a commission of $100, or some such figure, and "charge" the other $100 to offset the salary. That way, when 10 sets of cabinets are sold, the eleventh and subsequent set will pay a direct commission of $200. The beauty of that type of program is that most of the direct cost of establishing the contacts and market development for the office cabinets, our primary objective, are covered by the secondary but shorter-term products.

But if market conditions and the salesperson's predisposition are such that the primary objective becomes in essence personal objectives, sacrificing the short-term recreational home cabinets and building for the larger commissions of the office job, then the salesperson must make the conscious decision to live on $1,000 a month. If the salesperson does in fact take that option, you should not modify the compensation package just to accommodate. After all, the purpose of the secondary objective was to keep afloat until the office jobs began to pay. You do have a big decision to make, however. Can you, never mind the salesperson, afford to forego the secondary objective and concentrate entirely on the primary? If not, you may wish to require, as a minimum job performance standard, a level of secondary sales sufficient to pay the light bill.

Now that we have paid the rent and lights as a result of sufficient sales of the secondary cabinets, let's refocus our attention on office cabinets. The reason for the office work being the primary objective was due to the larger size of the jobs, the better margins possible as a result of controlling raw material inventory and less competition, because few firms are capable of and most haven't spent any appreciable effort on marketing. With that in mind, we can establish some profitable figures for the situation.

Gross profit margins are nearly 30 percent before overhead and sales expenses. A typical job runs close to $15,000 for cabinets for a medium-sized law firm all the way to $50,000 for a full-floor insurance firm, down to $5,000 for a small professional office. But the margin stays relatively constant.

Should the secondary product in fact cover the direct costs for the primary sales program, then we should be in a position to reward the salesperson commensurately. For purposes of discussion, let's consider paying a fixed percentage of gross margin higher than for the secondary product. In this case we'll use 40 percent of the gross as the commission margin of the item. The higher commission rate and the higher dollar volume of each job should be sufficient to encourage the salespeople to concentrate more effort on the primary product, once the "floor" is covered.

With specific numbers, a $25,000 cabinet job should gross $7,500 for the firm and pay a commission of $3,000—not bad for a morning's work. But at that rate and with a penetration rate of 50 percent of the new offices, the total dollar volume over the two to three years that the growth is expected should be substantial and contribute greatly to profitability. If there will be 200 new offices, we are able to sell cabinets to 100, and the "average" sale is $25,000, the three-year volume will be $2.5 million, in excess of $830,000 annual rate. Admittedly all these numbers are blue-sky but illustrate the point. There is more longer-term, less cyclical, and less seasonal profit in the office cabinets, the primary objective, than recreational home cabinets, the secondary objective. Therefore the rewards for the salesperson are structured accordingly.

Another example of primary and secondary products objective is the case of selling one item that results in *subsidiary sales*. It's the case of the razor sales resulting in blade sales or the camera selling film or communications equipment selling service.

Other similar situations would include a special group, such as computers. The hardware differs between alternative suppliers. But within a class or power range most of the units are similar. But there is significant difference in available software packages. Further, some firms have developed some semicustom software, which may fill unique requirements of a customer group or industry. Packaged software is not available, due to the small size of the particular group. There is a golden opportunity. The firm that recognizes and responds to this need can then price the software to return a substantial profit, also selling the moderately well-margined packaged software in addition to the tightly margined hardware.

Therefore, the sales compensation package should be structured to reflect these differing margins. The easiest method is to pay on gross margin. But be sure that the salesperson understands the relative margins and dollar volume possible in all three categories so they will sell what is most profitable.

The *razor-blade or camera-film* situation is a little more complex, however, but gives us some greater opportunities to do more than just sell profitable items. It helps create a steady, fairly predictable cash flow. Any relatively infrequent-sales item that requires, or at least encourages, customer use of "captive" supplies fits in this category. Examples also include such things as private clubs with initiation fees and dues, communications equipment that requires monthly service, even engines and machines that require single source parts and service. In all these cases there is one common problem, that is, how to encourage the salespeople to maintain contact with the customer long after the "romantic," infrequent, relatively high-ticket purchase has been made. The supply items are perceived by most salespeople as not challenging and worthy of their efforts. Of course, the result of such an attitude is declining use of the product, with consequent decline in the supply items sales. Eventually the customer resells the item or banishes it to the junk heap. The net to the company is that not only do supply sales diminish but also the customer is unhappy with the entire unit and doesn't mind telling associates, further damaging the reputation of the company selling the product. The last step in the chain is ever diminishing sales of the product, and the downward spiral is underway.

What can be done to prevent this impending disaster? For our firm we are convinced, as our studies of our profitability confirm, that the supplies generate profit as well as being a source of relatively constant cash flow with little effort to realize recurring sales. The one-time sales are barely profitable after considering all the direct and indirect costs and overhead contributions. We need to continue selling the item to get the real profit, supplies.

Sales Force Organization

Now that the problem has been defined, what are the practical and profitable options available? How can we maintain sales of adequate "initiations and dues"? At least two alternatives are possible. One is to have *separate sales forces* dealing in initiations and another dealing with dues.

Separate Sales Forces

In this type of organization, one sales force spends all its time developing leads, qualifying prospects, closing sales for the initial purchase of the product or service. That sales force, because it is dealing with relatively high-ticket items and working with fairly sophisticated customers, becomes expert in financing packages, understanding and selling the rate of return on the customer's investment, etc. In general, the salespeople are well educated and sophisticated.

The second sales force is more use-oriented. The salespersons tend to be more concerned with the operation of the machine or service and less concerned with the actual benefits of the original purchase. In machines they probably are former mechanical or technical people who wanted to move into field sales but who have not developed the experience and self-confidence to make presentations and close larger orders. Their function is to serve the customers' recurring needs.

An example of this situation is the marketing director for the private club who contacts prospective members and signs them up for membership, collecting the initiation fee. The club pro, then, and the pro's staff are responsible for the regular use of the club by the members and work with the members to develop their enjoyment of the game.

Another example is machines, whether office machines, heavy equipment, or anything in between. Machines consume supplies and wear out parts. Machines are designed to produce goods or services for the customer. To operate machines correctly requires training and supervision. And for the machine to operate correctly also requires supplies and parts generally purchased from the organization that sold the machine new in the first place. After-market or "will-fit" replacement parts represent a fairly small percentage of the market for parts, although a large dollar volume. But the machine dealer would like *all* of the parts and supply business.

One sales force sells the machines, heavy trucks as an example. The other sales force sells parts and service for the trucks. The truck salespeople contact a relatively few number of customers in a given month, whereas the parts sales contact 10 to 15 customers in a given day. The parts sales is a profitable operation in its own right but also serves the function of providing communications of the technical information from the service department and the customer. The result is trucks that operate correctly and profitably for the customer, causing the customer to buy additional and replacement trucks from the dealer.

The parts salesperson also knows more intimately the condition of the customers' trucks so that the truck sales department will know when new trucks may be needed. One department profitably feeds the other. It's a nice system that works well for many machine dealers.

A similar system is the office machine variant. In that scheme the principle is the same as the truck dealer with a notable difference. The parts, service, and supply salespeople repair or maintain a machine, deliver supplies, and discuss the machine's operation with the customer's employees. They can sell additional supplies and service contracts and can also be a source of leads for the machine salesperson.

This system works well because it takes advantage of the personality traits that do best in each job. The machine salesperson won't like to spend the time on relatively small tasks dealing with details and the actual operation of the machine. The parts and service salesperson won't be as inclined to spend the time selling machine benefits and probably won't be able to arrange financing, etc.

The real reason that this system works is that one group of salespeople doesn't relate as well to details, and the other doesn't do as well relating to people needs. There are gradations of both types, but the structure is built on the general trends. That general tendency on the part of both groups goes a long way toward explaining why a good parts and service salesperson almost never makes a good machine salesperson.

One Sales Force

Let's return to the basic question of how to sell "initiations and dues" profitably. Many firms have successfully used one sales force to sell both types of products. This works particularly well when the "dues" or supply items do not require much additional sales effort or when the supply items do not require any special technical training or information. Cases include communications services, life insurance, and similar instances where the customer makes the initial purchase and the subsequent purchases are fairly automatic. Communications services require a deliberate decision to purchase or make a long-term lease for equipment. This could be residential telephones, mobile telephones for the business person, or radio pocket pagers. The basic unit doesn't provide any benefits outright unless connected to the system, the switched telephone network, for example. The salesperson's direct involvement on a regular basis is through when the equipment is installed. Subsequent contacts would be for purposes of checking satisfaction and providing use education only. But the company profit is in the recurring services.

The salesperson selling this type of product or service then should be encouraged to continue selling the equipment (initiation) but needs to maintain some contact with the customer to assure continuing sales (dues). Simply demanding the duty as a requirement for employment doesn't work. But the object is to retain a high percentage of customers on recurring service, even though there isn't much romance in that type of sale.

Educating the salesperson as to the importance and profitability to the company is an important aspect. The salespeople need to know that the company objective of profitability can be fulfilled through this type of service. An otherwise happy salesperson doesn't want to look for a job just because the employer went broke.

Perhaps Figure 5–7 will help. Assume that a salesperson should earn $20,000 a year. A common practice is to pay 25% of gross margin on equipment sales (30% margin), and 10% of monthly recurring charges.

By adjusting the percentage and/or mix of compensation, you will naturally effect changes which should reflect your objectives. An exception might be when, due to the marketplace, the item carrying the lower percentage is easier enough to sell so that the volume potential will overcome the per unit commission deficit.

The last piece of the puzzle is the compensation package. Borrow a page from the life insurance industry. Pay a percentage of the recurring billings as a commission. At least two benefits result. The salesperson is rewarded for the customer who continues to use the recurring service, in addition to the commission for establishing the equipment sale. The salesperson is more inclined to see that the customer is educated in proper use and encouraged to increase the usage. More regular sales contact between your firm and the customer occurs. The other benefit is that the income of the salesperson builds up as more customers are added. By that means you can come as close to buying loyalty as possible. The residual payments terminate when the salesperson leaves the firm, of course.

This type of system encourages the future-thinking salesperson to accept a somewhat lower initial compensation than otherwise required simply because the real monetary rewards to successful continued sales are substantial over time. The salesperson who is doing a good job naturally obtains more customers. The more customers, the more value there is to the company because of the familiarity with the customers. When this type of system works well, it is good for the salesperson and the company.

To give you a flavor for this system, consider paying the salespeople a commission of 10 percent of the recurring billings for that salesperson's accounts. Pay a reasonably good commission for the one-time charges, say, the equivalent of 30 percent of gross margin. If the unit sells for $1,000, the margin is 25 percent; then the salesperson gets a commission of $75 one time. But the monthly service of $25 means that at 10 percent, the salesperson doubles the commission in 30 months and reaps the rewards of longevity. In 15

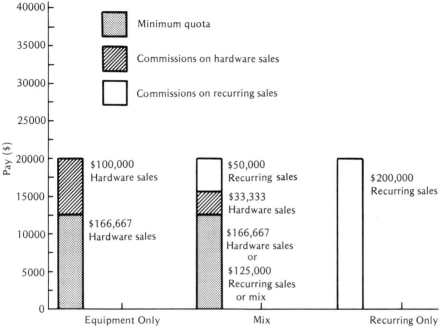

FIGURE 5-7. Compensation Analysis

months of adding two a month, the salesperson receives more in residual commission than one outright sale. And yet the residual commissions won't make the salesperson rich, and because some customer attrition is natural, continued efforts to get new customers are necessary.

Using two separate sales forces works best when the customer base is fairly small and the supply of recurring service is frequent and requires some expertise on the part of the customer. The single sales force tends to work best when the customer base is large and little expertise is needed by the customer to use the recurring service. You probably find yourself somewhere between those extremes. The best thing to remember is to examine your business in this light before assigning your gradient position.

Changes in the Compensation Plan

No matter how carefully you study the alternatives and no matter how carefully you determine the appropriate sales compensation plan, you will need to change it sometime. The product life cycle may change, the absolute and relative price may change, the product complexity may change, and risk and responsibility assumptions may change. Any or all of these considerations mean that a change in the sales compensation plan is necessary.

How the change is handled can be the difference between good salespeople staying or leaving. How the change is handled can also mean the difference between profitability and losses.

But change can be accomplished simply and fairly painlessly if you carefully keep in mind and follow these precepts. Never, except in the most desperate of circumstances, change the plan more than once in 12 months. A more desirable minimum is 24 months. If the plan is well conceived and the numbers worked out carefully in advance, the only more frequent change necessary would be occasioned by product development that changes your whole operation. I can't imagine what that would be. By adequate planning and the use of electronic spread sheets, there is no reason in the 1980s that you would need to change more frequently.

When doing the numbers crunching on the electronic spread sheet, try to keep the alternatives as simple as possible. Administration of the sales compensation plan must be simple and straightforward. Both the salespeople and the administrative people benefit from a simple plan and both for the same reason. A simple plan reduces the possibility of errors. Errors take far more time to correct and more direct expense than doing the task right initially. That shouldn't surprise anyone. But an error in the administration of the sales compensation plan costs either management or the salespeople direct cash. They and administration must take time to resolve the error.

A simple, easy-to-understand plan has other benefits for sales and management. Both sales and management are better able to chart sales performance. Sales performance is not just a measurement of individual performance, but significant deviations may be symptomatic of other causes. Those causes may be personal, company-related, broader economic or industry-related, but they need to be identified and either capitalized or corrected, depending on whether the deviations are positive or negative. But the salespeople need to measure their own progress.

A low-risk method of encouraging the salespeople is not to put a ceiling deliberately on their income. If they think that there is a ceiling, they will react negatively, even though the ceiling may be higher than they can reasonably reach. Many successful firms have top performing salespeople who earn more income than upper management. They've found that it pays off in the stability of the sales force, which of course means a more stable customer base.

Some firms have found a *graduated commission* scale to work extremely well, whether straight commission or a salary-commission mix. As an individual salesperson's production increases in a given time frame, that salesperson has recovered overhead expenses. Increasing sales, therefore, are more profitable to the firm and the salesperson should be rewarded accordingly.

An inverse scale whereby the percentage of commission goes down as sales go up not only effectively imposes a ceiling but also encourages and reinforces mediocre performance. The high performer looks for more lucrative opportunities as soon as circumstances permit.

The emotional impact on the salespeople of an error in compensation administration is hard to understand, but essentially it undermines the trust relationship between sales, management, and administration. In various stages of my career I experienced errors, but my reaction was constant. I thought that I knew how much money was coming and was devastated to receive something else. An error on the high side produced the same results because of the fear that the check couldn't be used and because of the time to get a correct payment.

When I was in management and not a direct party to the error, I observed the administration-sales interaction. I knew that an error was unintentional. I still had to spend considerable time defending both the salespeople and administration in the conflict and get it resolved quickly. People make errors but if the system is simple, the possibility of errors is greatly reduced.

Involvement of Employees

When you decide that a change is necessary for any reason, share the reason with the salespeople. Describe to them and get definite assurances from them that they understand why. Once their understanding is accomplished, ask them to give you some ideas as to how the plan should be changed to accomplish your objectives. If they only nod agreement but don't really understand why you're changing the compensation, they will not have any valuable contribution to designing the new plan. By the same token, if you think that they understand and they don't, but you follow their suggestions for change, their suggestions may not contribute to your attainment of the objective of the change in the first place. When that happens, you both lose.

The actual active *involvement* of the salespeople in the changing process is critical for more reasons than just helping you. By understanding your objectives they are better able to help you attain them. Also by including them in the process, their involvement is reciprocated by opening up your relations with them and by their adopting your objectives as their own. That may sound nice in theory and look good on paper, but unless you actually practice including them, you won't believe the results that are possible.

The stability of the compensation plan and the salespeople's involvement in its modification are extremely critical for one reason. Messing with their compensation does more to unsettle them and detract their attention from performance than anything else you can do. Remember that to them compensation as a direct feedback mechanism is vital to their success. By arbitrarily changing that system you are changing the most critical aspect in their environment.

Should you take the position that you don't want their participation and, if they don't like the results, they can quit, you'll pay for that. The manner in which you'll pay is simple, direct, and certain. You won't be able to attract good salespeople to replace the departed. Your lack of concern for them will be rewarded with their lack of concern for you.

The underlying objective of a good sales program is to make money, but in order to make money, you *need good salespeople*. The only sure way that you can get and keep good salespeople is to implement and maintain a program

101

that is profitable for you and them. Provide the rewards, both financial and emotional, that you both need. It is a partnership that is dependent on profitability for both of you. If that is your guiding influence, you won't go wrong.

Summary

Now that we've hired and devised a method of paying the salesperson, let's see how we got to this point. By determining our sales market position, we were able to define the type of selling job to be done. By making an accurate definition of the product and its life cycle, we were able to judge the primary duty of the salesperson in terms of what kind of information needs to be given to the customer. By arriving at an understanding of our product objective in terms of growth and profit contribution, we were able to focus the efforts of the sales force on the primary objective. Finally, where we have two types of products or services, and one is marginally profitable but necessary to generate the highly profitable sales, we can structure the sales program and payment plan to achieve our objective successfully.

The underlying necessity is to understand the exact nature of the sales job to be done and understand the customer completely. Along with this is the implicit assumption that you completely understand which products and services contribute most to your profit and overhead and which ones are absolutely necessary to support the profitable items. If you completely *understand your own business,* recruiting and compensating your sales force is easy, following the guidelines presented.

6

Sales Force Development: Motivation and Evaluation

How do you motivate salespeople? What is involved in getting the salespeople to work hard, "smart," and consistently? How can you evaluate their efforts to determine if they are doing the job?

After we answer all those questions, how do we decide on how many salespeople we need? Isn't figuring how many salespeople to hire a part of sales forecasting? How can a small firm estimate sales and forecast with any accuracy?

We may not have all the answers to these questions, but we will at least touch on possible methods for you to get the answers. Despite the efforts of scientific studies to quantify the aspects of sales, it remains more art than science.

All through school we are taught why one thing is beautiful and another isn't. We are told the elements of beauty, how tones mix, what to look for in artistic composition. But in the final analysis, none of us can say just what makes for success in art. For example, who is the better singer, Willie Nelson or Placido Domingo? Both sell out their performances and by monetary standards both are extremely successful. It is the same with two successful salesmen. We can analyze, poke, study techniques, and find as many differences as similarities. Like any art, there is no pat formula for success.

However, all artists study and practice the fundamentals. No performer just walks out on the stage and begins. Even some so-called natural artists who didn't have a formal education still went through some type of learning process. That process may have been nothing more than years of trying and failing until one day they finally hit on a formula of success.

Another example from music supports this concept. The late 1950s jazz pianists, Errol Garner and Oscar Peterson, were both excellent musicians and showmen. But their careers had different roots. Mr. Garner had no formal musical training. Mr. Peterson had many years of classical piano training. Yet they were equally well regarded by the experts and equally successful with personal appearances and record sales. Their styles reflected their backgrounds to some extent, but certainly not to the detraction of either. They both were excellent with the basics of music, rhythm, tonal quality, composition, melody, harmony, and expression.

The point is, even though there are many ingredients and many combinations for success, all artists must learn the basics of their craft. The same is certainly true for salespeople. By carefully analyzing the methods of different successful salespeople, we can learn enough to use in combination with our talents the marketplace to do a good, perhaps even excellent, job.

An orchestra conductor has a job similar to the sales manager. The conductor motivates, leads, and directs the musicians in the orchestra, with all their different talents and different instruments, to produce music. Could an orchestra conductor lead a group of musicians not knowing anything about music himself? Hardly. Just as the conductor must be a musician, so must the sales manager be a salesperson.

Many times the phrase *motivate salespeople* is used. How ridiculous! In truth, however, only salespeople motivate salespeople. No one else can do it for them—no more than someone else can motivate us to do anything. By re-defining motivation, maybe we can learn what to do to cause salespeople to motivate themselves. Because nearly all sales managers are responsible for motivation, we must understand what is involved and how we can develop the necessary skills.

We should put one other misconception to rest: Money is *not* the moti-vation behind top sales performance. Making a salesperson "hungry" enough does not guarantee sales. In fact it may have a negative effect.

When we described the sales compensation plan as closely interrelated with the specific nature of the sales job to be accomplished, we mentioned that some salespeople are well suited for long-term sales projects. These people work best with the security of a salary, although they still require financial feedback for their success. However, they are patient, good with details, and relatively error-free in customer and product application analysis. These salespeople work well with high-ticket items, because sales are relatively infre-quent. By the same token, if they didn't have a salary, making them "hungry" by depriving them financially would not work to motivate them. Probably the effect would be the reverse.

On the other hand for the type of salesperson who works best on straight commission assuming that the product and market position lend itself to that strategy, the lack of financial security serves as a part of the motivation stim-uli. But even with this type of person, money alone won't serve to motivate—it is only part of the total package. Other nonmonetary types of feedback must be used with all salespeople, regardless of the other components of the sales and marketing strategy. These include evaluation, training, and development, including them in planning and providing rewards, to name just those most easily used by small firms.

Starting with the basics and following the flow of ideas from inception, to description, to implementation, to conclusion is the most logical approach to the subject of sales motivation. Think about the general subjects that we covered in Chapter 5. We discussed the steps necessary to hire the right sales-people and pay them correctly for the job to be done. There is our first hint to motivate them.

Expectations

It is important to let salespeople know specifically what is expected of them. Salespeople aren't inclined to analyze the nature of the job the way you need to. They aren't likely to analyze the firm's market position, the segment

105

of the market, the overall marketing strategy, the resources available to the firm, nor any of the other considerations that you included when developing the strategy which led to their selection in the first place. They certainly are not going to study in much detail the nature of the selling job that they just accepted, the age of the market, the phase of the product life cycle, nor the product mix with which they will be involved. Those all are critical considerations when putting together the sales program, but salespeople probably won't know or care about that.

In the discussion about hiring salespeople, we mentioned that at least one interview was devoted to describing the sales job. But in one short interview you are not going to provide enough detail to let new salespeople know exactly what you expect of them. So, the first Monday morning of the job, schedule some time with them to let them know in *exact* terms what you want them to do. This is not as simple as it sounds. If anything, this post-hiring interview may be more difficult than all the previous interviews. During the previous interviews you spent considerable time, unconsciously perhaps, selling the firm to the prospective employees. Simultaneously the prospect spent considerable effort selling you on why they should have the job. That process is behind you to a large extent, although admittedly you continue to sell yourselves to each other throughout your relationship.

Now is the time to be *completely candid.* Otherwise you run the risk of spending time and money in the training process only to find that the job isn't what either of you understood, with disastrous results. At best they will quit or you will terminate them fairly early on in the relationship. At worst you both will continue but neither of you will be happy. That is the biggest danger because even though you and they are going through the motions, the sales effort isn't as effective as it should be. Both parties are then faced with the choice of making the most of a bad situation or deciding to separate. In either case strong emotions come into play and rational judgment could be sacrificed.

From a purely economic point of view both you and they could lose considerable opportunities to make money. They won't be working effectively and putting the concerted effort into the job that is necessary to achieve excellence. From your standpoint you do not get the sales possible. The cost of lost sales to a business is much more than the immediate loss of revenue. The bigger loss is the market penetration that should have been made, and that loss is truly incalculable.

During the hiring process we prepared an outline to guide us in our discussion of the sales job to be done. Use the same outline during the critical orientation interview on the first day of employment. The difference is that much more time must be spent on each item. Describe in detail your market position, strategy, opportunities, and competition. In addition describe in specific terms how you envision them performing their mission in your marketing strategy.

When you talk about duties and responsibilities, be specific. What hours do you expect them to keep at the office? If considerable time is spent away from the office, what provisions are available to maintain contact? Do you provide telephone answering, pocket pager, or mobile telephone? Or how does the person answering the phone handle messages? Determine ahead how you and the salesperson want phone messages handled to your mutual benefit.

In discussing your expectations of accomplishing the sales mission in your strategy, review carefully the method of reporting and how to handle sales. Is reporting to be formal, including memos for certain accounts or situations? Or do you have a simple call report form that they are required to complete every day or every week? Explain the reasons and advantages of whatever system you use, and be open to suggestions for improvement that new people may offer from their experience.

As silly as it may sound, make sure that they know exactly what to do when a customer wants to buy something. Understanding this step immediately is more important than understanding your business or products. This knowledge would come eventually once they have acquired product knowledge, but it is better to prepare them ahead of time. How many times have you tried to purchase something from a new salesperson only to discover that you know more about writing orders than the salesperson? You get so frustrated with the person's incompetence and poor training that you avoid doing business there again. The simple way to avoid that dilemma is to train salespeople to handle sales early in the orientation stages, even before they understand your company and products, so they can start to be productive right away.

Probably the only remaining topic to discuss with the new salespeople that we can address on a generalized basis here is the matter of presentation alternatives and terms of sales. This may seem simple, but a new salesperson coming into the firm needs to know your particular method of presenting the benefits of your firm to prospects, not only what verbiage to use but in what form. Do you have the support resources for elaborate written proposals, or do you use a standard proposal format? In the case of verbal presentations, have you worked out a standard script that assures that the whole sales story is told every time?

Let me correct one possible false impression. I do not believe in "canned" presentations as such. However, there should be a *standard outline* for salespeople to use with their own phrasing and words, possibly even changing the order to suit their individual preferences. But to start new salespeople, it is helpful to provide specific guidance until they understand the relevance of all the information that the customer may need to make a decision.

The last and most often overlooked sales consideration is the standard *terms of sale* for your firm. Do not assume that all firms in your industry use the same terms. Even if the terms are similar, make sure that the salespeople know when and under what circumstances they should quote prices and terms without management approval, whether that is always, never, or somewhere between. Most difficulties seem to arise from incorrect quotations of terms. You may not want to quote a lease-purchase option except on certain models. Or your credit manager doesn't want to do business with certain customers except on a cash basis or at most on a net 30. Whatever your rules are and however you make your various term offerings to the customer, make sure that your salespeople understand them completely. It may be more difficult to correct errors in terms than in pricing or even product application.

Mode of dress and transportation are part of the image of the firm. How do you expect the salespeople to project the image that you want? Are they to wear business dress at all times or are they permitted to dress casually? What may be standard for your industry and its customers may not be standard for the rest of the business community. Make sure that your salespeople understand your requirements, and that you can explain rationally why you have them.

If company transportation and uniforms are used by your firm, make sure that new salespeople understand that ahead of time. The same goes for expense accounts—don't assume that they know your expectations or your industry's normal practice. Are they authorized to buy customer lunches? Should they join civic and service clubs at your expense?

Expenses

Let's look closely at expense accounts for a moment. So much time is spent on discussing expenses not because of the outright monetary impact on the firm's cash flow but rather the *moral considerations*. Which is most important: the demoralizing effect on nonsalespeople if the salespeople have an overgenerous allowance or the demoralizing effect on salespeople if their expense account is inadequate for the job to be done?

Discuss expense account policies the first day on the job. Write down the salient points of your discussion to make sure all parties understand what is expected. A sure way to undermine sales efforts is to mess with the salesperson's money, whether compensation or expenses. A little time spent on this now prevents many problems later. If your salespeople are paid on a straight-commission basis, they generally are expected to absorb normal expenses, including transportation and entertainment. But if you want them to attend a function that is out of the ordinary realm of the duties of their assigned area or accounts, then it would be normal for you to cover a predetermined, reasonable expense account.

In all other cases the norm is for the firm to pay entertainment and transportation expenses, directly or indirectly. There are nearly as many ways to handle this as there are industries, and I have never been able to come up with anything at all scientific as to what and how much to do. But by looking at some typical methods, however, maybe you can find a system that fits your needs and is typical of your area or industry.

Let us consider transportation expenses. For most small firms that means an automobile. Three basic systems work well. The first is to pay a flat car allowance of $100 to $300 per month and have the salesperson be responsible for all car expenses. The advantages to the salespeople are that they have the latitude to economize on transportation or drive a luxury car, and that the allowance becomes a de facto income supplement that is tax-free. The advantage to the firm is primarily the ease of budgeting—you know in advance every month exactly what your transportation costs are. The system's main disadvantage for the employer is the fact that the allowance may cost more than a reasonable mileage payment would. Additionally the employer loses control over the selection of the mode of transportation.

The second main method is to pay an agreed mileage rate for actual mileage incurred while on company business. Usually the equitable rate is whatever is approved by the Internal Revenue Service. This system has most of the same tax advantages for the employee and the firm. The disadvantages to the firm are less certainty for budgetary purposes and lack of control of mode. The main caveat with this system is to agree with the salesperson at the time of hiring and to reaffirm at the time of any change in duties exactly what mileage will be paid and why. If you won't pay mileage for them to go to lunch with friends or to play golf, but will pay mileage for them to attend club functions representing the firm, those are the types of specific conditions that need to be clarified at the outset. I've heard some firms complain that this system allows for easy abuse and padding, but employee padding of mileage reports is the least of your concerns. They can more easily convert company money, fudge on whom they take to lunch, and, most importantly, make less than an honest effort to sell your products or services. The slight financial risk of this system is not enough reason not to use it.

The third method of handling transportation is to furnish company vehicles. Like the other two systems this isn't perfect, and again it is important to make sure that all parties completely understand the ground rules in advance. How much and under what circumstances is personal use of the company vehicle permitted? Are salespeople assigned a specific vehicle? Can they go back and forth to work or just pick up the vehicle to make sales calls? These are the types of questions that need specific and clear answers. The advantage to the firm for this system is control of the type and condition of the vehicle. Do you want it marked with the company logo? It's difficult to ask that of an employee using personal transportation. You can demand a clean and neat vehicle. In other words you maintain more control. The disadvantage is the cost of the vehicle and its operation. Whether this is more or less than the other systems depends on total mileage and use considerations. The cost is small if control is important.

One system that works well is a combination of all three. The company pays an allowance to the employee for transportation, but the vehicle selected by the salesperson must meet preset parameters suitable to the company. The salesperson then keeps track of business and personal mileage, and any personal mileage over a predetermined limit is paid by the employee. The major disadvantage here is the system's complexity. It has many of the advantages and disadvantages of all three systems. Some firms with this system allow employees to pay a small monthly fee for unlimited personal use. This system is particularly attractive to reward high, sustained sales efforts with a luxury car and perks.

One expense system that defies classification but has merit in many situations involves sharing the responsibility with the salesperson. Make a determination ahead of time as to what expense limits are appropriate for a given period, typically a month, or for a special event. This works well for attendance at trade shows or out-of-town sales meetings. At the end of the period, if the salesperson exceeds budget, that's the individual's problem. On the other hand, if expenses come in under budget, the savings are split between firm and employee.

Expense advances must be dealt with on an industry basis. There seems absolutely no consistency as to when and how much, nor do the use of advances seem to correlate with a firm's expense policies in general. Do what you think best and reasonable but *be consistent* with all your salespeople.

Check with your accountant first to see which system offers you the most economic advantages. Weigh those carefully against the relative control that you would retain or give up. Consider what would be best for your employees, all things considered. Longevity is important, so don't risk your profitability needlessly. But there are ways to pass some benefits on to employees without having them treated as taxable income, such as having salespeople with company vehicles charge a tank of gas on their personal credit card each month so they can show that they don't have unlimited personal use of the company vehicle. But you should check with your accountant before designing and discussing *any* system with your employees.

These same types of systems would apply to the other expense items, such as travel and entertainment. Pay a flat allowance, pay only predetermined items, or pay up to budget limits. The payment up to a budget limit passes control to the salesperson, but by the same token heavy spenders will be using their own money after exceeding the limits. A flat allowance may encourage the salespersons to limit expenses, but usually at your expense—since they stand to make money on the allowance, you may not get the customer entertainment for which you are paying. Above all, decide and discuss in advance and clarify specifically what is included in entertainment expenses. clubs, drinks, recreation? at what level? first class or coach? steaks or Big Macs? Don't assume. Discuss.

Sales Performance

So far we have talked in terms of informing the new salespeople, and presumably the existing ones, about your expectations of duties and some nitty gritty details of operation. But we haven't talked about the most important aspect of the job: sales performance.

Many inexperienced sales managers are for some reason reluctant to talk about sales performance. And yet what could be more basic in terms of describing your expectations of their work? Your description of your expectation of their performance says a lot about you. Let 's dwell on the ramifications of discussing performance.

If you downplay your anticipations of their performance, they will assume that performance isn't important to you. If you minimize the efforts necessary and make the job seem too easy, they will probably feel that you think the sales job is easy or, at the least, that anyone can meet your requirement levels. There will be a lack of a challenge to their ability, and they will think that they can coast.

The other extreme is to make the job so difficult that they are overwhelmed with the magnitude of learning the business and developing the territory for their own clients and still maintaining an adequate level of sales from the outset. If they are overwhelmed, they will be so in awe of the job that they won't be able to function at all. In the process they may not only get an insufficient level of sales, but also be confused to the point that they never understand the basics of the business, its benefits for the customers, and the mechanical knowledge of pricing, terms, and execution of ancillary duties.

To say that you should steer to the middle ground is such a gross oversimplification that some additional time must be spent determining exactly where that middle ground is. At issue is not only fairness of your expectations but possibly even the success of your whole sales program.

To determine the middle ground, start with the salespeople's personal earnings. They can relate to this. During the course of hiring you probably discussed with them the job's potential, and they no doubt shared with you their financial expectations. If this exchange of expectations was candid and realistic, it should serve as the basis for charting sales. The key words are *candid* and *realistic* from both of your points of view. If you indicate that the job has a reasonable potential to produce $25,000 annual income but the salesperson feels that $40,000 was a better reflection of abilities and desires, then you may have some basis for mutual concern. No one could reasonably assume that those income figures would be attained early in the relationship unless the salesperson is coming from a competitive situation and has a developed clientele. Otherwise the need to develop product information and a clientele list consumes considerable time and energy during the initial stages of employment.

If in your opinion the salesperson is capable of earning $40,000 but the job can be expected to produce only $25,000, you both are better off to face that issue squarely. On the other hand a salesperson who wants $40,000 but doesn't seem to have either the ability or desire to achieve that kind of earnings will probably fall far short of even $25,000.

In essence this discussion with the salesperson, whether a new employee or someone moving from another job within the firm, is the basis for the critical goal-setting task. A salesperson without specific goals will probably not succeed. As we discussed earlier, salespeople by their nature need direct feedback as to their performance. That feedback works best if it is some form of direct compensation, whether salary, commission, or perks, but it must exist. Therefore, without the feedback mechanism, the salesperson won't know whether sufficient progress is being made.

Goal-setting

The simplest and most effective way to approach goal-setting is to request the salespeople to submit their goals to you in writing, spelling out specific achievement levels by specific points of time. You and they should each retain a copy. Be sure to file your copy with their other confidential records, not in the general file where other employees have access.

Because the goals are theirs, rather than ones imposed on them by you, they are more likely to attain them. They will be committed to reach the goals for their own satisfaction and also because they have mentally already spent the money. However, you must encourage them to reach their goals by helping them throughout the period and expressing a sincere interest in their attainment.

One phenomenon that no one seems to understand does work. When the salespeople set goals for themselves, they almost invariably set higher standards than you would reasonably expect them to achieve. Pride has a bearing, no doubt, and yet if you are profit-oriented, you want them to attain a profitable level of sales and contribute to company overhead and profit.

There are two logical explanations as to why they set higher standards than you would impose. The first assumes that management doesn't have any sales experience. Therefore the sales job looks difficult, and even modest success seems hard. The second assumes that management in fact does have a sales background. But due to management's strong ego the perception is that no other salesperson could possibly attain the success that management enjoyed. Therefore management sets lower levels than would be reasonable. Against both of these backgrounds is the salesperson's own ego. Salespeople want to achieve, and they must achieve. Therefore, they set higher standards than either type of manager, whether sales-oriented or not. At any rate, let salespeople set their own goals. It's unlikely that you will be disappointed if you did a reasonably good job of recruiting and hiring.

Having determined what the salespersons' goals are, expressed in personal earnings, in gross sales, or in gross margin produced for the company, the next step is to develop a chart to trace their progress. This chart should be expressed in either gross sales or gross margin produced. Design the chart to show their goals and their intermediate objectives. Allow the chart to accommodate a small margin for overachievement. That margin should be kept small to encourage them. A wide margin would tend to demean their honest goals. If they do overachieve, they then get greater satisfaction from "going off the chart." Clearly show their goals. Keep the chart up to date with the latest sales figures so that progress against intermediate objectives shows as well.

Also, by seeing that the graph is current, you are indicating to them that you think goal setting and attainment are important and that their work is important to the company. Obviously, failure to maintain the graph and data accurately conveys to them that you care little about their work.

Because we are still operating on the assumption that your sales force is small and there may be little direct competition among your salespeople, *avoid* a chart that places them side by side for performance. It is sufficient merely to have the charts for each salesperson displayed in your office or the sales office. Salespeople compare them even though the graphs are designed to depict only *their* goals and achievements. The underachiever or poor performer sees quickly the relation to the other salespeople. A chart should be a reflection of personal goals and expectations based on service time, territory, or product line potential and other personal factors that affect their performance for that period.

Also make it perfectly clear that the graphs are not the final report card. There could be legitimate reasons why goals and performance are at less than a profitable level, and those should be discussed between you and the salesperson in confidence. Of course, you don't want a sustained period without profitability.

At the outset we said that no one can motivate salespeople (or anyone else, for that matter), but can only provide an environment in which they can motivate themselves. With this goal-setting technique we in effect let them motivate themselves and get their commitment to a satisfactory level of performance.

Achievement of Goals

Starting with goals set at a satisfactory but attainable level, let's see what it takes to achieve those goals. This is an area where you and the salespeople can get a big jump on the competition in most cases. Practically no small firms have an organized program to reach goals and objectives. At most they write down their goals, prepare graphs, do all the other parts of the exercise described earlier, and then quit and wait for results. Few have an organized plan to accomplish the objectives and reach the goals within the prescribed time. They may talk about goals, have short bursts of activity that make the goals look attainable, and then don't follow through.

The Sales Lead

To get sales, you must first get leads for prospects. After the prospects you must qualify them, make the presentations, close the sale, and collect the money. Let's study how we can develop these steps from management's viewpoint. We won't talk about the mechanics of performing the various steps for the simple reason that there is an abundance of articles, pamphlets, and books on sales techniques. But we will address the process from management's perspective.

Whether you are operating a retail store that is dependent on advertising or a commercial or industrial firm that relies more on direct sales efforts, sales leads must be generated. Advertising should do that for the retail store, except for more expensive goods or services. Then the advertising may be institutional to remind customers of your existence. At any rate the advertising may arouse the potential customers' interest in your product or establishment. What happens next is up to the salesperson. But no matter how the sales leads are generated, it's helpful to understand how to measure sales effort and predict results working from the sales leads.

When you receive a sales lead, whether in the form of a customer coming to the premises of a retail store or a phone inquiry to a commercial or industrial firm, record the lead. This recording process should include the source of the lead, the product or service in which the customer expressed an interest, and whether that is in fact what is best for that customer. Finally indicate the volume of business that you anticipate the firm doing in the near future, say, 30 days and the probability of your getting that business. By compiling the data, you begin to develop some trends as to lead sources and products that arouse interest.

When taking data on an informal basis such as this, don't let early trends cause you to jump to premature conclusions about your lead generation process. Additionally don't let the process of developing this information take so much effort that the actual sales presentation gets short shrift. I have observed cases where the employees of the firm have been so concerned with filling in a survey form correctly, that they've lost the customer due to lack of attention. But make every reasonable effort to gather and compile the data consistently.

By studying the sources of your leads, you can determine if you are reaching the market audience that you feel has the most potential for your firm. And you can probably draw some inferences if the source of your leads or the nature of the customer is considerably different from what you had expected. If you do encounter substantially different results from what you anticipated, you may want to reexamine the message itself or the target that you had selected. At the least you will want to gather as much data as possible before changing your tactics or your strategy.

But this "research" is also great help in evaluating your sales program, whether it or the advertising is responsible for developing the sales leads. Along with the information about the lead source and the product drawing the interest, you can measure the success of your sales rate. If you receive 100 sales leads, but you close only one sale within a short time of receiving the lead, you will want to delve further into the disposition of the 99 leads. Did they purchase comparable products or services from someone else? Why? You need to know why they stated an interest and then purchased from someone else or didn't purchase at all. Naturally a fairly large portion of leads does not develop into sales, but certainly you should have better than a 1 percent success rate. Be as objective as possible evaluating the customers' stated reasons for not purchasing. It may give clues as to the real reason or maybe the clue is that your lead generation program is aimed at the wrong prospect.

If the salespeople are directly responsible for generating their own leads, you can use the lead measurement indicator as a device to determine their effectiveness. Or, to put it in the other context, how many leads they generate should be an indication of their efforts, both as to quality and quantity of their contacts made.

Qualification of Leads

To tie this into their goal setting, you should be able to quantify the leads to such an extent as to predict sales accurately. Some examples may be helpful to illustrate the point. If the salespeople generate 100 leads every month, at least 10 should become qualified prospects. Of those 10, 2 should result in sales within the month. Five or 6 won't buy for two or three months, and the balance will buy from your competitor. But if your sales goal is 4 units a month starting with the first month and working up to 8 within a few months, then let's see how this progression would work with sales leads as the starting point. Figure 6–1 illustrates how to track the efforts and results.

To reach a sales goal of 2 units a month requires 100 leads, as shown in the previous example. If you need 4 units a month starting with the first month, and continuing to build at a progressive rate, 200 leads must be generated. This could be expressed in units or dollar volume. Because dollar volume is the important final measurement, you may wish to convert the units. If

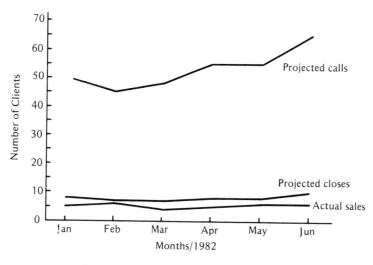

FIGURE 6–1. Performance Review: Jane

you are dealing with multiple products at various price levels, the principle stays the same; it only requires some subjective data as to the dollar potential of each qualified prospect.

There are some valid and consistent ways to change the equation, although the basic formula remains the same. The numbers cited are based on cold sales leads resulting from advertising or sales contacts by mail. The salesperson then follows up the lead with a phone call to try for an opportunity to see the prospect and make the presentation. If the product is low-priced and simple, even the presentation could be done on the phone. But that probably won't work well if you're selling to other businesses or professional offices.

This program works well and produces consistently the types of numbers in the equation that I've cited. By the same token I've also seen the formula modified so that the numbers are different but it is still successful. The use of advertising, whether printed media such as magazine or newspaper or the use of direct mail, with the target audience well-defined in either case, is the starting point.

Next the salespeople need to contact by phone as much of the target audience as possible. This need not be as formidable as it might sound. By working for 60 to 90 minutes at a time, three times a week, starting the first thing in the morning, they can call 20 to 30 contacts a day, or up to 90 per week, and leave plenty of time for coffee, golf, expense reports, and sessions in the hall, along with other comparable critical duties.

The purpose of the phone calls is simply to gain either appointments or other opportunities to make the presentation of your firm and product. To make life as simple and unconfusing as possible for the target audience, try to limit the message to one product or service or groups of services. This isn't the time to try to impress prospects with your full capabilities. You'll confuse them and lose their attention altogether. When calling, the salesperson should suggest a specific time to meet but let the prospect suggest an alternative.

At least 10 percent of the leads contacted by phone should result in opportunities to make the presentation. If your success ratio is significantly higher, you may have more sales potential then you realized, and significantly lower would tend to indicate either something wrong with the advertising message or the technique of the salesperson. Any reasonably articulate salesperson should easily realize a 10 percent success ratio. Although this isn't a book on sales training, make sure that the salespeople have a "script" outline to use while they are phoning. Otherwise they tend to lose sight of the objective of the phone call—opportunities to make presentations.

With the names and addresses of the opportunities for presentations, the salesperson is prepared to go forth. But those presentation opportunities are a long way from closed sales. The next step in the process is to qualify the prospects. By qualify, consider two categories. First, does your product or service truly benefit them? If the customer is a business, you should be able to show direct rewards for the purchase. If the customer is a retail consumer, then other, less qualifiable benefits must accrue to the purchaser. But benefits must occur, and sufficiently to warrant the purchase. Otherwise the prospect is not qualified. Second, can the customers afford your product? Can they pay for it? Their reactions to your presentation should answer that question. If you don't have a clear answer by the end of the presentation and after asking the closing question, the answer probably reveals itself when you ask for the money or a credit application. If customers tend to pass over that subject, they probably don't want to pay. This area requires considerable judgment and maturity on the part of the salesperson; but a good, paying, solid, credit-worthy customer never is upset by this line of questioning.

If after the presentation and qualifying of the customer the customer still won't place an order, but the salesperson has by trial closing determined that the sale is assured, only the timing is in question; that particular customer may not buy during this month but may be a future sale. That doesn't mean to imply that all reasonable efforts to close the sale or to follow up with later meetings at the customer's request shouldn't be made. But if after reasonable effort delay is inevitable, then repeat the whole process with another lead. Future sales won't pay the light bill, but it takes a backlog of futures to succeed in the present.

Of those prospects to whom you made presentations, at least 2 of 10 should buy almost immediately, 2 or 3 will probably buy from your competitor, and the balance will generally split evenly between buying from you later or not buying from anyone.

From management's point of view the key to the process is for the salespeople to generate or follow the leads to begin with. During the goal-setting process, once the sales goal is defined, begin showing the salespeople the efforts needed to attain their goal, and show how they can attain their intermediate objectives, presentation opportunities, working a reasonable amount of time with moderate success ratios. If they think that they can exceed the normal success ratio, don't discourage them; maybe they can, but make sure that they stick to the plan, no matter what ratio they actually achieve.

By using this step-by-step process you do more to motivate salespeople than nearly anything else you can do. They need to set intermediate goals and objectives in terms of lead follow-up, presentations, and the other steps, but those should be figured out with the final sales goal in mind. Setting a sales goal without working out the necessary intermediate steps and objectives generally results in sales goals that aren't achieved, at least not on a consistent basis. Figure 6–2 presents an analysis of how such a plan works.

Program Variations

Let's look at variations of this program and why the variants work and when. Salespeople probably want to make personal calls, rather than phone calls, in most cases. Their argument is that they won't get many prospects to make presentations as a result of a phone campaign, whereas personal calls achieve a much higher success ratio. And they're absolutely right.

However, there is a catch that they choose to overlook. They find that it is impossible to make a sufficient number of contacts working with "cold"

	Percent of above				
Contacts		200			
Appointments	10.00%	20			
Demonstrations	50.00%	10			
Closes within 30 days	25.00%	2.5			
Average system cost		$7000.00	Add $10,000/month for residual		
Total sales		$17500.00	$27500.00	$37500.00	$47500.00
Commission		$1700.00	$3100.00	$4500.00	$5900.00
Salary		$800.00	$800.00	$800.00	$800.00
Expenses		$100.00	$100.00	$100.00	$100.00
Gross income		$2600.00	$4000.00	$5400.00	$6800.00

FIGURE 6–2. Sales Projections and Commissions

calls. No matter how many prospects are available when the salesperson arrives, it takes at least 15 minutes per contact just to set up a later presentation meeting, even if the prospect agreed to the presentation at the time. Working at that rate, starting at 8 A.M, taking one hour for lunch without breaks, and working until 5 P.M., they can make contact with only 32 prospects, or 4 an hour. But stop and think how impossible it is to follow that schedule. In the first place, 8 to 9 A.M., 11:30 to 1:30, and after 4 P.M. are poor times to see customers without preset appointments. That is 3 hours gone or 12 prospects not contacted. During those time slots the salesperson needs to do reports, organize the next round of work and tabulate previous efforts; it's not likely that the salesperson is on break during those hours.

Even with the ridiculous assumption that the salesperson does make 32 contacts and finds that 25 percent or 8 presentations can be made, that probably results in no more than two sales. Most salespeople and sales managers find that averaging six calls per day requires considerable concentration and luck.

But there is a time when personal contacts to set up presentations are absolutely necessary for two reasons. First, high-ticket items, by their nature, require more personal contact with the customer. Second, if the market is relatively small in number and geography, then personal contacts are necessary to increase significantly the success ratio cited earlier just to survive.

The method and mathematics of developing leads boil down to considering the number of sales to be made to reach the sales goal, the size of the perceived market in quantitative terms and geography to be covered, and the amount of time needed to make the presentation. In other words, simple logical application of time segments provides all the direction needed. No sophisticated program is necessary.

Personal contacts to establish opportunities for presentations may be a suitable alternative to phone calls, but make sure that the numbers justify the means. Requiring a simple daily tally of activities helps the salespeople recognize which sales tactic will work best for their particular circumstance. That may be the secret of motivation. Make sure that they know what efforts are required to attain their sales goals and provide the mechanism for them to measure their efforts themselves.

If salespeople are not encouraged to measure their own efforts and results, the tendency is to ignore the intermediate steps necessary to make sales until late in the month. Then the realization hits that their sales do not approach their monthly goal. To avoid that, have them keep track of all their activities from lead development to presentations as well as closes.

Provide them the means to chart their intermediate objectives in both shorter time frames and preliminary steps to make the sales. That way they won't be surprised, and by monitoring their own progress, or lack, they are far harsher and more effective at getting themselves on track than if their sales manager is scolding or finger-wagging.

Lead Generation Program

An organized, concerted *lead generation program* (LGP) is the key to sales success. Beyond the purely quantitative results cited earlier, let's look at some subjective values to the salespeople. A lead generation program that requires a specific number of leads generated in a given time frame, leading to a predetermined level of anticipated sales prospects, which leads to actual sales closes, provides extremely valuable direction to the sales efforts. Otherwise salespeople tend to get off track, get busy doing simple customer training or follow-up that others should be doing, and spend their time in other nonproductive matters and manner. The LGP gives structure to their activities.

Another value of a concerted LGP is the phenomenon that activity breeds activity. Work hard calling on customers in one group or end of town, and another group springs to life. Sit by the phone and nothing happens. Go to the second end of town and start working hard; the first end of town starts calling. There is no completely logical, plausible explanation for this occurrence because the events are too close together to be entirely attributed to the synergistic effect of one customer contacting another. It just happens. Use it. Don't try to understand.

Because of the carefully structured time of the salespeople working an organized lead generation program, they use their presentation time more effectively for two reasons. First, they know that they must see so many prospects within a given time frame. Instead of letting the socially amiable customer waste time, they concentrate on making a good presentation and closing the sale. They focus their best efforts on their sales techniques. Second, salespeople on a program qualify the prospects quickly and use their time with more qualified leads. In both instances it's a matter of time utilization, which results in a better sales closing rate and more time with the customers that are qualified. Figure 6–3 is another look at tracking efforts and results.

That makes it seem so simple. But unless you have been in sales full-time, dependent on your sales ability to make a decent living, it is hard at best to understand and feel the frustrations that salespeople experience daily. No

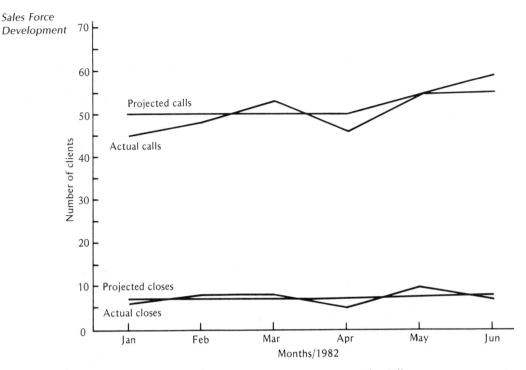

Number of clients

Projected calls

Actual calls

Projected closes

Actual closes

70

60

50

40

30

20

10

0

Jan   Feb   Mar   Apr   May   Jun

Months/1982

FIGURE 6-3.   Performance Review: Bill

matter how carefully you plan or how effectively you work, the fact is that something approaching 95 percent of the leads don't turn into sales. Just to get at a reasonable number of prospects that still need to be qualified and to make a good presentation requires hearing no many, many times. Usually it's not no but maybe or later, which still comes out in the final analysis as no.

Much earlier in analyzing types of personalities that make good salespeople, the subject of emotion came up. To handle this much rejection and yet still have the self-confidence to continue asking customers for the order requires a high level of emotional commitment to the selling profession. To go against those fantastic odds and still succeed takes more emotional effort than nearly any other occupation. It certainly isn't logical to take that much abuse. That's a simple explanation why frequent closers tend to be less stable emotionally, which usually comes through in their personal life style and habits.

Rewards

One other area of motivation bears consideration, that is, the psychological needs of the salesperson. Salespeople must have sensitive but large egos to do their job. But one area that is often ignored by sales managers, and managers in general, is praise for a good job. Write notes; go out of your way to compliment good performance, good appearance, or just good sustained effort; and the boost to ego is immeasurable. This is particularly true of salespeople. They need their self-confidence boosted more frequently than other skilled labor. As should be well understood, salespeople are in the sales profession for the recognition more than any other single factor. The money is only a measurement of recognition. Praise from a boss can go a long way to satisfy their recognition needs.

There are many books on the various aspects of sales as a profession. Some deal with the psychological concepts of priority of needs, based on Maslow's theories, and others work on the concepts of comfort zones. Still others deal with setting and reinforcing goals and many more ideas. You should find and read one or two books that make sense to you. Adopt the system that the particular author develops as the basis for your sales understanding. The books won't take the place of living the sales profession, nor will the books guide you on a daily basis in the conduct of your sales and sales management activities, but you will gain insights that will help you understand the phenomena that you observe daily.

You will probably want to set up some specific rewards for goal attainment. These rewards can be small and inexpensive, but they should be tangible and lasting. Salespeople should be able to display the reward in their office, home, or car, wherever they will be reminded and can in turn remind their peers of their success. Success breeds success.

Successful salespeople need more than a nice payday to continue success. Praise helps, but there is something more that will meet their needs, reward them for outstanding performance, and also pay you dividends: *professional sales training.* If you are representing a manufacturer that holds sales schools periodically, annually send the top salesperson to one, assuming that the top salesperson was in fact profitable.

One system that seems to work well for some firms is setting rewards for predetermined levels of achievement, for example, for $20,000 monthly sales, or a gross margin of $5,000, a dinner for two. For a level of $15,000 a month margin, or a figure that is profitable for you, reward them by sending them to a professional sales seminar, preferably one specifically for your industry. The farther the trip, the better the reward is. The additional air fare won't amount to much over the cost of the school and living expenses. These types of schools are quite often expensive, but the high-performance achiever will get a great deal of benefit, which will pass to the firm.

Above all, don't send the underachievers with the hopes of making them into sales performers at a school. It won't happen often enough to justify the risk and expense. Sending the achievers will reward them, and they are more likely to learn enough new ideas and further develop their old techniques; then the school will be extremely profitable for you both. They will learn as much from associating with other successful people as what is discussed in the classroom. Consider sending the spouses, as well, to increase their interest in your company.

Carefully establish the requirements to go to the school in terms of specific sales performance over a considerable length of time, say, at least a quarter but more likely six months. A more expensive, prestigious, or distant school may require a year of sustained performance before you can afford to send the achiever. But don't announce it at the last minute. Let the salespeople know well in advance the reward and requirements for attainment.

Another similar reward that works well but is much less expensive is attendance at your national or regional trade show. This is not working your booth, selling your products, but going to your own trade association meeting, where they can get other ideas from within your industry and see the latest products and programs. They will get just as much and sometimes more benefits from attending a meeting like that as you do.

Sales Meetings

The effect of rewards and seminars are all short-lived. The best job of training and developing your sales force can be done by you together with them at your place of business on a regular basis: the company sales meeting. Is this a meeting with lots of hype? or a boring meeting to voice clichés and review the excess inventory on hand? That isn't necessary.

The single most important key to successful sales meetings is *preparation*. Preparation is another word for planning. The second most important key is merely an extension of the first: *commitment,* commitment to regular meetings with nothing to interfere with the schedule. Sales meetings that can be delayed and postponed and don't stay on the schedule are sales meetings that are not considered important by management. There is no other way to interpret that course of action or inaction. If sales force development and growing sales are not important to you, the easiest way to communicate that fact is to let something interfere with the sales meeting schedule.

As we look at how to set up regular meaningful sales meetings, try to keep one fundamental in mind. Salespeople tend to be more sensitive to their working environment and interpersonal relations. Therefore they tend to give more importance to words and actions than you may like. For example, no matter how seemingly logical to you, rescheduling the sales meeting seems to them that you are demonstrating a lack of commitment to the sales force. Keep their sensitivity in mind.

As with any planning process the first step is to set the *objective of the sales meetings.* You most likely have both a near-term and a longer-term objective for the sales meetings. The near-term objective might be to redirect their efforts from one product or service to another, possibly by examining another of your products or by discussing competitive offerings. Or there may be opportunities for some other products that have been ignored by the salespeople. On a longer-term basis your objective may be to establish an organized lead generation program or to raise the professional sales techniques by establishing a sales training program.

There is no reason why all these objectives can't be accommodated simultaneously. You will have more success by *structuring your sales meetings in relatively short segments,* simply because salespeople, more than most, tend to concentrate on any one subject for shorter periods of time.

Regularity is even more important than the content or length of the meeting or *frequency,* for that matter. But frequency requires some special considerations. Frequency should be a function of logistics. The meetings, to be meaningful, should be at least monthly and at most weekly. In small business there is no good reason not to hold to that frequency. Distance should be the primary consideration. If the salespeople are spread over several hundred miles, monthly meetings may be all that's practical; but if they're primarily in the same city, weekly meetings are ideal. You must acknowledge local considerations in your planning. What is easy driving time in one part of North America may be considered grueling in another. Driving for several hours is acceptable west of the Rockies, while much shorter times for transportation are the norm in the Northeast.

The other part of logistics is *scheduling.* There is no hard-and-fast rule to follow, but logically you should schedule the meetings during the least disruptive sales time as possible. For most commercial and industrial firms this translates to Monday mornings. Many firms find that starting with breakfast or coffee before the normal business day lets those attending the meeting use and apply what was discussed. Other commercial and industrial firms have nearly equal success on Friday afternoons. The information retention rate may be somewhat less, but that may be outweighed by consideration for disruption of productive selling time. In most areas Friday afternoons are not good times to see customers. If your salespeople don't live in the same city, traveling Thursday evening or Friday morning for a Friday meeting to return home before the weekend works well.

The guiding consideration should be the least disruptive time possible. The reason to avoid disrupting productive selling time is twofold. First is the obvious direct potential effect on sales when the salespeople are in a meeting instead of making sales contacts. Second, and nearly equal in importance, is the salesperson's perception of the importance of time utilization. You need to reinforce by word and deed the critical time utilization concept of concentrating on the most productive task in any given time frame.

Whether your meetings occur every Monday, with salespeople who all live and work in one city, or monthly to bimonthly, for firms with salespeople somewhat distant, the most frequent schedule possible should be established. Schedule at least several weeks, if not months, in advance for you and the salespeople with written notice. That helps communicate the importance that you place on the meetings.

When you are establishing for your own guidance the objectives of the meetings, both long-term and near-term, write down those specific objectives. For at least two to three meetings in advance, sketch out the subjects to be covered at each. Develop a flow of ideas, and that way you can work toward a conclusion. Don't try to communicate all that you think is important at the first meeting. Start a train of ideas, all linking together, that will form the essence of knowledge. Remember your own education. Use the building block concept of adding a little new information each time but also reviewing the old. Requesting the salespeople to prepare and present the reviews is also a helpful device to get them involved in the process.

It is important that each sales meeting have an agenda. In building the agenda, try to limit the subjects to three areas: product information; operating, credit, financial, or administrative subjects; and sales technique training. Nearly everything that you want to discuss falls into one of those three areas, although perhaps not cleanly. But keeping those three areas in mind, you can raise the general interest level by not spending all the time on one subject or one area each meeting. By nature salespeople do better if they are given an opportunity to deal with a variety of subjects.

There is another clue in that paragraph: agendas. Write and distribute well ahead of time copies of the meeting agenda for all attendees. Then stick to the agenda. Invite all the salespeople to suggest ideas for the agenda.

When starting a program, take one form of pressure off yourself. Ask the salespeople what subjects they'd like to explore in the areas of both operating and credit considerations and sales techniques. The meeting is supposed to be for their benefit, rather than a chance for you to preach. Let them tell you how they think their meeting time can be spent more effectively. Avoid asking them individually or in private but seek participation from all.

No one expects you to be an expert in all areas. If they'd like to discuss a sales technique, or they feel weak in prospecting or closing or presentations, let them lead the discussion, sharing with the others what they are doing and why they think it works or doesn't. The other salespeople have perceptions and experiences to share on the same subjects. It would be helpful, of course, if you had sales experience so that you can more easily relate to their concerns, but serving as a good moderator is extremely important.

By letting the salespeople as a group help build the agenda and participate in the review process, you give them the opportunity to develop further their presentation skills as well as getting them more deeply committed to the subjects. It does take courage; but if you provide a framework for their growing process, you both benefit, and anytime you and the employees benefit, you probably are the bigger beneficiary.

Although few salespeople enjoy the process, role playing is an extremely effective way to practice and develop sales skills in presentation and closing. Don't spend a large portion of the sales meeting in role playing, but give all an equal opportunity to participate. Describe the scenario including the specific skill to be developed. Then let the salesperson address the prospect. In time the role playing becomes more realistic. The observers learn just as much as the participants, if not more, but make sure that all play all roles.

Time management should remain a central theme around which all the other subjects revolve. Salespeople, more than most, need to concentrate on time utilization techniques. By providing them the structure for their time through the development of the lead generation program, and establishing specific task goals under that program, they have the tools to utilize their time effectively.

By actively communicating your concern with time utilization, their awareness levels are raised significantly. You can communicate your concern by some simple devices. When you schedule meetings and personal conferences, are they during prime selling time? Do you emphasize the importance of doing the most important task that needs to be done during any given time frame? Have you made available a book, tape, or seminar on time management?

One of the chief values of the sales meeting is the opportunity for informal conversations. Selling is a lonely job. Salespeople find it extremely valuable to be able to share their daily experiences with their peers and to seek guidance from management. Don't try to schedule so tightly that some time isn't allowed for informal interaction between the salespeople and management and among salespeople themselves.

Review the lead generation program at each sales meeting. Ask for reports on their results from each salesperson. They should be able to develop excellent data as to quantity of sales calls necessary on a daily rate basis, along with resulting closes and prospecting calls to focus on the task.

Review and Evaluation of Performance

The lead generation program data should serve as the basis for your review and evaluation of the salesperson's efforts and performance. This review and evaluation should be done at least on a quarterly basis. It can be an extremely valuable tool in the salesperson's development. The review process also has a profound influence on performance and interaction between the salesperson and the other departments.

The review and evaluation process that I've found to be useful has several elements that can build the relationship between your company and the salespeople into a solid alliance. As mentioned, this review should be done for salespeople at least quarterly, although for other employees annually or semi-annually is frequent enough. The quarterly review should not be just your written report and evaluation of their performance. They probably know their performance. The review should be a learning experience for the participants.

Schedule an hour, slightly more if necessary, but certainly no less time. Meet in private with the salesperson, preferably away from the place of business. Before the meeting, review and become familiar with the salesperson's sales reports and performance. You should know what the actual sales for the period have been and have a clear understanding of the nature of accounts or territory for which they are responsible.

The focal point of the evaluation conference should be the evaluation form. Figure 6–4 gives an example, but you should design one that emphasizes

125

Field salesperson _____ Date _____

QUARTERLY EVALUATION
SELF/SALES MANAGER

OBJECTIVES

1. To identify individual contributions and capabilities—assess present job performance.

2. To improve individual performance.

3. To assist in personal development by preparing for advancement.

INSTRUCTIONS

Sales manager and salesperson each complete a copy. In conference, the two are compared item by item, particularly differences. Hold conference in private without interruptions. Allow 60 minutes maximum. Then review quantitative performance data:

1. Evaluate individual performance relative to job objectives

   a. Include both negative and positive specific examples

   b. Analyze specific significant objectives:

      (1) Objectives met
      (2) Objectives missed
      (3) Objectives exceeded

   c. Factors that helped or hindered job performance

   d. Specific examples of opportunities for improvement given by both supervisor and employee.

2. Prepare a development plan outlining objectives that the individual and supervisor agree will aid the employee's growth.

Performance Review Form

1. ORGANIZATION

	Always	Usually	Sometimes	Rarely	Never
Responsive to customer/prospect					
Paperwork timely					
Paperwork complete/accurate					
Uses time effectively					
Effective territory coverage plan					
Car and office organized for efficiency					

2. IMPRESSION

	Always	Usually	Sometimes	Rarely	Never
Dresses appropriately for customers					
Punctual for appointments/meetings					
Conveys positive attitude					
Courteous to all					
Honesty and sincerity exhibited					
Personally neat and clean					
Car and office clean					

3. RESOURCEFULNESS

	Always	Usually	Sometimes	Rarely	Never
Creates new leads from existing contacts					
Uses literature and written proposals appropriately					
Pursues leads diligently					
Creative application of products and services					
Looks for hidden opportunities					
Familiar with competitive programs and offerings					

4. SALES TECHNIQUES

	Always	Usually	Sometimes	Rarely	Never
Tailors approach/presentation to specific situation					
Is sensitive to customer's desires and objectives					
Questions prospect carefully to determine applicable product/service/combination					
Presents feature/benefits to prospect					
Exhibits pride in company and specific product/service					
Tough, forceful closer					
Asks closing questions frequently					

FIGURE 6–4.   Performance Review Form

the issues and traits that are important to your firm and the salesperson's development and profitability. At least a week ahead of your conference give the salespeople a copy of the evaluation form so that they can complete one rating themselves. Then when you get together, compare the results of the two forms. Go through item by item. Where your ratings differ, discuss and determine why the differences and resolve each before proceeding to the next. During this conversation you both find that the avenues for good two-way communications are opened.

The next part of the evaluation conference should be devoted to discussion of actual performance and effort measurements. Each of you should try to learn the why and why not of the performance characteristics. The salesperson's strengths should be discussed first; then move to weaknesses. Volunteer the company services or your personal attention to help correct the weaknesses. If the salesperson is genuinely interested in improving and is willing to seek remedial guidance, be sure to encourage and help all that you feel is reasonable.

The latter part of the conference should be used to discuss any operational or product questions that the salesperson has and for you to help determine whether product knowledge is adequate. Perhaps the person has been covering a lack of knowledge while in the group but may be more willing to ask questions of you in private. With that or any other issue, make sure that the person understands why, not just rote memorization of the product information or operational procedures.

As a conclusion to the conference, sum up briefly the important points discussed, but be sure to end by reviewing and expanding on strengths and positive contributions. A short note or memo confirming the conversation and highlighting the information that you need to convey is invaluable as a reinforcement device. Make sure that you and the salesperson retain a copy of the evaluation and self-evaluation forms. Subsequent meetings should also review the progress or slippage from the previous review period.

The overriding consideration should be that the evaluation and review conference is not a counseling session for reprimands or the basis for disciplinary action but a true sharing of information between management and salespeople. If management and sales honestly approach the sessions that way and both are prepared for the meeting, it is a positive learning experience for both parties.

Scheduling and preparation are the primary ingredients for the success of the review and evaluation meetings. It shouldn't require any special training, but, including preparation, about two hours per salesperson per quarter at the most is required but may be some of the most valuable time that you have spent in terms of results.

If you have several salespeople, make sure that your efforts are expended as equitably as possible. Don't let the high performer or the most likable dominate your time or become the de facto spokesperson for the group.

Counseling

With all these ideas on goal setting, ways to assure adequate sales, and concern with motivation, what happens if despite your best efforts, the salesperson doesn't maintain a profitable level of sales? Assume that you have convinced yourself at least that the fault is with the salesperson, not the company or the product. How do you deal with that?

For a surprising number of managers, this aspect of sales management seems to escape them completely. A huge percentage of the time, one of two equally bad characteristics seems to come out in the manager. Either the manager won't face squarely the fact that a problem exists or will face the problem with glee, for someone else can be blamed for the manager's troubles. Either set of reactions is destructive.

What should be done? Spend some time privately with the salesperson, *review goals and intermediate objectives* set by the salesperson. If failure to reach those goals represents substantial losses to the company, share that information also. But stress the lost opportunities for the person and the company that may not be recoverable due to the poor performance.

The final phase of the discussion is critical. Having made perfectly clear the successes and shortcomings, ask why performance is slipping. Listen to the reason. Don't arrive at the discussion with some predetermined ideas for the slipping. There may be some legitimate reasons that can't be helped, even though that particular salesperson is the only one experiencing difficulty. Make sure that the person understands the cost to the company and self for the present level. *Then give a specific time frame in which to attain a specific level of performance* that you consider moderately satisfactory and also serves as an indicator that the salesperson is getting back on the track.

Let the salesperson tell you what specific courses of action are necessary to achieve the sales level that you consider necessary. If the person doesn't have a direct and specific plan of action, devise one with the salesperson that is agreeable.

Put in writing the quantitative standards, whether sales, lead development, or whatever, that you think should be attained; also put in writing a clear definition of the date by which the objective must be accomplished.

Termination

If the salesperson can get performance back up to satisfactory levels, you both win. Often a salesperson who doesn't feel able to make a valuable contribution will quit before you need to terminate. Should it become obvious that the salesperson cannot perform adequately, spend time discussing why and helping the person find another job, perhaps outside of the sales profession.

Moving from a mediocre sales career to an extremely successful career as service manager has worked in two separate cases with which I'm familiar. Sales training and experience are invaluable in dealing with customers. If these people had been dismissed outright for poor performance, their employers would not have excellent service managers today.

Failure to succeed in sales does not mean by any means that people don't possess valuable talents that you or some other firm can use profitably. My reason for helping such people find another job is simple. Not only do I think that we owe some debt to our fellow humans, but also we must share in the blame for their failures. Perhaps if we had developed a well-organized sales program and spent the time counseling them and guiding them in their development, they would have succeeded. Helping them, even on the way out the door, is the least that we can do for our part in their lack of success. Don't lie on their behalf, obviously, but let your peers know the person's strengths when making recommendations.

Another benefit may accrue to your firm if you are a genuine help. Word will get around that you are humane and want to help your employees and also that you require specific performance, which will gain you respect among prospective employees and make recruiting for the replacement somewhat easier.

These last few paragraphs make it all sound so simple. And yet it seems a difficult process to execute. Managers won't face their roles in the failure, or they let emotions override rational approaches to the problem, or they can't bring themselves to set down standards and enforce them. Whatever the reason, this simple procedure of setting performance standards and then enforcing them seldom is carried out rationally, at a large cost to the company and a waste of human resources.

Let me tell about one client. I was brought into the firm to find what was wrong with the sales program. The firm's owner and one full-time salesperson were the sales force. After interviewing and evaluating, it seemed questionable whether the salesman should be in sales at all. Further, the owner didn't want to direct the salesman; he just wanted sales to happen. Instead of using me as the opportunity to set performance standards by which to guide the salesman, the owner chose to have me directly counsel and instruct the salesman. The most that the owner would face was that he wanted the salesman to be selling at a certain rate within 60 days, or at least be making progress in that direction.

The owner lost twice: he lost sales and he lost what he paid me to work with the salesman. The most that was accomplished was getting the salesman to a marginally profitable level, but short of the potential for the firm. By the time the owner paid me and the salesman, he broke even, which was an improvement but short of the possible results. This was primarily because the owner didn't want to set guidelines and enforce them. The irony is that the salesperson involved was one of the most teachable, hard-working people I've ever known. He tried nearly everything I suggested and made great strides. But the fact remains, he just didn't have much natural talent.

Summary

The small firm needs every area to be profitable. Sales force development is especially important for the small firm and should be the source of high returns. The most important investment for this sales return is to implement and maintain a concerted and consistent program that includes forecasting, recruiting and hiring, training and education, and review and evaluation. The final result will be a highly efficient, productive, and profitable sales force. The small firm cannot afford to have less.

7

Advertising

NIGEL HERE SPECIALIZES IN ADVERTISING FOR SMALL FIRMS

T ell people what you sell. Let them know where you are. That is advertising. It isn't anything more complex or mysterious than that. Don't let
anybody tell you otherwise, and don't let this discussion leave you with any
other impression. Those two things and only those two are the purpose of advertising.

You may need to deliver both messages or only one. You may need to
emphasize one and secondarily mention the other. As we proceed, it should
become obvious to you what you need to do.

We will look at some of the considerations as to which message you need
to deliver, how to deliver it, how much money to spend, and when to deliver
the message. Let's correct one wrong impression that may have already crept
in. This chapter is not to be a "one-source" reference for small business advertising. Rather it is to serve as a guide adequate for the needs of small business
managers who have little background in advertising techniques and little time
to spend on the process. Should you want to study the subject in more depth,
included in the bibliography are some books that I've found helpful, but there
are many good specialized books including college-level textbooks. Following
this chapter is a glossary of terms that people in small business should be familiar with so you at least get the drift of conversations with agency and
media representatives.

This chapter is written on the assumption that you *don't spend much time in
developing your advertising program.* As the generalist manager of a small business,
your time is spent on the areas with which you have expertise; for the areas in
which you're weak, you rely on your employees and key staff to fill the gaps. If
your background is the technical end of the business, you place most of the
bookkeeping and cash management responsibility onto the bookkeeper and
office manager; you hire salespeople and maybe service people. In all probability you oversee even the functions with which you're not familiar or experienced; but you still need to understand what is happening in those areas, even
if you can't do the work yourself.

With this assumption we will try to do a good job of defining the questions and showing you how and where to begin to find the answers. Because
you may get answers to any given question that conflict, we will try to help
you determine which answer to use for your particular situation. Usually the
conflicts are because the question and all its implications weren't correctly
understood, so redefining the question may be all that's needed.

Frequently, small business managers, whether wholesale, retail, commercial, industrial, professional, or manufacturing, all say the same thing: "I
can't afford to advertise much" or "I can't advertise like the biggies." Both are

true statements and should not be changed. But we aren't trying to compete directly with large firms, or at least we shouldn't. We should be concentrating on a small market segment that the biggies can't serve effectively.

A Start in Advertising

Let's put aside the question of how much to spend until we have a chance to understand our situation in the advertising context and what to include when determining on what we want to spend money. You can't decide how much money to spend on an automobile or even a residence until you decide what you want to *accomplish* with the purchase. Do you want luxury, utility, or size to accommodate a large family, or is style to reflect your tastes the important consideration? All are ways of saying the same thing: What is the intended use of the car or home? After the purpose is understood, then you can decide how much you want to spend. That may even be the most important factor in the final analysis, but it certainly is not the first question to ask.

Definition of Your Business

Understand the nature of your business. Forget for a few minutes all the assumptions about your business that have been guiding you. The assumptions may be correct, but let's see how all the pieces of the puzzle fit together.

Start with the *basic definition.* Is your business normally classed as retail? Do you sell directly to the end consumer? Another way to look at that question is what happens to your product or service once you sell and deliver (and presumably are paid). Does your customer use the product or service exactly as is or use it, along with its own products and services, to sell something? That may not be as complicated as it sounds, but the same products could be used in several ways, over which you have little control.

An article of clothing, say a blazer, could be a retail or commercial product, depending on its use. After the blazer is purchased from the clothing vendor, is it used strictly for business, or is it worn to social, religious, and entertainment functions? What happens to the blazer physically? Is a patch sewed on, or embroidered, to represent the logo of a company or organization, thereby tagging the blazer for specific rather than general use? You can go through the same exercise for personal computers, typewriters, autos. To decide what kind of business you have is best answered by seeing who your customers are and how they are using your products. Harry Homeowner could buy a garden tractor to maintain his own residence or to maintain rental properties in which he has an interest. How the item is treated for tax purposes by the purchaser may be another clue.

Commercial firms, which comprise one of the fastest growing classes of small businesses, are firms that deal almost exclusively with other businesses. *Almost exclusively* is used because you may sell 90 percent of your products to other businesses for their use in selling to their customers. Maybe the rare person comes in off the street and buys a personal computer or typewriter for home, nonbusiness use. Because that purchase does not represent even a large minority of your total business, you don't make any significant advertising or sales effort to get that customer. (Maybe you should. See Chapter 1.)

Business periodicals do not agree on the definition of industrial firms. But to remain consistent with the rest of the book, I've chosen the interpretation that industrial means, in fairly specific terms, the heavy construction, logging, and agricultural businesses. The definition used by business periodicals to include manufacturing firms in basic industries isn't applicable to small business. The types of products and services aimed at commercial and small industrial firms are unique enough to warrant the separate classification. Additionally the tools that they use, the equipment, is normally called *industrial equipment* when describing the construction, agricultural, and heavy highway transportation machinery. Their sales and advertising are decidedly different from that of the traditional commercial firm.

The large firms manufacturing in basic industries could well be and quite often are *customers* of small business, but by their scale would not get much benefit from this book. We are concentrating on the specific challenges of small business advertising.

Having decided what kind of business we are in by knowing who our customers are in general terms, we can look at the other facet. What does our business do? Are we primarily providing services or using services to sell products, or strictly selling products, the only service being to help the customer out the door with the purchase? Each type of business has different objectives for advertising.

Service-oriented businesses obviously use advertising to talk about the quality and experience offered. If you have a service department to support the sales of a product, the objective is to talk about the product; even when mentioning the service department, take the assumptive tack ("Of course, we have the best maintenance service in 10 counties"). Products as your only basis are more difficult because you are a somewhat easier target for your competitors.

Your type of business determines the objective of your advertising, but it could also complicate the message that you want to deliver and make the measurement of the results of your advertising more difficult. As we proceed, you can begin to decide how to take advantage of your own situation. Service is hard to talk about in advertising, sales and service combinations have the potential for implying problems with the product, and product-only situations are vulnerable to explicit competition.

The Customers

Although we have talked about customers at some length in other chapters, we again need to take a look to see who our customers are. We defined our business by category; but within those categories, we haven't yet discussed the total markets and the people who make the decisions in those markets.

We need to understand the people in terms of their duties and responsibilities
for their employers, the demographic, geographic, and socioeconomic groupings so that both media and message reach them most effectively. In addition to those considerations, we must consider the application of our product or service, whether it is frequently or infrequently purchased by the customer, and, for both cases, whether the purchase is discretionary or mandatory. To begin to plan an effective advertising program, all these factors must be known accurately.

When trying to determine the nature of your business for developing the advertising, try conducting your own simple research using information readily available to you. Review your sales records or, for new products and services, your anticipated volume and profit by product. Examine your customers, keeping some quantitative information as to category, so that you have a fairly accurate profile of what products sold and in exact terms who purchased. This is essentially the same information developed for your original marketing plan and further discussed while looking at marketing strategies for growth.

Objectives of Advertising

With that simple yet basic work done, we can begin to investigate and develop various advertising alternatives. One of the first steps is to define the objective of the advertising in simple terms. Incidentally, although our advertising objectives may change frequently, we will be successful only by focusing on one at a time. Unlike our planning objectives, advertising objectives may not change frequently; they may change in reaction to outside influences. Therefore, we must have the advertising objectives clearly in mind before we can intelligently decide on the message and media.

Our marketing objective is included in our basic plan. The marketing objective defines what we want to accomplish with our total marketing mix, which is the interaction of all elements of marketing: advertising, sales, pricing, and distribution. Our marketing objective is relatively fixed, as far as the objective and mission of the company itself are fixed. Our advertising objective is relatively unstable and reactive, rather than stable and directive.

Just now we passed over the concept again of the *marketing mix*, but let's take a minute to see how that works in small business. At the moment we are concentrating on the advertising component of the mix. The distribution channels and our pricing strategy assumedly are stable at this point. As we study the various methodology and objectives of advertising, it is extremely important to consider how the advertising will interact in specific daily operational terms with the sales efforts. Look again at what the salespeople do and their role with the customer. Do you expect them to present the benefits, close the sale, and do postdelivery follow-up? Or do the salespeople make a brief presentation, deliver the product, and go to the next customer? Do they have a relatively complicated task of matching the products with the application and arranging the appropriate financing? Or do they hand over the product, collect the money, perhaps only helping with the selection? All of these possible roles must be considered so that the advertising objective fits with the sales role. If the advertising does all the selling, or merely keeps the name in front of the customers, it must mesh with the sales effort.

When we define the objective of our advertising, the alternatives fall into *three basic categories;* in each of those categories, we need to direct our efforts in one of two directions. These categories of objectives are to inform, persuade, and remind our audience. Each of those objectives further needs to be directed toward either conveying what to buy or conveying where to buy it.

The categories of objectives could be a function of the product life cycle but certainly are dependent on your tactic with the product and the competitors' strategy. Which is the determining influence is irrelevant, but try to define clearly in your own mind which category of objective you want your advertising to fulfill. You will intuitively know which is appropriate without spending too much time on research. Any vestiges of doubt as to which to do should be eliminated by the end of this section.

Objective 1: To Inform

To inform, as an advertising objective, implies that you have found that the marketplace is not aware of your product. No matter how you reached this conclusion, you structure the advertising to tell the target audience about your product, what it is, and the benefits that will accrue to the user of the product. That is all you do in the advertising. Don't try to do anything more. Talk only about the features and benefits. This objective implies that the message is couched in fairly generic terms. That will be more obvious when we look at the other objectives. You may wish to focus on this objective for new products or products that are relatively unknown in the marketplace.

Occasionally you can adopt this objective as a tactic to place your product in the leadership role by taking the assumptive stance that yours is the only one available. That will only work if it is fairly new, even if well known, and you find that market penetration is low. Sometimes you can use this objective as a tactic when your competitors have not advertised the product for a considerable length of time, as if it is the forgotten product in their product mix.

This objective can be employed in either of two directions. When you are trying to tell the marketplace that the product exists and about its features and benefits, your purpose is either to tell what product to buy or where to buy the product. If the objective is to inform, then what do you want to inform the marketplace? Is the objective to inform what or where to buy? The two tactics are executed entirely differently, though for classification they appear to be mere variants of the same thing.

Telling the marketplace what to buy and providing basic information about the features and benefits implies that the product is new to the market or, at least, has not had wide acceptance as yet. When you use the

Objectives of
Advertising

same tactic to try to inform the marketplace where to buy the product, the purpose becomes only one of establishing identity with the product and the features and benefits of buying the product from you. In the latter case the objective of advertising is not to talk about the product but where that product can be obtained. That tactic is quite common for outlets near the end of the distribution channels when the product itself is well known. There is certainly no need for the local dealer to describe to the market how Cadillacs are a quality American sedan. The dealer knows that the message is established and only needs to make sure that the target audience knows where to buy the car.

Perhaps there is some confusion. We have been describing categories of objectives and directions that those objectives can take. While it is impossible to be effective trying to deliver too many messages and we have concentrated on the advertising objective, we don't mean to imply that the advertising could not mention a secondary objective. For the small business it does little good to talk about why the product is beneficial and then not provide information as to where to obtain it and vice versa. But the common mistake is to put nearly equal emphasis on both what and where, so that the message gets diluted and confuses the market, losing its effectiveness. In that case neither message registers with the audience. Concentrate on one objective category at a time for a campaign and focus on either what to buy or where, and only secondarily mention the other. However, that doesn't mean not to mention the secondary message.

Objective 2: To Persuade

In the category of persuasion the message is decidedly different. In this advertising objective there is more competition, and the effort is to differentiate between and among the competitive products. Sometimes the competition is not another product but apathy or other demands for resources. If that is what is happening in the market, one tactic is to use the "inform" objective of advertising. But normally the course to follow is to persuade the market that your product delivers the most benefits. For the small business the safest way to meet this objective is to *focus* the advertising on the *benefits* that the competition does not have. It should be relatively easy for you to establish benefits if you have done your marketing planning well and know the competition.

Direct comparative advertising is a high-risk mode of advertising. If not implemented in the right way, the comparisons can easily backfire. Either the comparative results won't be what you want or the competition will claim that the features compared aren't important. This is such a tricky area that unless you have a large budget and a top-flight agency, I'd stay away from the tactic altogether. Even the national agencies working for big business are having second thoughts on this tactic.

Once having persuaded the audience of the benefits of your product by demonstrating and describing the advantages over competitive offerings, then the direction must be where to purchase. When the objective is to persuade the audience, choices are implicit. That is true whether you are trying to establish what to buy or where to buy. To continue the pursuit of the where-to-buy direction, you operate on the assumption that the product is the same from multiple outlets but that your outlet has superior sales and application assistance or that the service department is the best. At any rate you need to put the message into the marketplace that the delivery and support of the product are superior. A Cadillac or a Caterpillar purchased through inventory liquidators may be the same product, but the authorized dealers aren't likely to give as good support if it was not purchased from them.

Objective 3: To Remind

The third category of objectives is to remind the audience. Again, starting with what direction, this strategy assumes that the product has been on the market and well accepted for some time and that frequent purchase patterns have been established. In order for this category of advertising objective to succeed, the product does not need to be introduced. Nor do you need to inform the audience of its existence. For any reason you may decide that market penetration or share is likely to remain relatively constant at the current levels, so you would not have much reason to "persuade" your audience of your superiority or the benefits of use. As the name implies, the objective is to keep the name in front of the audience in a favorable manner.

In this category the objective could also be to remind the target audience of the location of your business or the outlets for your product. The most frequent, but by no means exclusive, use of the where reminder is the local retail store's name and address advertising in proximity to product advertising done by the manufacturer or distributor. Another variant is done by groups of dealers, particularly in cars and appliances, sponsoring the advertising of promotional specials in a trade area.

With the objective of your advertising clearly in mind and defined in simple terms as one of the three categories, and the direction or emphasis to be placed on either what to buy or where to buy it, you can move to the next level of decisions.

Media Selection

Media selection does not need to be as complicated as most people claim, including, unfortunately, some insecure advertising professionals who might discover the secret. Further, the best and most reliable information sources, provided that you have time to do your own investigation, are free.

There are two main sources of media information, depending on your market. One is the media salespeople themselves. They know who their audience is in fairly precise terms. They can cite surveys that are conducted on a regular basis. These surveys show the market covered by several categories.

First is geography. You need to know what area is covered, whether a part of the city, the whole city or county, the whole state, region, or nation. More is not necessarily better. Too much coverage may generate more sales leads than you can handle or may exceed your capacity to produce. Broadcast media—whether radio, television, or cable television—know their area of coverage by empirical data and ongoing studies. Printed media, such as periodicals, know their areas of coverage by virtue of knowing their circulation. No matter how the periodical is distributed, the publisher knows where it goes through physical distribution (paper carriers and newsstands), subscriber lists, or a combination. Printed and broadcast media nearly always are members of an association or rating bureau that authenticates the information that their salespeople use.

Second is audience composition. The audience is measured in terms of age, groups, marital status, spending habits, occupational groups, socioeconomic groupings, special interests, and on and on. Whether you are trying to reach the low-income housewife under 40 or the high-income professional of any age, the media salespeople can tell whether theirs will do the job. They probably won't phrase the information in negative terms, so you must know whether you want to reach upper-income households residing in the suburbs with children 12 to 16 years of age and then look at the media salesperson's information to see if that medium reaches a substantial portion of that market.

Practically all the media salespeople can provide statistics on market segment penetration in percentage terms. Don't be fooled by data that says that one medium, a radio station, for example, has 40 percent penetration of a segment that you want, and another station 30 percent, and a third 40 percent. None of them is lying, but the overlap represents the audience moving from one medium to another—dial turning—which underscores the necessity to buy advertising with more than one. The same is equally valid for printed media.

Commercial and industrial marketing of products and services has the easier job of selecting media. Almost any business or trade has periodicals published precisely for that business or group of businesses. These periodicals may have regional or national circulation and in some cases may be targeted for employee groups within that business. They could be written primarily for the benefit of the equipment service departments, for the salespeople, or even specifically for top management. Another reason that commercial and industrial advertising is easier is that there may be more media potentially available, but the audience is numerically smaller than the consumer audience, and the segments are more easily identifiable. Media selection then becomes easier for both reasons.

The other principle source of information about media audience, and rates for that matter, is a reference set of books published by Standard Rates and Data. It has all the information that you need to decide which media will work best for you. Included is a statement from the publisher about the mission, type of articles or programming, and the intended beneficiary, the target audience. Editions are published to cover virtually any media that you are likely to consider, including radio, television, consumer magazines, newspapers, business publications, and farm publications. These books are generally available only by subscription, but most larger city and university libraries subscribe. Many small and medium advertising agencies subscribe also.

Direct mail is an extremely valuable medium. But the cost is higher than the other media in most cases, on a per-exposure basis, but obviously no medium targets an audience better than direct mail with less waste. Mailing lists are available for purchase or rent by firms that specialize in nothing but the brokering, compilation, and sale of mailing lists. The lists can be almost as general or specific as you need. The more targeted, difficult to obtain, and higher financial potential of the audience is the principal determining factor in cost. Lists may also be available from trade associations or periodicals, but those lists may be the most expensive because they are targeted and verified.

If you are considering direct mail as a medium, whether or not you have access to a mailing list that you feel will be adequate, take time to study what techniques are going on in your market. How are the letters, brochures, and flyers actually executed? In addition, spend a little time and money (extremely profitable) and read books and magazines aimed specifically at the direct marketing industry. Because it is the most expensive medium, a great deal of study has been done and the results are readily available. Unlike the other media, direct mail is something that nearly anyone can do using a good printer and possibly a graphic designer specialist. But the trade-off is that you need to be better prepared because there is less free advice and direction available. The few hours necessary to develop an effective campaign or even to use mail as a supplement to other media will be well spent.

Now that you know the composition of the media audience both quantitatively and qualitatively, we can begin to consider other information as to media selection. This primary information that we just discussed was essentially a process of "overlaying" our customers onto the "profile" of the media to judge the match. Actually it's easy, assuming that we know who our customers are or should be.

Determining which media to use and when and how is simple once you start with the understanding of your target audience and apply some common sense. Several factors should affect your decision, no one being necessarily more important than another but together forming the basis for deciding with the highest potential for success.

Timing

The first consideration is the calendar. By looking at the buying patterns for your product in seasonal terms, or for new products anticipating the buying patterns, you can begin to plan the media use. As you watched what the big firms do nationally, you probably have already figured out that the objective is to anticipate when seasonal purchases will be made. Waiting until after the season has started forces you to play catch-up, which is as hard in marketing as in football or basketball—not impossible, but requiring considerable effort and luck to succeed. Toys are an example. Their sale is largely seasonal so the advertising for the Christmas season begins in the late autumn and reaches a peak in early December. How long to continue into the season is usually dependent on whether sales are meeting expectations or the advertiser is trying to increase market share. Advertising suntan oil in the Pacific Northwest in January isn't wise unless the medium targets the audience that is headed south or to the islands.

On the other hand, if your customers' buying patterns are not seasonal, there is a good case to be made for not advertising during the Christmas season for the simple reason that the media will be near saturation with seasonal advertising. The audience is being heavily bombarded. Time your advertising to receive maximum attention. Advertising during political campaigns is another situation to avoid.

Cost

The second major consideration is the cost per exposure. When you were gathering the basic data on media, one of the factors mentioned was rates or costs. Another factor was audience. Both are simple, straightforward concepts involving grade-school arithmetic. How many are in the total audience? In that audience how many are in the target group or market segment that you want to reach? Divide that amount by the cost of exposure. That term *exposure* means just that—how many times your audience is exposed to your message on a per audience member basis. For example, if one medium reaches 30 percent of the purchasers of commercial typewriters in your geographic market area, and you know that there are 1,000 customers in that area and an ad costs $250, then the exposure cost is 83¢.

Compare all three factors when deciding which is the most cost effective, and don't overlook production costs, as they are in addition to space and time costs. Media salespeople tend to talk only about cost and exposure for a total audience but that won't help you if the segment that you want to reach doesn't use the medium for information or entertainment.

Budget Limits

Budget is another consideration. We'll deal later with the process of planning your budget and even determining how much to spend. But how much money you have to spend has an obvious bearing on the medium selection. Because most small businesses are "bootstrap" operations, you must carefully select the medium that will deliver the most for the money. If you have only $1,000 to spend, and you are in a small or medium-sized market, you may find newspaper the best, almost no matter what your product. If you are selling industrial or commercial equipment or service in that same market, you may consider putting your money into high-quality printed brochures and let the salespeople carry most of the message. Perhaps in the final analysis that is more expensive, but the trade-off is that the message is targeted better.

If you don't have the cash for the medium that is really best for you, do second-best, but do something. Many firms feel that they can't afford to advertise as much in one medium as they should, so they wait until they have their pennies saved. It's better to do second-best carefully, so as to generate sales, to generate money, to generate positive cash flow, to generate money for advertising, so the cycle can be enlarged and quickened. However, it must *start somewhere.*

Competition

The third major consideration is the tactics of the competition. By no means am I suggesting that you should "me-too" the competitors' advertising tactics and media strategy. But if they are established, you have reason to believe that they are good operating companies, and they appear to be growing at an equal or better rate than you, consider whether what they are doing makes sense. Do not dismiss what they are doing just because of your negative feelings about the competition, but neither should you copy them in lock step.

The point is to consider carefully what and why they are doing their advertising and when and where they are doing it. Make a rational decision whether they are right or wrong. Just because you or your employees use a particular medium for information or entertainment and your competitor advertises in that medium does not necessarily mean that the competitor's advertising is reaching the target audience for sales. Maybe the competitor uses the medium for the same reasons that you do and has convinced himself that the medium is good, whether the facts and figures bear that out or not. Your own advertising can make you feel good about your own firm, but is that a good use of your money?

Message

A fourth media choice consideration is the nature of the message that you want to deliver and the market position that you have. That really is not two things but two ways to say the same thing. It is almost, but not quite, a logical conclusion from studying the audience data of the media. The right choice borders on the intuitive. One of the questions is whether the medium can convey the message you want to send. The other part of the consideration is whether your positioning strategy lends itself to using a given medium to convey the message.

You may be able to answer this yourself; after seeing what your competitors and similar businesses in other market areas are doing, consult with the media salespeople. They have creative staff people who may help you decide, either by recommending against use or their failures at attempting to convey the message on a trial basis (ad proofs or unbroadcast tapes). They want you to be successful and are not likely to give you false information. As a matter of fact, they need your success.

The fifth major consideration is the nature of your product or service itself, as differing from the message that you want to convey about the product. This consideration also requires you to look at the objective of your advertising itself. Do customers purchase frequently or infrequently? How many people are involved in the decision-making process? If a consumer item, do the kids and the husband have anything to say about what kind of milk to buy? or what kind of dessert? In commercial firms who are involved in the decision process for company vehicles? computers?

This then is another factor of knowing your customers and common sense. If the product is purchased frequently, then advertising must be frequent. For infrequent purchases, however, you can't be forgotten between purchases; the purchase cycle, the time between purchases for the average buyer, will be filled in by other buyers on various cycles. The important point is that for frequent purchases, advertising should be frequent but the correlation is less predictable for infrequent purchases.

Geography

One last factor affects media selection and usually doesn't make its way into textbooks or seminars. Particularly important to retail and commercial firms is the impact of media from adjacent market areas. No matter whether you are trying to reach a small, medium, or large population or geographic area, you must study carefully and understand the role of media from adjacent markets. If your market is San Jose or Oakland, both are large cities in their own rights, yet despite their own local broadcast and newspaper media, they are heavily impacted by the San Francisco media. Even more common is the medium-sized city that is close enough to a larger city that little attention is paid to the local media because for entertainment and even many purchases both consumer and commercial customers go to the city. But a city that same size located by itself has well-developed local media. Don't overlook the obvious when selecting which media you will use.

Common Sense

One consideration that is the function of the interaction of all the others in the process of selecting the media is old-fashioned common sense. After you have carefully considered all the factors discussed here and looked at your objectives, the final remaining element that many small business people seem to ignore completely is common sense. That is all the more surprising because most of us in small business have tended to pride ourselves on common-sense solutions derived from having to be generalists, rather than ivory-tower specialists. These systems of marketing, and other management systems as well,

145

are little more than a systemic approach to understanding why our intuitive decisions work. Use common sense.

Advertising Agencies

You may have concluded that you do not need to use an advertising agency. Nothing could be further from the truth. Whether to use an agency is to be decided almost entirely on the basis of costs versus benefits to you. But whether you do or don't use an agency, it will make your advertising more effective if you understand these simple concepts of setting objectives and knowing your target audience, the media available, media selection, and the message to be delivered. If you do your own work, you need to know how to get the results that you want. If you use an agency and you are familiar with the concepts, you will lower your costs because less time must be spent learning to communicate with the agency representative.

Services of Agencies

Advertising agencies perform several vital functions in the development of your advertising. All these services are done at your direction, but the actual execution of your instructions is handled by the agency.

An agency plans your advertising. It lays out what advertising is to be done on a calendar or schedule. This is particularly valuable to see graphically because you may want to schedule around special events in your business or that affect your customers. In addition, planning your advertising eases the personnel planning required to provide response to your advertising. That applies to any type of business. Advertising without providing the facility to respond to inquiries is permanently damaging. And the planning includes how to spread the advertising resources over a period of time and among multiple media—scheduling and coordination, in summation, with all phases of your operation.

After the plan is developed and approved by you, the agency selects the media and actually contracts for the space or time to run your advertising. Because the agency has at its fingertips the information about the audience using the media, it can select times and locations best for your needs. Because it represents several clients, it stands a better chance than any one client of the media getting the time or location preferred, although practially no medium will ever make any advance guarantees to an advertiser. The agency can work directly with the production and scheduling people at the media, whereas you would work through the media salesperson.

Agencies also develop the theme of the advertising in terms of the nature of the message to be delivered. They develop the advertising to meet the criteria that we discussed earlier, beginning with objectives. After these concepts are discussed and methods devised to portray the concepts, you and the agency decide which ideas are the most valid to use and develop further. Then copy, layouts, and sketches are done so that you can give final approval of the direction of the creative efforts.

Once the direction is finalized, the agency produces the actual advertising material in finished form, as required by the media. This may be the tape with special effects and the announcer telling your message for radio use, or the videotape of the television advertisement, or the camera-ready ad for the newspaper or magazine. You are then asked to give your final approval, usually by signature or initials, before the use by the media.

An agency also provides the recordkeeping function. It keeps tracks that the advertising planned gets executed the way it was conceived, verifying the placement of time and space of the advertising in the media according to the prearranged schedule. This is a relatively simple clerical function comparing the plan with the actual, except that the reporting formats used by the different media usually are different enough from each other that only someone familiar with the reports can decipher easily what happened. *Easily* is the operative word.

Another aspect of the planning and recordkeeping functions that are extremely valuable to a small business operating with limited advertising funds is the cash scheduling that most agencies gladly do. They sketch out on a calendar or similar format the anticipated total costs and when the billings are due for all aspects of your advertising program. This is invaluable for you in the cash-flow management of your business. Once the scheduling and expenditures are agreed, the agency then compares the actual with planned so that your unpleasant surprises are minimized. If there are variances, the agency can quite often, but not always, anticipate those variances and notify you so that together you can modify your plan if necessary to meet your cash requirements.

An advertising agency is a *service* business, selling only labor. But how it is paid helps you understand whether you can use it. The principal source of payment is from *commissions* paid to the agency by the media. Generally this is 15 percent. Most media, but not all by any means, give a discount (commission) to agencies for placing advertising on behalf of clients. The advertiser is not eligible for this discount unless it owns an agency. The media give the discount or commission because the agency relieves them of some of the work normally associated with developing and placing of the advertising.

In some cases agencies supplement their commission income with *fees and retainers*. Then they in essence become like other professionals, charging for their time expended managing your account. This type of charge is fairly common among agencies dealing with small firms for the simple reason that to do a good job requires certain overhead, and they, like any business, need to generate cash to pay the overhead, stay in business, and continue to provide the service. Larger advertisers may not pay this fee simply because commission revenue is substantial and the production and scheduling are done simultaneously for several media at once, which normally lowers the time required per operation.

Most agencies charge according to a preset fee schedule for the actual

147

time and materials used to produce the advertising for use by the media. This may include the services and materials for developing brochures, mail pieces, and specialty items in addition to the conventional preparation of the advertising for media use. Art, copywriting, photography, and specialties within those areas are usually charged by the time spent to do the work, in addition to photostats, etc.

In some cases your advertising agency may do work that is not directly related to the production of the advertising, nor the management of the account or the purchase of media time and space. Such cases would include arranging for marketing research, clerical time for special projects, and a wide variety of similar services. These vary from agency to agency as to what they include or contract on your behalf. But the agency must pay the supplier and make the arrangements so the agency marks up the invoice and charges you. In most cases it would be difficult at best to contract for those services on your own, so there is little opportunity to beat the agency markup. You probably wouldn't know how to buy the service advantageously, so the markup may be well spent.

Finally, consider how much time you have available to develop your advertising program. Then, aside from time, how much education and experience do you have, or your employees have, in the field of advertising? Remember what functions the agency performs and how it is paid. Decide about how much you plan to spend for advertising in the next 6 to 12 months.

Agency Selection

To complete the decision making as to whether to use an agency, start the process of selecting an agency. The two processes overlap and the results of one usually provide the answer for the other. To put it more simply, tell the agencies candidly what you want to do and see if the agencies are interested in your business.

Selection of an agency should be done just as carefully as selection of any other professional or supplier. With an advertising agency it may take one to two years for you and it to reach maximum effectiveness working together, so you need at least to start with a solid foundation for the relationship.

By whatever combination of tactics works best with you, check the *Yellow Pages,* ask your business colleagues and managers who are successful whom they use, find out whom your competitors use, and use any other source of information that you think may be reliable. You should come up with a list of at least five or six firms that have a good reputation, seem to produce good results, operate with a high level of integrity, and are solid financially. From this list eliminate those that work for your competitors, although those under consideration should have experience advertising for the same audience as your customers. Agencies won't work for competitors; if they know you are shopping, which implies that you may change your advertising, they will probably inform their client of your action. For comparative purposes, you should still have at least three or four firms to investigate.

Although you may want to give them an edge, do not automatically go to those agencies that may have been soliciting your business voluntarily. They may be who you want, and you probably want to include them in your list of agencies to contact and screen.

Before you contact any of the agencies, further reduce the list by establishing whether they have been in business for several years, or if new, how long the principals have been in the community and in the advertising business. In that same vein learn as much as you can about the financial stability and credit worthiness. If you are in a business that offers credit to your customers, whether commercial, retail, or industrial, the credit-reporting agency that you use will probably be able to provide a preliminary credit report. Alternatively your banker may be able to provide information or do the financial research for you, but the bank may be limited by an operating policy from divulging negative information. Your accountant is another possible source of information. However you get the information, determine the financial stability and credit worthiness of all those you are considering. If they are unstable or don't pay their bills promptly, you could possibly pay the agency for advertising and be liable to pay the media for the same advertising. Your own credit exposure is important, but their financial standing also gives clues as to their overall management and responsibility.

Being completely honest about the amount of money that you are in a position to spend in the next 6 to 12 months for advertising, contact the agencies and ask if they are interested in your account. Make sure that they are capable of handling your account. If you go to a small agency and your advertising expenditures represent more than they can handle, they may not get the work done on schedule, they may not have the working capital to see that outside services are done, and they may not have the staff to do the work that you require. On the other hand the agency that specializes in handling accounts that routinely spend far more than you can afford would not be interested in your business, or even if they do solicit it, they won't give it the attention that it deserves and you need. Matching the agency size with your anticipated expenditure is important.

The extent and sophistication of their presentation to you vary according to the agency and the potential size of your account. But when the agency makes the presentation or pitch to you, you should learn why it feels particularly qualified to handle your account, by virtue of experience with your customers, preferably. You also will want to learn about the experience, background, and stability of the principals of the firm as well as the salesman (account executive) who will handle your account. They will no doubt tell you what benefits will be yours for selecting them, but get a clear understanding of their overall business philosophy and advertising philosophy. They will gladly and probably voluntarily show you examples of projects or accounts that they have handled. See if the work appeals to you. Don't be afraid to ask if the example of work represents current accounts or recent accounts. You may want to check with the firms represented, particularly if you know the management, to learn positive and negative reactions. Agencies quite often

149

show work of which they are most proud, but it may not be recent. You don't care about the past, only as a reference. You want performance, not history.

The most important consideration in the selection of the agency must be done last for total effectiveness. After all the steps in the exercise of selection, carefully keeping and rejecting possible agencies at every step, you probably have two or three firms from which to choose. Now that the hard part is done, the easy and the fun part comes. Choose the one that you like and feel that you can communicate with most easily.

You must be able to communicate easily, quickly, and effectively with the agency to be on the same wavelength. If it doesn't understand you, and you don't understand the agency, not only do you waste time trying to communicate, you may inadvertently miscommunicate to the point that your advertising does not attain the objectives you need. You may communicate to your target audience either wrong information or irrelevant information, either of which will be a waste of money.

If you find that no agencies that meet all your requirements are interested in your business, then the decision will be not to use an agency. By spending a little time and thought and working with the media salespeople keeping your objective in mind, there is no reason that you can not develop an effective advertising program and get good results.

Advertising Evaluation

One area that seems discussed far out of proportion to its importance is the subject of advertising evaluation. Advertising, despite attempts to systemize it as much as possible, remains an imprecise art. You cannot measure art, only the results. But because money is involved, many people want to evaluate in money terms whether their advertising is effective.

Evaluating advertising for effectiveness can be done several ways. Your media salesperson or your ad agency is glad to help you choose the method best for you. Among the possibilities are coupons in printed ads. If the customer brings a coupon, offer a discount on a certain item. Another possibility is to key advertising in different media to slightly different products. Then note (actually write down) which products receive the most inquiries. With direct mail, prepare part of the mailings with one type of information, and another group using different information or method of presentation. Make sure that the sample is large enough to be meaningful, and simply measure which mailing provided the best response with all other factors constant.

Some of these simple evaluation techniques can produce information not only about whether the media are delivering the message to the target audience but also how effective the message is in getting the audience to take positive action for your benefit. Large national advertisers conduct surveys to determine the effectiveness of their advertising, but they spend far less proportionately in the process than most small firms. Perhaps the reason is lack of self-confidence in their advertising on the part of the small firm; whatever the

Maintenance of Continuity

No matter how much money you have available for advertising, spread it out. The advertising needs to be on a sustained basis for a considerable period of time to be effective. Some media require more ads over a longer period of time than others, but that is also influenced by the message. The agency or media salespeople can advise you as to what may be likely requirements for your particular situation. All competent, experienced advertising people, whether they work for an agency or the media, stress the need to spread out your advertising. If you have $500 a month to spend for advertising, spread it out throughout the month and by the same token, maintain that level for several months, at least a quarter for most businesses.

Another aspect of this spreading it out is to use as many different media as you can afford. Take the $500 and use a well-planned campaign for two different, or possibly three different, media. Rarely does the situation exist that only one advertising medium is available to reach the target audience effectively. By measuring the profile of the audience using the media, as discussed early in the chapter, you can determine which should be your primary, your secondary, and your tertiary media purchases. Your cash situation may be such that you can use only small amounts of advertising in your secondary media, but even that will multiply the effectiveness of both dramatically. Don't try to outguess the results of large agencies and large advertisers. They have confirmed this many times over in the expensive research they have conducted. Don't reinvent the wheel.

Above all, don't do your advertising in spurts. The high-powered professional experts say that even for items that aren't purchased frequently, thereby implying that you don't need to advertise as frequently, you still need to maintain your presence in the marketplace.

One other consideration is vital. During the recession (depression?) of 1979–1983, many firms made a classic mistake. They quit advertising. Studies have been made repeatedly evaluating various advertising tactics before, during, and after recession, going clear back to the depression of the 1930s. The message from all those studies is that, even though the market may contract, those that maintain their advertising, or increase it in relation to the competition, increase their market share. When the market starts expanding again after the recession, the increased market share that you picked up during the recession when the market was smaller is retained. The firms that continue to advertise and increase their relative advertising make most of the gain in share by taking over from the firms that decreased their advertising, even if the decrease was caused by the firms' withdrawal from the market.

If there is any secret to the process, and the most profitable cash management approach to timing of advertising expenditures, it is to increase your advertising just before your competitors and also just before the market begins

151

to expand. The catch is that no one ever knows for sure well enough in advance to plan on the turn arounds. The safest tactic then is to maintain your advertising, always trying to increase it in *relation* to your market share position and the competitive advertising. This must be done even if your cash situation requires you to give up the country club or the luxury car to sustain the advertising.

Incidentally this phenomenon does not occur only during a recession. It may also occur during some localized economic events caused by something external to your business but affecting either your geographic area or just your customers. No matter the reason for the downturn, no matter how localized, and no matter how long the market is likely to be down, always maintain your relative advertising position, and do everything possible to increase your advertising.

There are also cases where due to evolutionary developments, you do not have a viable product with which to compete. You may even be telling some of your customers about that situation in personal conversations. But no matter the state of the economy, and no matter the product cycle in which you may be trapped at the moment, *maintain* your advertising. Not all your market may know that the product is inferior or technologically behind the competition. Or if things are really desperate, you may want to use institutional advertising, saying nice, generalized things about yourself or aligning yourself with good causes to keep your name before the public until you are ready to resume a more directed advertising campaign.

Projecting an Image

Large corporations spend much money, time, and effort to project a corporate image. Some even teach their executives how to write with a writing style and language dictated by headquarters. They all very jealously guard and protect the corporate logo or the brand logo. Everything that emanates from the corporation has the logo somewhere.

Image synergistics is a *discipline* that few small firms practice, and yet the results can be fantastic. The word *synergistic* means working together. We talked about the concept when looking at the marketing mix. In many cases it doesn't even cost money and in fact may save money. It's getting your act together and taking it on the road.

You have many opportunities to put your image before the public and particularly your target audience. Every time you use that opportunity, you should apply consistency to the message. Everything that goes public delivers some kind of message, no matter how subtle or even subliminal, and those are all opportunities. Your letterhead, purchase orders, sales orders, invoices, brochures, note pads, vehicles, building or door signs, specialty gifts, newsletters, point-of-sale displays, product packaging, shipping labels, public service announcements are all opportunities, but by no means the only ones to display your company name and logo.

Let's start with the simple things. The first step is to adopt a *logo*. The logo can be anything from a particular type style, whether common or unusual, that you use when writing the company name. For that matter, some large firms do nothing more than use their initials or their name in reverse type (white on black, rather than black on white). On the other hand you may wish to invest a little money and have a professionally conceived and executed logo. A competent professional graphic designer or advertising agency can do one that accurately conveys the desired company image.

The next step is to decide, usually in concert with a graphics designer, the color of the ink and the color of the paper to use for your stationery. A graphics designer or an experienced printer can help you develop a combination that works for many applications, such as envelopes, business cards, and other everyday uses. Your local printer probably has a good feel for what colors are popular, so that you can choose something else that is unique but still attractive.

Then go through with the designer or printer all the printed forms and documents that you use in the conduct of the business. As each supply comes up for reprinting, have them done in the logo, ink, and paper colors adopted for your standard.

However, the process goes one step further to be totally effective. Put together, either by means of samples or even cutting out appropriate portions, the *standards* that *all* your printed material must meet from that point forward. This would include the use of the name, logo, address, and phone numbers for advertising purposes as well. In this *style book,* you will want to include displays of your name for both horizontal application and vertical stacking and make a definite statement in writing which mode you want to use as standard and under what circumstances you will accept the alternate mode.

This effort doesn't take much time (little more than it took to read about), and yet it is important to take advantage of your logo. If you are doing enough advertising that several people could be involved in the creation of visual information, it probably pays to have the style book executed by a professional, whether an independent graphics designer or the advertising agency. In either case the money is well spent.

Having gone through this process for your conventional printed material and setting the standards for visual advertising, also decide, with the help of your agency or the media salesperson on whom you rely most, how you want the name displayed audibly. Describe how to say your name? You bet. Adopt a standard for pronunciation, emphasis, word order, and all the elements that are audible to convey the message of your business name, product brand name, and where to find it. Try to use a unique order, of course, to set yourself above the throng. You may be able to take audio one step further without spending much money, if any, and find a "voice," a single announcer to do all your audible advertising for both radio and television. Your ad agency or media representative can help with this. Avoid using your own voice as the company voice, unless you have been announcing or in theater professionally.

You may think that the process is completed, except for applying the concepts to other media, but it's not. In the first place don't overlook the possibility of displaying your logo on all your company vehicles. Depending on the number of vehicles, their nature, and how long you normally keep them, you can get the logo and signs put on with paint or silk screen by a professional sign painter and truck letter shop, or your quantities may be substantial enough to make vinyl decals economical. Avoid magnetic signs if you want to look established and quality-oriented. I tried expensive thin magnetic signs, and they were only a slight improvement over the conventional type and proved expensive after some were stolen, lost, or damaged in the car wash.

The other reason that the process is not complete is the fact that the process is never complete. Despite your instructions to the designers, printers, sign painters, they are artists and each will try a version of your name and logo. Make it clear in advance that you will only accept the way shown in your book and nothing else. Even your ad agency may not be as insistent on conformity as necessary; but if you make it clear to the agency what you want, it can be the heavy and tell the other vendors that the work is not acceptable. Agencies know and understand the importance of the concept; but in the press of managing your affairs along with other clients, sometimes details slip through the cracks. That's not really a sign of incompetence for a small agency; just that the staff is human. Remind them that they are the enforcers.

Spend as much time as necessary—which doesn't represent money, only your thinking—to decide on the logo, typeface, style and all the other elements. Then, no matter how large or small your business may be, stay with that logo and style for a minimum of 5 years, preferably 10. Use that logo, style, and name on everything you do. Even if you start another business or service, use the same logo and name, if legally possible.

Why spend so much time talking about the obvious? Few people make the effort to develop their image. It's like keeping the premises and vehicles and the customer items that have been serviced neat, clean, and well signed. You would think that small detail would be automatic, but it is not.

The monetary value of working hard to maintain a uniform image is incalculable because of the synergistic effect. By using the interaction of all the visual and audible material delivering the *identical* message, the effect of each separate message, whether building signs and vehicles, stationery and advertising and all the other possible combinations, multiplies the impact of each one individually. Considerable in-depth academic research in advertising has been done, trying to definitely quantify the multiplier effect. The results are different for each set of combinations, but one thing is consistent. The message has a demonstrable multiple impact on the audience greatly in excess of a single, isolated medium message. That's the real reason that it can save money, because you can have more impact on the audience for less expense if you make the effort to project a consistent image. Every time the audience sees your logo they are reminded of the specific messages you have sent. Consistency is the key to take advantage of the synergistic effect.

Types of Advertising

Public service advertising may not be advertising, even though those words are used. Or it may be extremely valuable advertising. The best suggestion about evaluating public service advertising as a means of making your firm or product known is to understand who your customers are and whether they are likely to hear your name used in a public service context. Or you may consider it support of civic, artistic, or athletic endeavors. You want to do it. There is little pure commercial value, but you enjoy supporting the activity. Make sure that those expenditures represent a truly small percentage of your total advertising and don't let peer pressure cloud your judgment.

Memberships that are sold as advertising tools, such as some clubs, directories, etc., should be weighed on their own merits. Let any advertising benefits that are possible be plus benefits. Keep such types of expenditures in line with your overall spending. The club may be fun, a good place to make contacts, an excellent place to develop leadership and organizational skills, and contribute to the community, but clubs are not good advertising media. I have been involved for many years in a wide variety of service, civic, visual and performing arts support groups, trade associations, education and self-improvement groups (and on and on), but they have little intrinsic value for my business life.

Trade-out advertising is a trap. Many media offer you opportunities to trade advertising for products or service. In and of itself, that is good for both parties. But what usually happens is that one party or the other ends up with more than it can economically use and so the resources spent in trade are wasted. Trade-outs work well for both parties if they both truly need each other's services or products and have agreed ahead in writing the amount of exchange for a given time period. Putting it in writing clarifies things for both bookkeepers and causes both parties to look at what they're doing.

Institutional advertising does not fall in the "marginal" areas that are being discussed, but many people think so. The real reason that true institutional advertising can be beneficial is that it keeps the name in front of the audience in a favorable light. Earlier we talked about some of the ways institutional advertising can fill in when you have a temporary market disadvantage, but institutional advertising can also be a preplanned message that you deliver consistently in an appropriate media as another way of establishing position.

Newsletters are a special category. They use direct mail media but usually are less targeted than direct mail advertising. Newsletters are normally an institutional device. They also establish a leadership position if none of your competitors is doing any. But to be effective, they almost must be done professionally. If you feel that you can take advantage of this tactic, commit to putting an issue out at least four times, and preferably six times, annually. Make the cash commitment to publish the letter for at least two years. Get the form preprinted so that they are all the same in appearance, and change only the copy each issue. Getting them professionally done saves you from the labor of writing, printing, and mailing. Those seem like simple mechanical things, but they can be a real burden to you for time; if the newsletter doesn't appear consistently, effectiveness diminishes.

One exception to this process does work well in a particular set of circumstances: seasonal businesses such as agriculture. They may be newsletters by the nature of their nonspecific advertising message, couched in institutional or generic terms, but they really are direct-mail advertising. Due to a seasonal rush of business requiring many hours of time by the customers overseeing the operation and working in the fields themselves, they may not welcome a salesperson, even though at other times that salesperson is welcome. But you as their supplier may have critical time-sensitive information that you need to get to them but don't want to interrupt their activities. Then a "news bulletin" works effectively. But it works only if you have established relations with the recipient and are delivering vital information, not just selling products. In other words, you are using the trust that is established.

The Advertising Budget

Repeatedly over the years I've tried to get an advertising professional to tell me how to set the advertising budget. No answers fit in all situations, but I'll share what seems to be the best ideas. For one thing, what your competition is doing naturally has some bearing on your advertising tactics as to the amount to spend in addition to the considerations we reviewed earlier. Objectives of the advertising have a large role in determining amount of expenditure. What to class as advertising affects expenditures planning.

Before we discuss specific money considerations, for the sake of emphasis let's review some basics. Advertising should represent a steady pull on the marketplace, not spurts and jerks. To gain maximum benefit requires a commitment of advertising over a considerable length of time. This length of time varies according to the purchase cycles or seasonal nature of your business, although advertising may contribute to a flattening of the cycles or working counter to the purchase trends. The length may be a year, a quarter, a season, again depending on your business cycles. Because of tax and accounting calendars, annual planning probably works best in most situations. Whatever your particular circumstances, the anticipated advertising expenditure must represent a commitment for a length of time, not a spurt.

Part of the advertising objective determination involves the role of advertising vis-a-vis the sales effort. Which part of the marketing mix are you relying on to deliver the message to the marketplace, and what is the message? If your product and customers require a heavy emphasis on personal sales, then your advertising expenditures may be less than the cases where advertising is doing everything except hand the product to the customer.

Another part of the objective determination is ascertaining the nature of the message. Is the product new, and therefore the emphasis of the advertising is to inform, or is the product established and you need only to remind the marketplace? This has considerable bearing on determining the amount of money to spend on advertising.

How long has the product or service that you plan to advertise been in the market? How long have you been in existence? That not only determines your advertising objective, it also has a significant bearing on how to set expenditures.

Advertising is an investment, although for accounting purposes it is an expense. Like all investments, two things need to happen. You must get a return on the investment to stay in business. And you need to make the investment in advance, cash up front or committed. With that in mind let's see how much you need and can afford to spend.

What are your gross sales or revenue for a year? If the business is new, what are your projections? Working from that base you can "annualize" your advertising expenditure. The appropriate amount to spend in a year probably varies from 1 percent to 10 percent, and in extreme cases even slightly less and slightly more. But for mature, stable businesses to persuade and remind, most advertising professionals suggest about 2 to 3 percent of sales as a starting point. On the other hand a new product or business introduction that ultimately will not emphasize personal sales in the marketing mix may approach or exceed 10 percent of anticipated revenue.

It is an investment. Therefore, when you pencil out how much you are to spend, also pencil out how you plan to recover that investment. Are sales likely to meet projections and, if so, will gross profits support the advertising expenditure? Alternatively, what will sales be without advertising, and can you afford to run the risk? Advertising should be a relatively small part of your operating requirements and overhead expenses and can do more to reach the market for less money than any other method, including direct sales.

How to spend the money is another important consideration—not just media selection but the peak and flow of the expenditure. You may need the help of your media representative and advertising agency to answer this question. They can tell you whether you should start with a peak, such as a new product or service introduction or you intend to reenter or reassert yourself into the market, in contradistinction to merely "keeping your name in the public." With the remind objective you must maintain a level over a period of time.

Let's look at it another way. On a calendar, pencil in what you plan to spend in advertising for a given month. If you are in the inform mode, this may be a short burst. What are you to do the second month? Don't spend all the advertising money for bursts; but even if bursts are appropriate, hold back something to keep a maintenance level (remind mode) for the balance of the period. Follow bursts with a steady but lower level of advertising. If you are in the remind or persuade modes, you are more likely to find that continual, steady advertising is most productive.

Discuss your plan as candidly as possible with someone in advertising whom you respect. Review your overall marketing objectives and objectives of your advertising. See how they evaluate your situation and whether it is significantly different from your assessment. Even though deciding what to do, when, and how is fairly logical and involves basic common sense, getting an outsider's perspective could be helpful.

By the way, include in your advertising expenditure, for purposes of establishing the budget, everything that advertises your business, but don't include the costs of operating the sales force. Include stationery, art, brochures, open houses, point-of-sale displays, special promotions, building and door signs, advertising specialty gifts, vehicle signs, in addition to the media production, time, and space costs. This list may not be complete, but don't mix up the expenses of the sales force with advertising. Both are investments that require a return and both represent costs, but you should be as accurate as possible in assigning costs so that you know whether you are under- or overspending.

The key word in setting the advertising budget is *commitment.* Make sure that you can meet the commitment for the appropriate length of time and that you can maintain the predetermined level. Chart out, pencil in a calendar, or use whatever to project cash flow requirements, but planning and committing are the key.

Sources of Advertising Ideas

Advertising in all its various forms is relatively simple. There is much about planning advertising that is much more scientific than artistic, but the overall execution of the creative function is an imprecise art. But art is still a process of using logical techniques and skills to produce a preconceived message, even if the actual message results in somewhat unpredictable behavior by the audience. But by studying actions and reactions, you can significantly increase the predictability.

Advertising does not need to be mysterious. This brief chapter gives extremely broad brush strokes to the whole picture but should be adequate to guide the small business manager to know where to find the answers and understand the process sufficiently. Nearly each topic that we looked at has been the subject for books in their own right, so we certainly don't mean to imply that this is all the information you need; however, it will help you get started on the advertising information gathering process.

I have found two simple, cheap, quick devices extremely valuable over the years. First, any advertising that you like for any product, brochures that are impressive, press releases that were effective, and anything else that *you* like or admire—put them in a carton. It doesn't need to be organized in any way, shape, or form, and the effectiveness of the collection may be raised by being a mess. That is counter to everything else that you should do in management, but this is part of the creative process. When you think that you need a new ad, brochure, or anything in that line, paw through your collection and let the ideas flow. Something that you have may be adapted or may trigger an even better idea.

The second device is to build a scrapbook of all the advertising done by all your competitors and similar businesses in other markets. There is no need to try to organize the pieces; just keep them together in a scrapbook as a reference source. Like the junk carton, this scrapbook may help your flow of creative ideas. But the scrapbook serves one other important and distinctly different function. By studying the competitive advertising, you can learn what their marketing strategy may be and watch for gaps in their product line that signal new things. Additionally you can understand their position, what segment they are trying to develop, and from those observations develop a strategy that will give you a unique position and help you focus on a segment that is being missed by all the competition.

Included in the bibliography are some of the books that you may find helpful, but several are available in local book stores, to say nothing of the city and college libraries.

So long as you keep the advertising objective and the message that you want to deliver in mind, you won't get into too much trouble or waste much money.

Most importantly, if you thoroughly know your customers and understand the life styles, interests, traits, and reasons that they purchase from you, the foundation is solid. Knowing your customers and your products and responding affirmatively to that knowledge greatly increase your advertising success.

There are plenty of opportunities for the person in small business to learn about applying advertising to a particular market without spending lots of time or money or for that matter to learn by wasting time and money. Nothing worthwhile is free, but neither should you waste your most valuable resource, time. Learn as much as you have time to spend learning, but rely on professionals with whom you have confidence. Your success is their success.

Advertising Glossary

Account executive. Person representing the advertising agency to the client and the client to the agency; agency employee.

Advertising allowance. Payment by manufacturer or distributor to retailer for advertising the product.

Advertising goals. Specific attainable, measurable accomplishments of the advertising, irrespective of other marketing elements.

Advertising objectives. Generalized statement of tasks to be accomplished with advertising.

Advertising specialties. Gift items imprinted with product, company name, or logo.

Art, artwork. Broad term referring to layout, sketches, photos, illustrations, etc., done by graphic artist.

Bait and switch. General tactic whereby one item is advertised at a low price, but another, higher-priced item is really intended to be sold.

Bleed. In printing, where ad, copy, or art exceeds normal border dimensions.

Broadside. Oversized folder, usually direct-mail piece.

Camera-ready. Art, paste-ups, type, etc., suitable for camera shooting for offset printing.

Campaign. All advertising designed to focus on a product, service, or firm, with a predetermined advertising goal.

Canned spots. Radio or TV commercials taped or script for use by local retailer or distributor who adds local identification.

Column inch. Print media measurement of ad size, 1 inch by 1 column wide.

Cooperative advertising (co-op). Manufacturer or distributor subsidy of advertising by firms at end of the distribution channel arranged by prior agreement and terms.

Copy. Verbal or written messages in advertising.

Copywriter. Person who writes ad copy.

Cost per thousand. Standard measurement of cost of media to reach 1,000 viewers, readers, or listeners.

Classified (ads). Separate section of small advertisements arranged by category in printing media; the "want ads."

Cut. In printing, the photoengraving. In broadcast production, the switch from one scene to another. In audio, the process of making a recording.

Dealer imprint. Space on literature for local name and address information.

Demographics. Description of statistical study to determine quantity, ages, sex, marital and family status, etc., of population segment being examined.

Die-cut. Pattern cut into printed matter to create a shape or slot.

Direct marketing. Advertising and sales of goods direct from producer to consumer, such as direct mail, direct ad response, and door-to-door.

Display advertising. (1) Advertising used in the editorial content sections of printed media, usually containing art or graphics designs; (2) also called point-of-sale, the advertisement in conjunction with product displays.

Drive time. In radio advertising, the time when potential listeners are driving to and from work.

Focus group. A technique using a small group of people representative of the target audience, with homogeneous interests, who are interviewed in-depth as a group to test measure suppositions, for marketing planning.

Four-color process. The printing process that results in full color; each color—yellow, red, blue, and black—printed with separate plates.

Frequency. The number of times an individual is exposed to an ad within a given time frame.

Half-tone photography. Reproduction process to shade or vary intensity of image using one color.

Institutional advertising. Designed to improve or change company image but not sell directly.

Layout. The sketch or drawing showing the arrangement of the component visual elements for print; a rough preliminary or smooth detail as needed.

Line drawing. Art used to depict an object, instead of photography; does not require half-tone for reproduction.

Logo. A trademark, name displayed uniquely, or other identifying symbol used to mark ads, printed material, signs, and products as to source or company.

Market research. Study of market conditions, reactions, potential, and characteristics to be used for marketing decision-making process.

Marketing goals. Specific measurable goals to be achieved within a predetermined time frame through the use of the various marketing components.

Marketing mix. The planned use and interaction of the marketing components or elements; advertising, sales, pricing, and distribution.

Marketing objectives. Broad statement of direction to be attained by the use of the marketing components.

Mats. Reproductions in papier mâché of ads or graphic designs for use by letter press printing process, particularly newspapers.

Media. A generic term referring to the means of communicating information on a mass basis, specifically including broadcast and print, i.e., radio, TV, magazines, newspapers.

Offset. Most commonly used printing process, using thin plastic (quick-print) or metal plate, which carries the image, which is the result of photoengraving from camera-ready material.

Plate. The medium of plastic or metal carrying the image for use in printing.

Point of sale. Advertising by means of a display or product packaging itself, signs, banners, etc., to attract attention and sell the product.

Positioning. The conceptualization of a desired uniform, distinct identifying image for a product, service, or entity; the image conveyed through the interaction and support by components of marketing.

Premiums. Reduced price or free items used as inducement to attract customers.

Press release. Typewritten article or announcement, specially prepared for use by news media containing information about product, service, or organization.

Production. Process of executing advertising concepts in finished, usable form for media.

Proof. An impression of the material prepared for print, to be approved as a last check for arrangement, accuracy of information, etc., before printing.

Public relations (PR). Information used as a planned effort to convey desired impression of product, service, or entity.

Publicity. A device to gain recognition for the benefit of a product, service, or entity through the news media, free.

Rate card. Broadcast or print media's published rates, conditions, etc., for purchasing advertising time or space.

Reach. A means to measure and record unduplicated times that an advertising message is exposed to an audience in a given period, usually by weeks or months.

Retail display allowance. Funds paid by manufacturers or distributors to retailers for use of most desirable display areas in the stores.

Reverse. In visual media, when the normal background and letter colors are reversed.

Sales promotion. Special short-term efforts used in addition to normal activities to stimulate sales, such as premiums, contests, discounts, special displays, trade shows, etc.

Saturation. High-level frequency and coverage of media advertising to achieve maximum short-term impact.

Screen. Commonly used term to describe photoengraving process employed to create half-tones.

Self-mailer. Direct-mail advertising piece designed to be used alone without an envelope.

Separation. The process of separating colors to make the plates for each of the four colors in full-color printing.

Slick. Graphic design, complete advertisement, or other material produced on slick paper camera-ready for use in printed media; often furnished by manufacturer or distributor to retailer for use with local identification.

Shotgun (approach). Strategy of using ad aimed at general audience with no regard for market segmentation.

Socioeconomies. Description of statistical study to determine education and occupation, income, social groupings.

Spot. Broadcast media commercial.

Tear sheets. Pages from newspaper or magazine showing advertisements used as proof of publication.

Test market. (1) The representative cross section or small segment of a total market used to validate marketing mix and product; (2) the act of testing a product or service in a small segment of the market to measure results against goals.

White space. The space without printing in an ad to focus on information presented.

8

The Small Manufacturer: A Special Case

All businesses are unique. But one of the most unique, challenging, and exciting fields for small business is manufacturing. The small manufacturer incorporates all elements of the multinational billion-dollar corporation but on a microcosmic scale. In this chapter we deal with understanding the marketing functions and the various components' role in getting the product to the user profitably.

Unlike the other businesses discussed in this book, the small manufacturer must more nearly emulate the larger cousins to succeed. Small and medium-sized retail or service establishments or those catering to commercial and industrial markets are mostly part of the distribution channel. Those firms' primary function is to sell and deliver goods and services produced or conceived by another. Occasionally a small firm develops a new and unique service and attains financial success. But, by and large, small firms find most of their challenges and rewards in the area of operations or marketing, not innovation and production.

Because there is such a variety of definitions of *small* and the definitions change according to the type of business, let's clearly define what is meant by small manufacturer. Admittedly, government agencies variously define it as a firm employing 250 or even 500 employees. But when I say *small,* I mean *tiny.* In my definition of small manufacturer I am including only those with at most five full-time salespeople. No effort is made to describe in quantitative terms the total revenue or production facilities or payroll. The concentration is on the marketing of the products.

Many times the small manufacturer makes only one or at most a limited number of products. An idea for a product or product line evolved from experience with an occupation or avocation when there has to be a better way was translated into a product application. Frequently it is just that simple and straightforward filling of need with a single product that could eventually become the basis of a larger corporation, or even an industry.

Limits to Success

Far too often the excellent idea or the well-conceived product does not produce the income or profit that the conceptualizer should have realized. Whether so many don't succeed because of lack of adequate financial analysis guidance or lack of marketing guidance is pure conjecture. Financial consultants, bankers, and accountants feel that a lack of proper financial controls and measurements is the cause of failure for a large percentage of small manufacturers with a well-accepted product. Marketing consultants, advertising, salespeople, and graphics designers feel that poor marketing is the cause of failure most of the time.

Both poor finance and marketing are to blame for failures and "fingernail" success. But whichever is the weaker area, the one common trait is a lack of planning, both financial and marketing planning. Most small manufacturers are product people, idea people, and not marketing or financially oriented. What's more, they seldom think in a systematic way about the results of their actions or do any formal anticipating of the future.

This is not the place to look for answers to the financial puzzle. Many excellent books are available on identifying and controlling costs. Applying the tools of financial analysis to small business situations is critical. For example, doing simple cash-flow projections, itemizing all expenses, making reasonable assumptions of production capabilities and costs, and considering the various concepts of discounted money to allow for interest and finance charges are too frequently ignored.

Here, however, we concern ourselves only with the marketing process; naturally some gaps that can be filled by financial planning and analysis are partially done. By definition, *planning* and *marketing* are nearly synonymous, so much of the skeleton on which to hang some numbers is in place by addressing only the marketing aspects.

Marketing Methods for Small Manufacturers

Many of the same concepts of marketing planning that we explored in Chapter 1 naturally apply to the small manufacturer, nor should I imply that small manufacturers don't need to study those concepts. But the special case of the small manufacturer is such that our discussion considers those issues that need to be decided, and we discuss the methodology for the decision process. This should prove to be a learning experience on two levels.

Clients of mine and other individuals and firms with which I'm familiar are the basis of this entire discussion. Some of the incidents, tactics, and priorities are reflected in the examples that follow, along with my preferences. The practices of the firms mentioned are so far out of line with normal logical processes that you may think that they are fabrications. Unfortunately they are not.

Product 1

One example is a special tool for use in home kitchens. The inventor was physically disabled and unable to leave home without help, except for short periods. The spouse was the sole support, along with a small disability pension. The inventor had at one time operated a service business in another town in another part of the state. That firm had no more than a half dozen employees at its peak. Because it was located in a boom town and had been established for some time, it had done no advertising or selling as such, receiving all the referrals and walk-ins needed to survive for a time. But with the onset of the disability, combined with rapidly changing business conditions—price competition primarily—the service business shrank, and the couple moved to another town.

When I became acquainted with the inventor, the product had been in the marketplace about one year. Its use was seasonal, although service life was expected to be three to five years before replacement would be necessary. The inventor and his family had developed the manufacturing procedures to simplify assembly and packing, after considerable experimentation. Simultaneously the product was improved, greatly reducing the quantity of faulty units they had been experiencing.

Product 2

The second example is a product developed for use with heavy industrial equipment. The inventor and his family were second-generation operators of a successful industrial firm. They developed the product for use with their own equipment. When interest was shown by other firms, they applied and received a patent. None of the principals in the firm had any sales or marketing experience and didn't want any. They were in no way dependent on the item to produce income but looked at it only as a curiosity with some commercial value. One or two improvements were made in the product after inception; then production was arranged with an outside firm, after trying several alternative firms on a trial basis. Some years before my involvement, perhaps six or seven, they did arrange for a commissioned representative to show and sell the product to the suppliers and end users. But that arrangement lasted only a few months. They received some referral business and responses to the few advertisements that they placed in a trade periodical.

Product 3

The third example is a product specifically designed for use with home computers, whether for business, education, or entertainment use. The product was made by a local company for sale through distribution channels without wholesaler, manufacturer representatives, brokers, or their own retail operation. My client had direct marketing rights only to the product and was prohibited from competing with the manufacturer in the distribution channels. The client's interest in the project was to prove to the manufacturer that by correct marketing the client could attain a higher sales level for the products. The other products were aimed at a totally different market, not even end-user oriented, but were required for use in retailing of certain items. Although the client wanted a return on the investment in marketing expenses and a profit from the sale of the item, there was no necessity to derive an income from the project per se.

The fourth product example is a direct result of having underutilized capacity and finding a product that could be produced and sold without significantly increasing capital equipment, which was expensive. Most of the available cash resources were invested in the product development and the marketing effort as it existed before my involvement.

The product was designed for the gourmet home consumer. The principal of the firm was a skilled craftsman of European background. As an independent craftsman, he had done fairly well financially until the recession of the 1979–1983 period, when his business volume fell by several hundred percent. He went from a busy shop with several helpers to working by himself with a grown son working part-time. His wife was employed but that provided only direct living expenses—and minimally. They had a huge debt for real estate as well as shop equipment, and they had hocked everything of value, in addition to taking a second mortgage on the real estate. They had no leveragable assets left.

The principal's only sales experience was handling the adequate supply of referrals when his craft shop was in full swing, but the customers were definitely coming to him. All he needed to do was quote prices and delivery.

As we explore the special case of the small manufacturer, we'll analyze each of these examples and the decision-making process at each major juncture. All the traditional components of marketing (advertising, sales, pricing, and distribution) are examined in some depth, as well as the rationale for the decision made for each of our example products. The methodology used should be transferable to nearly any situation but particularly the small manufacturer. Large manufacturers can and do use similar techniques, but they have staffs of experts dealing with each area and specialists working with only a limited number of aspects within their area.

Determination of Capacity

Contrary to most practice, the first task for the small manufacturer is to determine the total manufacturing capacity. Every firm with which I've been involved and those that I've read about and heard about indirectly do not accomplish this task first or even early. But determining the manufacturing capacity doesn't limit this bit of internal research to how many units can be turned out in a month. Many other considerations enter. Not only your own equipment and facilities need to be inventoried; you need also to inventory the necessary labor. Can you get the raw materials? Where can you put the product when it's ready for delivery? Do you have working capital?

Production and product development are not my background. By not paying strict attention to the marketing implications, you can inadvertently create a real monster that will not only lose money but also automatically underwrite your competitors' success. We will look at these considerations, not from a technical standpoint but an operational one with impact on the marketing function.

Physical Facilities

To commence the inventory of production capacity, the easiest place to start is with your physical facilities. Measure in specific quantitative terms exactly how many product units are capable of going through each step of the process. How many units can the the lathe produce? How many cases can the plastic casting machine produce? Go through your entire plant using this method. When you finish determining your machine or work station capacity, then re-examine the figures for possible glitches. Does your lathe produce 10 units an hour, but both casting machines together produce only 8 units? Are there any other imbalances? Be sure to add in a reasonable factor for breakdowns, scheduled maintenance, machine operator shortages due to illnesses, coffee breaks, etc. Don't just project the hourly production rate by multiplying by 8 hours by 5 days, etc. Be conservative, but base the estimates on actual experience, not what the machine or work station "should" produce.

Availability of Labor

Next determine from authoritative sources whether adequate labor is available to add more work shifts. Again, factor in additional equipment maintenance. You won't double production by adding a shift, even though logic says that you should. Consider what your maximum production capacity would be if operating 24 hours a day, again realizing that additional shifts do not bring directly proportional increases in capacity. Not only do you need to know whether there is adequate skilled labor available, or even unskilled or semiskilled for that matter, but make sure that you have on staff now enough people with supervisory experience and familiarity with your operation to operate additional machines or shifts.

Availability of Raw Materials

How many units worth of raw material can you get without paying a price penalty? how many by paying a premium? How long will raw material delivery take from time of reorder? What is the prognosis for supply in the near- and longer-term future? Can you control inventory so that you can purchase for quantity discounts sufficient to offset the cost of having your money and space tied up in unfinished goods and materials? Or is the control mechanism such that you can run with little inventory by proper reorder points?

Storage Facilities

What facilities do you have for storage of finished goods? Is it secure from weather, theft, vandalism, or other factors that affect the finished prod-ducts' saleability? Examine your finished goods storage space to see if it is adequate to handle a backlog of orders. If your customers prefer orders to be shipped complete, can you store the goods completed first while waiting for the balance to arrive from production? without clogging up production areas?

Working Capital

Working capital is critical. Determine in precise terms how much working capital you need. By examining your records or doing some logical creative analysis if you are just starting with the product, see how much cash it costs you to buy the raw materials; add the labor costs; maintain the machines; pay fixed and variable overhead; store the raw materials; unfinished goods, and finished goods; and float your accounts receivable for a reasonable length of time without any cash inflow. That is the extremely conservative approach, but too often small manufacturers don't allow for any, much less all, of those contingencies. They too often assume they will ship, bill, and receive money instantly as the goods come out of production. Sadly that assumption could be not further from reality. More than one company has folded due to lack of working capital, even though all other elements were in place, including long-term capital for equipment and facilities.

Decision Making for Product Examples

Product 1, the invention by the disabled person for use by home kitchens, was both easy and difficult to inventory production capacity. It was easy because it was entirely a hand operation. There were no machines or equipment involved in the production, only raw material and supplies. The only equipment as such was the tape dispenser to put together and seal the shipping cartons and the stapler (less than $25) used to seal the inner packs.

But the production estimate was more difficult because the labor was all family—husband, wife, two grown children, and their spouses. They had not determined the number of units that any one of them, all together or any combination could assemble and pack for shipment. When they got an order, they just went to the garage workshop area and worked evenings until the order was finished. A few were done ahead. When I became involved, they did some by-guess-and-by-golly production forecasting, but they had no payroll. My concern was not only that they know how many they could produce in a given time period, but also what the labor component was so they could compare with alternatives, such as sheltered workshop assembly, or hiring paid labor to come to their garage.

They finally arrived at an estimate.

With some prodding they obtained the price and delivery information for the raw material. A sophisticated, or for that matter even a written, inventory control system was not indicated. When they reached production capacity, both in terms of labor capacity and working capital capacity, they

169

planned to go outside for assembly, either to a contract sheltered workshop or, if higher capacity were needed, to a professional production firm, probably on the international market. For now, everything was done in the garage up to 50,000 units a season.

Product 2, for the industrial customers, presented a totally different problem. All production was done by outside firms. Inventory control consisted of ordering the raw material for drop-shipment to the producing firm and seeing that the quantity of finished products matched. Several firms were tried before one supplier emerged as better for price, quality, delivery, and administration. Because the product was relatively heavy, should sales exceed existing production capacity, additional alternative firms located closer to customers would be contracted.

Because the firm was profitably involved in another area, it merely "had a batch built" and was storing the unsold units at the facility when I became involved. Sales had been sporadic because virtually no sales effort had been made for several years. Working capital was not a problem. Raw material was readily available in essentially unlimited quantities. As a result of all these considerations, production capacity was of little concern, because multiple facilities were available to supply the wildest dreams of potential sales. Total known pieces of equipment that could use the product were about 20,000 mostly in one region and virtually none elsewhere.

Product 3, the computer-related item, had specific quantifiable production capacity considerations. Although the direct marketing of the item required virtually no working capital, the manufacturing firm had adequate working capital to support the production capacity for 60 to 90 days, which indeed is unusual for a small firm. (More typical is the situation where working capital is barely adequate for 30 to 45 days of production.) But this whole scenario is fairly unusual, with the production and marketing divided between two firms contractually. Of course, the manufacturer retained marketing rights through other channels, so we had to consider those needs as well as the direct marketing production needs. They could profitably produce a minimum 1,000 units a month up to 3,000 per month maximum.

Product 4, for the gourmet home market, was production-oriented, as you might imagine from a craftsman. He carefully designed the product for easy production, and the equipment necessary was already on hand from his original business. He had analyzed the production labor necessary on a per-unit basis for all phases of production from rough-cut through assembly to finish and packing for shipment. He based his production capacity on hired labor, taking twice as long as he did on a per-unit basis and adding in a fudge factor. He arrived at 100 per week as being the least he could produce profitably with hired labor; but with the equipment he had on hand, he could triple that rate with additional labor if pressed.

Products 2 and 4 introduce another consideration. You must look at not only the maximum production capability but also the minimum production quantity to utilize the physical facilities and labor efficiently. You could produce less than the efficient minimum if your labor were free, like your own, but you obviously could raise the per-unit labor cost so high as to price the product out of the market.

One other consideration when assessing your production capacity is the possibility of licensing the product for production by another firm, or you might approach the whole situation as a test-marketing exercise, looking toward selling not only the production licensing but also the marketing rights. If you should succeed with that tactic, then all you would need to do is review the royalty statements on your way to the bank with deposits. On the other hand there are production companies in North America, as well as Third World countries, that could produce many products or assemble and pack products for less than your setting up a facility for that purpose. As mentioned, consider sheltered workshops if any are located near you. Not only are their labor costs somewhat lower than conventional labor, but their employees are better suited for repetitive tasks, requiring only minimal dexterity skills. Charity and public agencies may provide the capital funding, but in most cases they are competitive for simple production and assembly labor.

Market Potential

The next part of the production planning assessment is to determine the market potential. To project the potential accurately enough in most cases for small manufacturers, try to identify the actual number of potential users of the product. By studying the prospective customer base in terms of demographics, socioeconomic groupings, types of business or industrial users, or the sum of all the various likely components of the customer base, make as accurate a quantitative estimate as possible.

Then, if you are confident that the resulting figure represents 100 percent of the potential, you can see what the 10 percent figure is. By 10 percent here, we are referring to the rule of thumb used by many market researchers that suggests that of the total market 10 percent is representative of the innovative leaders that will try anything that appears viable and answers needs, whether those needs had been defined previously or not—in other words the 10 percent that are brave and willing to risk something if they can improve their situation or get an advantage over their competition. The theory behind this concept is that if you reach the 10 percent of the total market potential, then the balance of your market penetration is dependent on the product, requiring the marketing function only to advertise, price, and deliver the product without the additional sales burden of providing substantial education or risk reducing information. (This product life cycle analysis has been considered in several contexts in this book.) If you never reach 10 percent, the product is doomed to failure; but reaching and penetrating the 10 percent is still no guarantee of success. How the 10 percent reacts and helps you sell the product spells the difference.

In other words you need to know what the total potential market is so you know when you reach 10 percent penetration. By the same token, once you reach 10 percent, your fate is largely in the hands of the market. If acceptance is good, then you can get off the 10 percent plateau so long as you don't significantly alter strategy or any element of the marketing mix. Some firms have reached the 10 percent plateau in a satisfactory time frame, then abused their position, and ultimately failed. Others are still trying to reach the 10 percent level but already have firmed their decision to maintain most elements of the mix. As a result they stand a better chance of succeeding than those that abuse their position. By moving slowly they may avoid many problems of quick success. One common mistake is to consider the 10 percent plateau as the arrival at success when in reality the 10 percent plateau is reaching only the threshold.

By understanding the total market potential and the 10 percent factor, it is then possible to segment the market to the smallest component, whether customer user group, demographics, geography, or other logical subgroups, to match the production capacity. The other part of the exercise in determining potential and matching capacity is to try to arrive at a time frame within which you can reasonably expect to achieve the 10 percent. From that decision you should be able to extrapolate how long it will take to reach your ultimate sales potential.

Product 1 was the easiest for this determination. Because the product was targeted for a clearly defined, special-interest user group, no further segmentation was possible, except geography. We determined that nationally 6.9 million households had purchased similar supplies and products the previous season. If you recall, our in-house production capacity was 50,000 units per season. Therefore, we couldn't even dream of trying to reach 6.9 million or even the 10 percent (690,000 units), because the purchases tend to be so seasonal. Our obvious choice was to segment the market geographically so that 10 percent would be well within production capacity.

Product 2 was the opposite situation because the market was slow acting and not seasonal. We needed to define the market potential to arrive at the 10 percent in order to achieve a minimum economical production quantity, and we needed to include the total potential market of 20,000 units. But due to the slow-moving nature of the industrial market, we needed to allow considerably more time to assess whether our plans were correct. Two years was seen as the adequate time frame.

Product 3 was again more a matter of segmenting the market geographically to match the 10 percent with production capacity. Alternative production facilities were investigated for future reference. The market was many millions nationally, so we had to segment geographically to match production and allow up to six months to measure our results. But because we were limited to direct marketing, it was easy to target a limited geographic area, and we operated on another principle in addition to the 10 percent guide. We determined that if we received a response rate of 5 percent requesting information or 1 percent placing orders within 30 days of the mailing, we would deem the test a success. So we could measure results and put out the quantity of mail that would generate the orders to match production capacity.

It was next to impossible to determine for Product 4 what the total market would be without research, which the firm could not fund, unfortunately. As a result the only thing that could be done was to present the product as often as necessary so long as the presentation process didn't cost more than the profits generated and make as many presentations as responses would permit production to handle. This was not scientific but, given the limited resources, all that could be done. But sales and production were balanced as carefully as possible.

The Roll-Out Technique

Earlier we alluded to another critical technique that small manufacturers too seldom use. It comes under the label of *roll-out*. It derives from the procedure named by large corporations. When they do their test marketing, they usually follow up by a roll-out process, which means that they add in sequence additional geographic areas to the marketing program for a given product. They may do large sections in each segment or small areas if they are still testing various aspects of the marketing mix. This technique works for a small manufacturer much as it would be for any small business, as discussed in Chapter 4. Add geographic areas one at a time as you add production capacity. How big each geographic segment should be is strictly arrived at by determining what incremental increases in production are possible, then weighing the market potential, the 10 percent, and the production capacity.

One special caution—sometimes firms carefully match their production capacity with the market potential and plan the roll-out to match production incremental increases and still end up in trouble—from logistics. Consider not only all the production requirements, as mentioned earlier, but also the additional requirements of the marketing elements. Do you have adequate quantities of literature to serve the larger market? How are sales to be handled? additional advertising placement? physical distribution logistics? These considerations are all part of the planning process but are often overlooked.

Having all elements of the marketing program in place, ready for simultaneous implementation gives a substantial multiplier effect over each element implemented sequentially. To proceed successfully through test marketing, product improvement, and the various other steps, only to not achieve total success due to lack of coordination of the elements is a mistake that occurs far too often, with disastrous results.

To apply the roll-out technique, consider adding a section of geography at a time that will not strain either your production capacity or your marketing capacity. To do this then requires that you know with some degree of certainty what the total market potential is for each additional section. In other words, you need to know who your customers are and how many. From the data generated by your test marketing, you should be able to predict accurately the potential for each additional geographic area, even if you hadn't done extensive research before introduction. You should know what the total population is for your test market. You know what your sales were for a specific time period. The result is your market penetration. Project this result onto additional, preferably adjacent, geographic areas until you reach the point where incremental increases in production or marketing capacity are necessary.

Population in this context does not mean the total human population of a geographic area. Population here is the statistical term referring to the total of a category. The population for the seasonal, special home kitchen tool was 6.9 million households nationally. The industrial product was aimed at a population of 20,000. Once the target population is quantified in toto, it is normally easy to segment geographically. If target population is expressed in relationship to any definable characteristic, such as census count, employment by industry, or other base data, then extrapolation is relatively easy.

Be cautious of the assumption that just because the 6.9 million households represented a percentage of total national households, you will understand your customer and product enough to know when you can mathematically apply a formula and when you will need to add in the factor to reflect demographics, socioeconomic group, regional usage, etc. One of the traps is that by assuming that the next geographic segment has the same proportion of target population as the existing segments in which you are marketing, you may overlook trends and use factors that will throw your projections off the bottom of the chart. Less target population in a given section means that the marketing cost per unit increases substantially, perhaps even beyond the point of profitability. Again, know your customer and product completely.

Segmentation and Positioning

During the course of discussing marketing strategy, we mentioned the techniques of segmenting and positioning. For the small manufacturer, particularly with an innovative product that has little precedence, this becomes both more critical for success and more intuitive to a large extent. To simplify, again look at our four example products to see how they accomplished this. We will ignore geographic segmentation because that was accomplished while defining market potential and planning the roll-out.

Product 1 had a clearly defined target market. Further segmentation of the market was impossible. All households with the special interest were the market. But we also could make some logical intuitive evaluations of some demographic and socioeconomic traits of the market, as well as some assumption about the life styles and personality characteristics. Our only research was our collective knowledge of the market, which was adequate. The position strategy was to place the product as performing a unique function. The only competitive product did not perform well. Our graphics design used line drawings showing the product in use and describing the benefits, and the product name further described its use. Our position then was that the product was efficient and effective, rather than performing the same function with "make-do" tools. Our pricing reflected this strategy by placing it with other specialized, good-quality tools but still keeping the price low enough to encourage the impulse buyers.

Product 2 also had a clearly defined market, but the composition of the market fell into three groups. However, it was necessary to address all three segments simultaneously so the message had to be multiple-targeted. The product application and benefits were the same. The only difference among the three segments was ownership of the equipment for which the product was designed. But due to the undercurrent of negative interrelationships among the groups as a result of their contractual relations with each other, each group would need to be addressed separately. But also because of their relations with each other, to select one as a target without including the other two would mean that the excluded targets would feel that we didn't want all three groups. That reaction would be emotional, but it would express a perception that the product wouldn't benefit them. Due to their philosophy of operation and perspectives, each group would have a tendency to place higher value on some benefit than others. To cover all bases, we simultaneously targeted for all three groups by using testimonials from representatives of the three groups in ads extolling the benefits most likely to appeal to that group—in other words one ad for each group. Another interesting facet was that to reach all three groups, we had to use the same media.

Product 3 required careful positioning. A wide range of quality and price offerings was available. As a result, particular care needed to be paid to establishing a unique position among a large quantity of similar products trying to establish identity. Because it was a new field, many firms that had production capabilities tried to market the product. But few had done even a brief examination of the competition to see what was offered and establish a position between and among the selection of products. Some were difficult to order from. Others had confusing advertising, but more than anything else, most didn't convey whether their products were price- or quality-oriented; some tried to be both. Our positioning strategy was centered on offering unusual value for money, being easy to order from, and having a product name that doubled as a position statement. Studying competitors' advertising revealed the market gaps available to be filled. A thorough analysis of the target customer revealed that most of the competitors were trying to sell the product function, not appeal to the customer.

Product 4, by being targeted for gourmet households, automatically positioned itself to some extent just by the fundamental perception of that customer. But in addition the product would appeal to gourmet households with certain life-style and residential considerations, specifically residents of small dwellings. That was the position statement, then: to attract gourmands residing in small homes, such as cabins, apartments, or condominiums. Space saving was the benefit that was unique among the products available.

Distribution Channels

After having determined production capacity, market potential, roll-out and segmentation considerations, and position strategy, we can turn to the basic day-to-day considerations. Initially in that category is the question of distribution channels. Physical distribution to a large extent also determines "message" distribution, that is, advertising media selection.

Selection of the distribution channel is determined by fairly obvious considerations, and yet often the wrong channels are selected for the wrong reasons. Consider first how similar products are distributed. If there are no similar products with which you are familiar, then check other products targeted for the same customers. Such considerations are as elementary as whether the customer is the retail consumer and, if so, what is being purchased in conjunction with your product. How are similarly used products reaching market? Are they being handled by specialty shops, of which there are few in your town, or is it like gum, handled by nearly every outlet handling packaged and prepared food as well as variety items? In other words, how many retail establishments handle similar products?

But if the product is for the business or industrial user, are unit quantities and purchase frequency such that sales are normally direct from the manufacturer to the user, or are intermediate steps through wholesalers, dealers, or unit assemblers indicated? In addition, is it a multi-tier market where the product is purchased for use with existing items as well as being fitted to new equipment by the assembler? Or is it a replacement product, either to substitute for a more commonly used item or to repair another product?

Following the lead of similar products is logical for at least a couple reasons. One is that if similar products have been moving through channels satisfactorily for some time, the channels are established and traditions may be firm. In other words, why reinvent the wheel if it is running all right? Another reason is that existing channels are an indication of probable quantities, and patterns have been established.

By using alternative distribution methods you may be able to reposition your product against the existing competition and gain attention with your uniqueness with the additional possibility of realizing more economical distribution. That strategy works particularly well if you have much difficulty getting into the established channels in the first place.

The overriding consideration through all this discussion is the quantity of units sold and the frequency of sale. Low quantities and infrequent sales would suggest that direct sales and distribution are most logical, so long as the physical distance between the production and the user were tolerable. If the product were low in price and simple to purchase and use, direct marketing is a viable option.

Product 1 was purchased relatively infrequently by consumers. But the consumers purchased other products for related usage through discount stores, variety and drug stores, and specialty stores. Some activity through supermarkets and home centers also occurred. Due to the sheer numbers of outlets and the total size of the market, even a small geographic segment, combined with the relatively low unit price, pointed to distribution from the manufacturer to the stores through wholesale houses or direct purchase by major chain operations that have their own distribution and warehouse centers.

Product 2 was a different challenge. Because the total market potential was relatively small—20,000—but regional, and products for use by the same customer and the equipment for which the product was designed were available from a multiplicity of outlets, sales to the user went from the manufacturer through industrial parts stores. In addition, the product could simultaneously be incorporated into new equipment. To serve that market tier, sales went from the manufacturer to the equipment assembler who actually sold to the end user. A push-and-pull strategy was used to get the product installed on new equipment, but the larger potential lay in retrofitting to existing equipment, which called for primarily a push strategy.

Product 3 was a direct marketing situation mandated by legal agreements with the manufacturer. But the manufacturer had retained rights to distribute to retail stores. The quantities of stores likely to succeed in handling the item were small, so the manufacturer sold to those stores directly on a local region basis but, due to distance considerations, moved a lesser quantity through wholesale channels. Quantity of units sold combined with distance to market was the determinant, then, resulting in multiple channels. The direct marketing and the store marketing actually seemed to help each other, even though the two products were finished, positioned, and distributed differently. Their differentiation and their similarity seemed to have a synergistic effect.

Product 4 was forced to choose the distribution channel by amount of financial capital available. Although the textbooks say that is a poor excuse, it nonetheless is a reality. Because funds were lacking for advertising or packaging, the product developer took some of the product and attended trade shows aimed at retail stores handling related items. Because the developer had neither money nor inclination to call on all the stores likely to handle the product, the trade shows and small fairs were the only alternative. At those shows the product was delivered to the store representative, who in most cases took only sample quantities, quite often on consignment. It would have been less expensive and more cost effective for other types of distribution, but meeting the store customers at the fairs did not require accumulation of money for a well-conceived advertising program. As of this writing, the developer is still struggling; but there still exists the possibility that the missionary efforts will pay off and demand will be sufficient to operate the shop at a profitable level.

Then with positive cash flow, the distribution strategy and advertising can be changed. Bootstrap operations are a gamble against tough odds but work often enough that others try.

Selection of Sales Method

Selection of the sales method is another area that is often passed over lightly. Many think that they can just show up at the customer's place of business, show or demonstrate the product, and go home with a sizable order.

For the small manufacturer, selection of the sales method, like other decisions, is dependent on several interrelated factors. The principal of the firm or a key employee may want to handle sales. Does the person have sales experience? How important is it that the person be on the premises every day? If the experienced person is available and free from daily operations, then handling sales directly is an option. But is it physically possible to call on all the people necessary to generate sufficient volume? Is it economically viable for both the manufacturer and the salesperson? Dollar volume becomes more important than unit volume at this juncture.

The Manufacturer's Representative

Product 1 was seasonal, with relatively low-dollar volume per unit but high-unit volume, and distributed through several types of stores located regionally. Those factors were coupled with the lack of availability of sales experience; because the inventor was disabled and the spouse employed elsewhere, a manufacturer's representative was the only viable option. A manufacturer's rep handles several manufacturers' products simultaneously when each manufacturer lacks sufficient volume in the territory to justify the expense of a sales force. The reps have established contacts with key buyers in chain store operations and specialty stores and can work in a multi-tier distribution situation. They in essence become the field director for the sales and distribution of the product. Manufacturers' representatives exist in almost all industries and are available to serve nearly any need, whether to call on small specialty stores or the end user directly or to concentrate on buyers for chains and wholesale operations.

If you have enough volume and your own sales force, read the section of the book dealing with sales force development, even if your sales force is one person, you. But if you choose to use a manufacturer's representative, consider how your rep is chosen.

The Selection Process

There may be several ways to select a rep, but the most effective is the simplest. Ask several potential customers, no matter what level you will be selling to, if they do business with any manufacturer's rep handling products related but not in conflict with yours. During this process you will amaze yourself how you can describe your product without describing your product, or at least you should. You do not want to be specific if the product is new to the market. On the other hand, if the product is on the market but without representation, being specific helps a person think of a rep that will be the most suitable for you. The reason for not divulging the product prematurely is simply to lessen the chance that someone will learn of your strategy and take countermanding tactics. By the same token, if you are thinking of switching representatives, you definitely need to exercise caution and may in fact want to use subterfuge or an intermediary to conduct the search. You need to maintain a continuity of reps and also maintain your reputation for integrity and stability. Whether you are justified in changing or not, letting your current rep learn on the grapevine that you are seeking a replacement only damages your reputation and makes it all the more difficult to get a good replacement. People need to make changes, but do it with sensitivity, no matter how you were treated.

After you have gathered a list of potential reps—and you should ask at least three or four sources, or more if necessary, so that you have four to six alternatives—you can begin the screening process. In nearly every segment of nearly every industry there are at least that many reps qualified and capable of doing a good job for you, but don't expect to find them anywhere but in the larger cities, say, the top 40 or 50 in North America. As your sources tell you the names of the reps or their firms, be sure to list them in the order in which they are given you. Repeat that process for all your sources. When the list is assembled totally and you feel that there is an adequate number of selections possible, make a composite list of the reps named and their frequency of mention. Only qualify the frequency if a source that deserves more weight than others gives different results.

In sequence contact the reps on the list one at a time. Do not contact several simultaneously. They all drink coffee together, so to speak, and word will get around that you are an amateur. Send proposal letters to reps only if they show any interest in your product. Make your initial contact by phone or in person, if possible. Don't waste your time and theirs by sending a detailed proposal letter if they are not interested. When you write them, describe the product, market potential, strategy, price strategy anticipated, and previous sales, if any. Demonstrate the benefits to a rep of handling your product. The benefits are sales and profit. Quantify those as nearly as possible, but also be realistic.

At this point in the game you are selling yourself and your product to them. You need to arouse their interest. Use common sense as to what it will take to accomplish this; but by the same token, don't give all the good news at first. Save some for later in case protracted negotiations are necessary.

Work your way through the list, starting with the first choice of the most customers. Not only must you sell them, but also see how they sell you. Are they quick to respond to telephone calls (they almost never are in the office when you call) and correspondence? Also judge the quality of the stationery, letter typing, and general business demeanor. Are they professional? Do they seem willing to step out a little extra with positive suggestions for you to improve your product, packaging, or pricing strategy? After this process you will probably be happy with your selection of a representative. Don't let one person snow you, but stick to your planned methods of evaluation if you consider several. Your business is at stake. Don't jump just because they jumped but only because they present the type of image and have the contacts that you need.

Communication with the Representative

Representatives are human. They like to be treated like people. But like most people, they like to take the path of least resistance. If your product is new and a pioneering effort is necessary, getting a rep may prove more difficult. But even that may be easy if you have other products that they can handle profitably while doing the pioneer work. They try to have each of their clients profitable. Most feel that when dealing with a pioneer effort, higher commissions are necessary, and many reps simply refuse to handle one-product companies unless there is considerable sales history or the companies in some other way demonstrate high dollar-volume potential.

More than one rep has also told me that most one-product companies are cottage operations or otherwise nearly totally dependent on their sales for survival. The result is that the manufacturer then puts too much pressure and harassment on the rep, so the rep isn't able to function efficiently for handling all the communications, which naturally detracts from the primary mission of making contact with customers. The reason for the manufacturer applying the pressure is understandable but is usually compounded by a lack of understanding of the sales process.

Once you have selected a rep with whom you can work comfortably and who seems to be responsive to your reasonable requests and maintains contact with customers, how can you tell if sufficient efforts are being made? Are sales at a level that you anticipated? That's as good a clue as any. Try to assess the sales effectiveness in relation to your original expectations based on the market potential.

Some time ago a small manufacturer asked me how to keep track and motivate the rep so that the product is getting the rep's attention. There is no magical answer but, for one thing, make sure that your sales literature is well designed and professionally executed. Keep your correspondence and verbal communications with the rep professional and businesslike. Return phone calls promptly. In other words, do to the rep that which caused you to select that person in the first place. Maintaining the attention of the reps in distant markets can be accomplished only by well-timed and spaced written communications. If that doesn't seem to get a response, contact them by phone. If you still don't get results and you have carefully and rationally analyzed your expectations and found the rep short of goal, then discuss that with the rep frankly, just as if the person were an employee. You can adopt and adapt many of the principles of sales force development when dealing with the rep.

If you have followed these suggestions for locating, selecting, and setting sales goals for your rep, and you have positively determined that the product or market is not at fault, you can assume only that something else has gotten the rep's attention or there has been a change in the rep's organization.

Advertising

The last major consideration is your advertising. Chapter 7 discusses the principles of advertising for a small business. But the small manufacturer has some other additional situations that other small businesses do not encounter. Advertising for the small manufacturer includes packaging of the product, possibly point-of-sale display, catalog sheets, and product information sheets for the rep, whether independent or your employees, ad slicks as well as the traditional types of advertising for the broadcast media and printed media, direct mail, and brochures.

It would be a duplication of effort to discuss the media selection, design, and other issues covered in Chapter 7 because they are essentially the same for all small businesses. But of special interest to the small manufacturer not selling to the end user is the preparation of the support production pieces. They need to be executed professionally.

Product packaging, especially if it is aimed at the consumer, should be attractive and display the product to advantage when competing for attention on the shelf along with related products. A professional graphics designer should develop the package to make your position statement consistent and to tie the graphics of the package with the other advertising. The cost for such work is small compared to the sales that you may lose by not displaying well. Even if the product is for commercial or industrial use, the shipping carton should at least have your logo. If you don't package your product at all, you don't need to worry about this detail.

For products that are being distributed through wholesale or distribution centers to the retail store, catalog sheets are necessary. These are put in ring binders in many cases by the reps and the buyers for easy reference. Product information sheets, as well, may be used for more detailed information regarding pricing and terms but usually are given only to the largest buyers.

Ad slicks are simply the graphics designs that you intend to use to advertise your product, whether packaging alone or multiple media. They are camera-ready renditions of the art. For manufacturers selling either directly to the retail stores, through rep firms, or through wholesale and distribution centers, ad slicks are expected. The store expects you to make provisions to advertise your product in their store advertisements. To control the image that you portray for your product and to communicate your position accurately, you must provide ad slicks.

In some channels of distribution, in some groups of stores, in some industries, and in many sections of the country, it is expected that the manufacturer pay an advertising allowance. You must give credit against the invoice price of the goods for advertising time and space purchased and used on your behalf by the retail establishment. If you don't make this provision, at best your product won't get any retail level advertising, other than what you do on your own, but more likely the stores won't handle products that are not well known without some provision for direct advertising. If the stores advertise your product in conjunction with their store ads, that quite often lends more creditability than your advertising alone. For one thing it tells the consumer where to find and purchase your product.

As with the process of negotiating with the representative, there are many variables for each industry and each section of the country; we are dealing only in generalities so you know what to expect. But be sure that you know in specific terms what is expected of your company and what you expect of the rep firm and advertising before you go to market. After you are in the market is too late to get your act together, because, for one thing, if you don't have all those details nailed down, you probably don't have all your costs under control and identified; your pricing strategy may be successful in the marketplace but may not produce sufficient revenue for your expenses.

By taking a quick look at the marketing elements and putting them in the context of the small manufacturer, we are doing little more than applying the basics presented in marketing books to a particular segment of the readership. But from my experience in sales and marketing, particularly while serving as a consultant to small manufacturers, I found that many do not anticipate some of the situations that occur routinely. By the same token, if you know what to expect, it is easier for you to understand the expectations of the marketplace so that you won't receive too many unpleasant surprises. This does not mean to imply that this brief chapter should be considered the source for all information but rather a practical overview of the marketing processes for a small manufacturer.

9

Marketing Professional Services

I n recent years and in an ever-increasing number of areas of North America, professional standards regarding marketing are changing dramatically. For years, no "legitimate professional" would advertise in the conventional sense. But the legal prohibitions are fast disappearing, and the professional ethics and conduct committees of the various associations are taking the stand that the option is up the individual. With more health care, legal, and business professionals advertising for attention, pressure that is not too subtle is being applied to those who choose not to advertise but nonetheless aggressively market their services. And those who do advertise need to understand the whole marketing process to get results from their tactics.

Surprising to me was the attitude of my own attorney, accountant, and insurance agent as to how they thought I should market my services. Even established consultants in personnel and financial areas didn't understand marketing. The thinking ranged from buying lots of lunches or spending time at the club to having articles published in trade journals or getting press recognition through releases and then waiting for the phone to ring. For that matter, that is the way most professionals have marketed their services.

In this chapter we look at some other marketing methods. If you've read the rest of the book, you'll discover that many of the same principles apply to professional services as to the retail, commercial, and industrial areas and small manufacturers. But the differences are enough to warrant a separate discussion. Many of the tactics and actual implementation processes are substantially different.

This chapter is based on my experience, not only with the marketing of my own consulting practice but also working with other consultants and professionals marketing their services. Many hours of conversation, reading, conducting, and attending seminars and workshops on the subject of professional services marketing provided the foundation for development of marketing for professionals.

In addition to my "scientific" study, my personal life is deeply involved in the professions. My wife works in health care, her father is a retired physician, her brother and uncle are attorneys, and my brother is a research consultant. Of my closest friends, one is a financial consultant and the other is an eye doctor. I live with professional marketing concepts on a daily basis.

The guiding precept for professional services is marketing. The two definitions of *professional* certainly exemplify that. As a noun *professional* means one who is engaged in an activity serving others as a livelihood; additionally we use the narrower definition referring to being engaged in one of the learned professions. As an adjective *professional* refers to one engaged professionally, in contradistinction to an amateur.

In common terms *professional* usually refers to making a living as a golfer, ball player, musician, artist, or consultant, in addition to the health care, legal, and business professionals. Because the professional is making a living at the occupation, the stature of a professional implies first-class, ethical, top-quality performance. I don't think that any quarrel is likely with those concepts, but by no means are they complete. But for our purposes they define the *professional.*

Marketing Objective

The initial step in developing the marketing of professional services is to set your objective. That objective might be in terms of the size of the practice or financial objectives but most importantly what you want from the practice in terms of work satisfaction or even methodology. Do you want to have a large practice with several partners and associates, or do you want to stay small? In either case what are your financial objectives?

Should you be in practice with partners, it is important that each of you determines and puts on paper individual objectives. If your objectives are either similar or are distinctly complementary, your practice will probably stay together for a while. Most partnerships that don't work see the principals taking different directions when they separate.

The group practice also needs to have the objectives set for the group as a whole. What does the group practice want to achieve, as differing from what each of the principals want to achieve separately?

Somewhat apart from setting the objectives for purposes of guiding the development of the marketing effort, the individuals, and group, if appropriate, should set out specific financial goals, if for no other reason than to set up the measuring stick to make sure that you are achieving your goals and objectives in the time frame desired.

Situational Analysis

Most of the work in developing the marketing for the professional services is in the situational analysis aspect. That part of development of your plan is the most critical and shapes the rest of the results of your efforts. In this stage of development we are inventorying our assets and liabilities, other professionals with whom we compete, and the condition and potential of the market that we serve. We need to spend some time in detail on the various aspects of the situational analysis.

Physical Resources

Physical resources are the easiest to deal with. Analyze carefully the strengths and weaknesses of your office location. Is it large enough and efficiently utilizing space? Is it located for the convenience of your clients? If the clients come to you, can they do so easily? Or is your location removed in terms of distance and life style from your clients? Do they feel comfortable at your office? On the other hand, if you work primarily at your clients' premises, can you come and go easily? Or did you select the office for prestige or aesthetic reasons? If you did—and there is nothing wrong with that—analyze what price you are paying for the office in terms of work efficiency.

Another aspect of physical resources is the equipment that you need for your practice. Whether it is just an old typewriter and the telephone, or a computer with electronic spread sheet, word-processing, and computer graphics capability, or the library of attorneys and consultants, what are the general strengths and weaknesses of your equipment? Is it reliable enough for your use or do you spend more time getting maintenance than using it? Are the books and reference materials adequate and current? Is the drafting table wobbly?

Does your whole facility package—office and equipment—present an image of professionalism and stability, if not prosperity? There is no necessity to have expensive or new physical resources to succeed. Normally the new and expensive equipment and ancillary items, such as decoration and furniture, are the trappings of success but not required to operate profitably. Above all, see that things in the facility are well-organized, appropriate, well-maintained, and neat. Sloppy appearance downgrades you in the eyes of the client, no matter what actual quality you deliver or try to portray.

Set up a schedule in terms of priority and time for changing of physical facilities. If machines need to be upgraded, such as replacing the typewriter with which you went through college for one of the new electronic machines with display and correction, or your phone system is inadequate, when will you change or replace them? If the desk is worn out so you can't open the drawers easily, when will it be replaced? Also schedule carefully the addition of physical resources after examining the positive and negative effects on the practice. Place a value to the practice on having the latest reference books or the largest bar refrigerator.

Human Resources

Human resources need to be inventoried and analyzed. If you have any hired staff, how do they contribute to the success of the practice? How do they detract? You need to analyze the staff not only in terms of their level of expertise and quality of performance, but also how they fit with the objectives for you personally and your professional objectives. This analysis needs to be done for your professional support staff, such as dental hygienist and assistants, trial and research assistants, appliance specialists. Also, your business staff, secretaries, receptionists, and bookkeepers need to fit your needs carefully, which is more than determining whether their education and experience is "adequate" for the position. If your staff is composed of several people, both professional and support, analyze how they fit together—not just how they get along but how they perform together and help you meet your objectives.

Many professional practices rely on either part-time or contract staff support. In many cases that direction is a means not only to reduce overhead but also to increase your professional flexibility by not limiting your practice to the capabilities of your own staff. Bookkeeping services, telephone-answering services, and secretarial services fall in this category. The selection of these outside services is just as important as if you are hiring your own staff. These services can also augment your staff during peak loads.

To select any outside support services, use the same process as you would in hiring staff. Write your own clearly defined objective to be accomplished. Spend some time analyzing your needs and making sure that the objective fits those needs. Don't let tradition in your profession or your vacancies subconsciously dictate the objective. Vacancies may be an opportunity to restructure a portion of the staff, whether full-time, part-time, or contract services.

Make a written list of the objectives to be accomplished. Interview the potential individuals or firms that may be eligible to fill those needs. The list of potentials should be drawn from a combination of directories with recommendations from your peers. Do not rely wholly on either method for the list, however. Try to get four or five alternatives, each with recommendations, before beginning the interview process. Then discuss with each what you want to accomplish and determine from their responses how they will fill those needs.

A common error is to talk to people about some need and have them convince you how best to fill that need. Then when you talk to other applicants, you restructure the need in terms of the first proposed solutions. That limits how others respond because they'll react to their perceived competition rather than applying their best efforts to satisfying your objectives.

Whether employees or outside services, these support activities do more to shape the reaction of your clients to your professional expertise than almost anything you can do by yourself. They have more frequent contact with your clients and, more than you, give final form to your communications. Consequently it is important that you select carefully and, after selection, make sure that they are fulfilling your wishes and doing the job that you need for your practice. In other words make sure that they understand and follow your instructions. If they suggest alternative methods of accomplishing what you want, make sure that they discuss the alternatives before the job is completed, not after. They may not have fully understood your objective so you probably will want to clarify that ahead of time.

Financial Resources

The next part of the situational analysis to deal with is the financial condition of the practice, whether new, recently independent, or established for years. Your accountant or bookkeeper can tell you your cash position and profitability, but for the marketing process you need to consider several other items, all of which can be addressed with nonquantitative techniques, although the results of this study are eventually translated into quantitative terms.

Accounts receivable is a particularly difficult subject for professionals. For one thing most don't like the unpleasantness of dealing with past-due accounts. Another consideration is the fact that you chose your profession because you enjoy the challenges and the work itself and would just as soon not spend time on business management or marketing of your own services. But it is important to establish an organized method of handling your billings to your clients and managing your receivables. It doesn't need to take much of your time, but lack of attention to this critical area affects your ability to continue to deliver services. This organized method should be done on two different levels. One is to establish on the calendar the dates when billings go out, the date when follow-up contacts are made on unpaid balances with (a) reminder notices, (b) personal contact, and (c) collection agencies, and finally the date when you will no longer perform services for that client due to lack of payment.

The other level is to determine the practice of a majority of professionals working in the same category as you for those various stages of receivable management. Can you collect a retainer in advance, receive monthly progress payments for a longer-term project, or bill by the job rather than by the month? Whoever is handling your receivables, whether you, your staff, or an outside bookkeeper, should prepare a report of the status of accounts that fall in any of the unpaid categories.

If your receivables are too large or you spend a good portion of your time trying to control them, the problem may be in how you are presenting your professional services and billings to your clients. Consider these ideas to improve your situation. Bill only on the prearranged schedule, as mentioned. Do not include correspondence with your bill. Make sure that your bill is readable and understandable. Describe the services performed briefly. Use specially printed billing forms, not just your letterhead. Do not provide preprinted spaces indicating past-due columns. After conferring with local legal advice, consider whether to preprint a service charge provision. You may unwittingly provide financing when you need the cash. Maintain frequent communication with the client.

Schedule out your cash flow requirements and projected income. Many opportunities to purchase equipment and join associations are excellent, but if they increase your overhead, even if just in the month that they are incurred, will your receipts be adequate to cover the expenditures? Working out the projections with allowances for fixed and variable overhead, as well as discretionary purchases, quite often requires you to give thought to longer-range financial planning. Are you making provisions for adequate insurance, retirement, loss of income due to vacation or illness, taxes? Review this with your accountant to be sure that all provisions are adequate for your particular situation.

For a group practice, or a practice offering a variety of services, determine which services are the source of the most revenue. Put that on a chart or graph. Then do the same thing for your biggest sources of profit. Arrange them in order, descending or ascending as you wish, but in order. Carefully consider the impact on your profit area if you were to eliminate the lower-profit revenue contributors. Most of us offer services that may not be profitable in and of themselves but are necessary to support other areas. Make sure that the profitable areas contribute enough to cover the loss areas as well.

External Factors

The next major part of the situational analysis deals with factors outside your firm. Those factors require more thoughtful consideration than internal ones because less objective data are available and more subjectively based conclusions need to be developed. Yet they are just as important as internal factors in delivering services to the market.

Who is your competition? List on paper all your competitors in quantitative terms. Include in the listing all those who compete for each category of service that you presently offer or plan to offer. If your practice combines more than one specialty, as well as a general practice, count all others that provide similar services. Should your law practice include general business practice, real estate law, and estate planning, don't count just other firms with that exact combination but rather firms that practice in each area. In medicine, if your specialties include family practice, a general category, and allergies, a special category, count others that do each.

When this tabulation is completed, then compare and express in some quantitative form, such as percentages, the total number of possible clients within your reasonable service area for each category. Weigh the findings of that study against the revenue potentials for each category. Another way to measure potential and capacity matches is to determine how long or complex the requirements of clients to whom you are delivering those services are. If the projects are each long and complex, obviously more professionals are required, although that may be offset by the relative infrequency of projects.

Now we need to study the competition in a different light. Who are their clients? Carefully and as accurately as possible, determine whether their clientele is based on a particular demographic group or socioeconomic group or, if business-related, with what types of firms they specialize. Categorize as many different ways as possible with quantities for each logical category. Do not assume, based on your perceptions of the competition, what their client orientation may be but try to determine as accurately as possible.

From the previous two analyses you may discover some gaps in the market that you may be able to fill profitably. But by no means should you stop your marketing efforts at this point. Several other items need to be considered and developed for your particular situation to help attain the objectives you set for yourself.

The balance of the market dissection relies even more on subjective analysis of data. The raw data are objective, but the relevance is subjective in relationship to your professional practice.

What population trends affect you? Is the area growing rapidly, stable, or even shrinking? If it is growing rapidly, for instance, more emphasis may need to be placed on providing exposure to the influx of people on the existence of your practice. If the area is stable or shrinking, developing and improving contact with the population involves different techniques and methodology. We'll look at the alternative strategies when we complete the analysis.

What other factors about the population may affect you? If a retirement center is being built nearby and you practice in geriatrics, what will your increased opportunities be? or your estate-planning practice? Will the changing population require more construction, which will involve architects and engineers?

When analyzing the statistical data to determine the relevance for your purposes, consider the comments being made in the general press, business press, trade journals, bank economists, chamber of commerce, public utilities, but do not rely on the coffee shop or club analysis. You need to seek actively as many different reliable sources as practicable to develop your own analysis.

It matters little whether your professional practice is for individuals or businesses. What are the trends for discretionary income in the area? (In economics *discretionary*, of course, refers to the positive cash flow that may become profit.) At any rate it is a fact that all professionals are subject to discretionary income considerations by the potential client population. Financial opportunities are much less for any professional, even health care, if incomes are low or on a general decline.

Marketing Strategy

Now we can begin to develop the overall strategy of our marketing plan. During the process of putting the information together as to the competition, you probably began to see some of the market potential that you could fill. You may have identified an excessive number of specialists in one field that you had considered for yourself but discovered another field that was practically wide open. And the wide open field also passed inspection in terms of potential for growth and revenue opportunities. The last may seem obvious but if you were practicing in pediatrics or orthodontics, the retirement center won't help you much.

Having selected what the market needs that you have the capacity to deliver, or capacities that can be easily developed, begin formulating strategy to convey intent to the marketplace, the potential clients.

Two overriding techniques should dominate your active marketing effort. First, whatever you do, do first class. By maintaining a first-class approach to your work, you build your clients' confidence in your professional ability. Do not let sloppy work habits show up in the form of sloppy jobs. This leads to the second thought: maintain communications with your clients.

Communications with Clients

Maintaining communication seems vague and grandiose sounding, or even bordering on the obvious. And yet so few professionals maintain communication with their clients that they are contributing to the undermining of their own professional status and perception by the clients as well as the more generalized negative image for the entire profession. To maintain communication seems so simple that it is difficult to see why that alone could be a key to success.

In the professions you are dealing with people, not machines. You convey most of your expertise by communication with your clients rather than by actual performance. Clients' confidence is established by you through communication. Your performance is usually so specialized that your clientele does not have the education or experience in your field to understand completely what you are doing, much less how. As a result your ability to maintain communication with your clients becomes even more critical than your professional ability alone.

All your written communications and all documents that leave your office should be pleasing to the eye, perfectly typed, well-written, and grammatically correct. All your verbal communications need to be understood by your clients, not showcases to display your esoteric vocabulary.

Calling or writing your client on a voluntary basis with follow-up information, providing information about developments that may affect the client, or informing the client as to status of projects, particularly when falling behind schedule, helps build your client's confidence in you to deliver what's needed. Providing the client with information about a project underway can do an unbelievable amount of confidence building that can't be done any other way.

There are books and pamphlets and flyers covering the art of written communication. We won't spend any time here teaching you to write. Your professional association may have information through its newsletter or national headquarters on writing techniques that apply to your field. My chief concern here is not the content so much as the frequency and appearance of your writing.

Critical to your success is the technique of keeping clients informed of projects underway. The first step is to agree with the client before commencement what time frame is encompassed by the project. Once agreement and understanding are achieved, the second step is for you to put that on your calendar as a checkpoint so you can see if you are on schedule. Third, let the client know that you are on schedule or, if behind, how far behind and why.

If the idea that you are so busy that you don't have time comes across to your clients, they likely will take their business elsewhere. If you are in fact that much in demand, you probably got to that point by having satisfied clients. You don't satisfy clients by not telling them what you are doing. Should you be actually busy on a sustained basis, you can afford to have your staff handle the progress reports or activity review communications.

Let me cite an example of each situation. Toward the end of every calendar year, my accountant calls me to review my cash position, my year-end profit and loss status, and other simple routine tax considerations. The calls take him at most five minutes. From the nature of his questions and the gen-

191

eral direction of the conversation, it is obvious that he does not have my file in front of him but is suggesting that I review my situation for possible tax implications. He did this voluntarily and didn't send a bill. Yet he is a senior partner in one of the largest practices in my city.

In addition his firm sends out specialized letters, from their word processor naturally but keyed to interests of their clients. I don't receive the information that their corporate clients do, but they don't receive the information that the small business and professional clients receive.

Further, my accountant has my quarterly tax forms prepared in advance, with guidelines as to when or if we need to modify our tax structure midyear; he has helped me develop the documentation necessary to complete my year-end reports and tax returns in a timely and economical manner.

The accounting firm has made so much effort in this regard that I have been impressed enough to send it clients that were with other large firms but not receiving this type of attention. Its fee structure is never questioned, even though it is among the highest in town, because the clients believe that the firm is performing and communicating.

On the negative side let me report the far too typical case that occurred with another profession. It may teach the lesson even more vividly. A situation developed in my business that called for the services of a professional in a specialized field of law. I went to the firm that I had used. It referred me to one of the partners, who had knowledge in the area that I needed and related experience. He understood my objective in the case, because he paraphrased, to my satisfaction, my wishes. Clearly everything seemed in place to get the project completed competently and in a timely fashion. My original understanding was in terms of days. On gaining a background in my particular situation, he was to conduct negotiations on my behalf.

After three weeks of not hearing about progress, I began an exercise in futility, trying to reach the attorney by telephone. His receptionist and secretary both said he was with another client, another attorney, or on the telephone, all of which said he was in the office, not in court or out of town—all the more mystifying when he didn't return my calls. After some days he finally returned my call. He acted as if I had not tried to reach him at all and proceeded to say that one of his clients had a critical problem, requiring urgent attention, which diverted him for a few days. He then said he had opened negotiations. We discussed negotiation strategy. But when the monthly billing came, the truth came also. Nothing had been done on my behalf for several weeks, commencing only coincidentally when I began trying to reach him by phone. After some more flailing about, he said that he would write the final document for my review and named a date two days hence. Twelve working days later, I received the document.

What I thought was an incident where I happened to be the unfortunate victim was later revealed as fairly typical of the whole firm. Now knowing that helps explain why the firm has had several partners and associates leave in the past few years and the firm is shrinking. If the attorney or his secretary had called to say that he was going to delay my work and gave me the option of using someone else in the firm or someone in another firm, I wouldn't have begun a search for a new attorney. Attorneys who seem to get the highest marks from their clients are those that charge the highest hourly fees but also keep on schedule and in communication.

In the health care professions the larger, successful practices are those that remind the clients when periodic checkups are due and inform the client promptly when reports from the laboratories are received. Practically no successful practitioner in any field waits for clients to call about progress. By initiating the calls to the client the professional practice not only does a good sales job but also is under better control of its time, rather than always having to react to clients on the clients' terms. The disruption is detrimental to work flow and actually lowers the client workload capacity.

With these two generalized recommendations, let's turn to some more specialized techniques of advertising and selling your professional services to your potential clientele.

Advertising

Name and Logo

Choose a name that is either descriptive of what you do or says something about your location. For example, if you are a group practice specializing in pediatrics, *X Street Children's Clinic* is descriptive. For that matter, if you are practicing alone, your own name and specialty are adequate. But be descriptive. Avoid *physician and surgeon* or *consultant.* Use a word or two about your specialty, whether thoracic surgery or engineering. If you use a logo along with your name, use it consistently on all visual communications, whether letters, billings, or the shingle by your office door. Single practitioners tend not to use logos, whereas group practices more often do. The custom varies from profession to profession and among various regions. But if you want to use a logo, have it executed by a professional in the field and have the professional set down on paper, where, when, and what colors are to be used consistently.

Should you choose not to use a logo, at least select a type style for your printed matter and stick with it for all uses. In addition, use a modern, clean typewriter with a style that is unique. There are dozens of selections in both electric and electronic typewriters, so having one that looks like all the others is totally unnecessary. Be unique but not weird. Consider using a colored ribbon. But some professions, as with law, have such things mandated by regulatory agencies or professional standards boards, so check before plunging.

Directories

No matter whether the listing is free or expensive, make sure that your name appears just like on your printed matter, complete with logo if appropriate. For professionals the *Yellow Pages* is a must, but also consider established directories that may be used by special groups. Before you buy space, however, learn the use of the directory, not the circulation. If you choose to buy space in the display section, have the ad executed by a professional and have it consistent with your other display advertising.

Media Advertising

Display and broadcast media advertising is becoming more widely accepted by professions. If you use this, have your advertising planned by a professional agency after you have clearly defined the objective of the advertising and the composition of the group at which the advertising is aimed. Is that group your target audience? your biggest potential? You may want to do institutional advertising, which does little more than mention your name in a favorable context or may consist of merely underwriting advertising for a civic or artistic event. Even then make sure that your name and logo are displayed correctly, and use your own professional graphics person if possible.

Press Releases

This is one of the more effective methods for any professional and many businesses as well. Press releases are not perceived as advertising by the general public and carry implicit creditability, which can't be bought. Consider whether you have the time or inclination to handle yourself or whether to contract with a public relations agency. They are surprisingly affordable and generally get more publicity for you than you can yourself.

If you do your own, don't worry too much about your writing style; just do it simply with proper grammar and punctuation, as with all written communication. In addition, treat the news media representative as you would any professional; ask for an appointment to hand deliver the information; submit to an interview if possible or asked. After the piece has run, write a thank-you note. Even if errors creep in, which they do, overlook all but the most blatant, so long as your "name is spelled right," to quote P. T. Barnum who "didn't care what they said." Try to develop an approach that is unique, more than just announcing staff changes or physical moves.

Radio and TV Talk Shows

If the nature of your practice is such that you want to take the time, talk shows, especially locally produced ones, are always looking for unique presentations and personalities. If you have something special to say or a new approach to an old problem or have identified a new problem that will affect a good percentage of the population, contact the talk show host. Writing is not as effective as telephoning because your projection of your personality is as important as what you have to say, and the host wants to judge that. Before you call, find out as much as possible about the audience of the talk show. Its advertising salesperson knows.

If you aren't a public speaker by nature, consider joining Toastmasters. Don't try to speak unless you are fairly comfortable. But with proper preparation and presentation, you can establish creditability and perceived expertise quicker through speaking engagements than almost any other method. As with the press releases and the talk show, develop a unique approach. Understand in detail who will be in the audience. Don't speak to the JayCees about estate planning or geriatrics. They may be interested, but those subjects do not directly involve them. There are many opportunities to speak. Contact your chamber of commerce for a list of organizations in your office community. Contact the organizations that are likely to have members who will benefit directly from your services. Organizations are constantly looking for programs, so opportunities are as numerous as you want, particularly if you are well received by your first audience; most people who belong to an organization belong to more than one.

Newsletters

Within the past two to three years I've seen some excellent newsletters published by nearly all kinds of professional practices, from health care, legal, construction, business and investment consultants, and on and on. But *do not* commence until you (1) have material for at least three issues ahead and (2) are financially committed to produce four to six issues in the next 12 months and can wait for up to two years for positive feedback. But given those conditions and an attractive newsletter that is well-written and aimed at your target audience with general information that doesn't directly advertise your practice, you will establish a high level of creditability and a position of leadership within your profession. Decide in advance what you want to accomplish with the newsletter, and build, or buy, your mailing list with the objective in mind. Consider carefully whether you want to send copies to your competition. There is much to be said both ways, according to your position and strategy. Think carefully about the possible impact of both alternatives.

Using a professional public relations firm to produce the newsletter has something to recommend it; it will be committed to the newsletter sticking to the preplanned schedule, and the probability of the quality remaining good is improved. The agency can probably also help with developing the mailing list as well as designing the format.

Brochures

These can take several forms. They are a necessary evil and may not be read closely by prospects, but take great care in preparing them for quite often they can do more harm if designed or executed poorly than any good from an excellent piece. A brief folder describing your services and qualifications aimed at your target audience, much as your other advertising, quite often suffices. A beautiful full-color brochure with lots of charts and graphs may be appropriate for your situation. Work with an advertising or graphic arts specialist to be sure that it conveys your image as you wish.

Another technique used successfully by many professionals is to have a brochure prepared that includes a short essay, either by itself or as part of a series, addressing an area that is of frequent concern to prospects and clients. The subject may be something that you take care of in your practice or could even be something closely related to but separate from your work. A cardiovascular physician may have a brochure on the effects of obesity or heavy drinking. A radiologist or possibly even a urologist could use the same brochure. But the subject does not matter, so long as it relates even indirectly to your practice. Attorneys could have one on estate planning or wills; other health care professionals may address care and maintenance of prosthetic and aid appliances. Above all, make sure that your professional name, logo, type style, ink, and paper colors are followed.

Conferences (*Professional and Trade Meetings*)

As a marketing tool, conferences are expensive and marginally productive. Go for fun and education, but don't expect to find many serious candidates for clientele.

Teaching

An excellent method to establish creditability, teaching is particularly helpful if you are starting your practice or have recently started on your own or with new associates after having been in another situation for several years. Teaching is also good for you as a device to review your own education. The low pay is offset by the other benefits, at least for a short time.

Referrals

Ask your clients and professionals in related fields for referrals. When you do receive a referral from them, reward them tangibly as a way of thanking them for their help. The size of the reward is not so important as the remembrance. If you choose to give a small gift, try to provide one with at least your name or ideally, your logo inscribed. The reward keeps your name in front of the referral source and may lead to other referrals. You'll have a problem providing a variety of gifts for frequent referrals.

Press Kits

These are a device that you should be familiar with but probably won't need. They in essence are a portfolio containing a resume, introductory press release, list of references, photos, brochures, etc., all to be used in the appropriate manner by the publicity person when you make public appearances. Although necessary when appropriate, they are expensive and presumptuous for normal use. Have one prepared if you are to present a seminar, workshop, or major address that is likely to be covered by several representatives of the media, even if only your trade press. Your public relations professional can advise you when they are appropriate and how to prepare yours.

Seminars

Seminars are probably one of the most successful devices that can be used by virtually any professional. Advertising and promotion of the seminar must be carefully designed to target the group that you wish to reach for further client development. Stay with the subject area that you are most familiar with and is most likely to appeal to your target audience. Make sure that people get benefits from attending the seminar.

Like teaching, seminars and workshops further enhance creditability but they serve one other important function: your prospective clients attend to seek specific information on your subject. If you do a good job of communicating with the audience, you will get excellent leads for potential clients. You'll need to follow up, of course. In addition seminars can be a source of additional cash income (don't ever do one free) and can be an avenue to expand your client base by approaching either different geographic areas or additional target groups.

Books, Magazines, and Trade Journal Articles

Again, these are all excellent devices to establish name recognition and professional creditability. If you don't think that you can write well enough, consider finding a ghost writer. Then all you need to do is prepare the outline in some detail, have an interview with the writer, then spend your efforts on editing and revising to convey your message. Naturally you must develop something unique to say; but if you are a professional, that shouldn't be too difficult. It is not so much what you say as how it is said or how it is presented to appeal to a specific target audience. Before you make some difficult commitments to editors, determine how long it will take you to produce the finished work in addition to taking care of your existing practice. Spend some time getting prepared before approaching the editors.

Telephone Campaigns

Despite the relaxation on the former taboos of advertising for professionals, actually running a telephone campaign, even if done professionally, to seek new clients, never seems to work. But using the telephone to follow up a letter campaign targeted at specific prospective clients works extremely well.

Letters

The letters fall into three classes: courtesy, solicitation, and proposal letters. None is more important than the other, although the anticipated action of the recipient is different. The courtesy letter would include sending a thank-you note for a conversation, invitation, or service well performed. Send complimentary letters to suppliers or other professionals when they do a good job; don't wait for the exceptional performance. By encouraging the good performance, maybe you will be the recipient of exceptional service sooner. So few people take the time to acknowledge a good job that you will be remembered for having done so. Also send appropriate congratulatory notes for achievements, promotions, elections, etc., for members of your target audience, even if you don't know the person, but particularly if you do.

The sales solicitation letter is just that but shouldn't look like that. Write a short, two- or three-paragraph, one-page letter asking them to think about one area of their life with which you can help professionally. Don't say that you are seeking new clients and don't ask them to call you. Voluntary responses, which are rare, are nonetheless extremely valuable as an indication of interest. After the prospective client has had the letter for two or three days, follow up by telephone to "see if we can chat a bit and kick around an idea or two" but have firmly in mind what you can do to help.

The proposal can take a variety of forms. There are books about this in almost any public library, and the subject is presented frequently in business magazines. But no matter how you choose to put together the information, be sure to include in all cases why you are qualified to serve the client, what you intend to do (but not how), what measurable, demonstrable benefit will accrue to the client only if your services are used, what the estimate of the costs is and what might cause the costs to change from the estimate, and in what time frame you anticipate to start and conclude your work. Anything else that you discussed or you know to be of frequent concern of clients should be included. Additional information that describes your expectations of the client and your perception of the client's expectations of you is featured.

Personal Contacts

In the final analysis it is your personal contact with the prospective clients that convinces them to use your services. Let's examine the selling process. It's no different for professional services than it is for any other product or service.

1. *Prospects for leads.* Define your target audience, approach them looking for openings that your services can fill. These leads may come as a result of your more aggressive advertising activities or as a result of referrals, but what you do next is the same in any case.

2. *Qualify the prospect.* You need to determine if in fact the prospect can benefit from your services. But you must also determine if the prospect can pay for your services. You may want to ask around informally, run a credit check, or make your own observations of the situation. If the prospect is leaving another professional who offers a service similar to yours, don't let your ego cloud your judgment. What caused the switching? Has the prospect left a large unpaid balance but in no other way expressed dissatisfac-

tion with your competitor? Learn as much as you can according to the financial risk you will assume.

3. *Make your presentation.* Describe what services you offer. Review the benefits for the prospect. Follow the same procedure as if you were sending a written proposal.

4. *Handle the objections.* A prospect may only want additional information and may not really be objecting to your service. By *listening* to the prospect's objections you can learn more about those areas of concern and can address them now, not later when you actually begin work.

5. *Closing the sale.* You must ask for business—a simple "How can I help?" "Would you like me to get you on my schedule?" or "If you have no other questions, when would you like to begin?" There are many books, seminars, and tapes on sales closing techniques, but most professionals can get by with simple methods of asking. If you have trouble in this area, take the time and money to go to a seminar or purchase a tape and take notes. Find techniques with which you feel comfortable and practice them frequently. People want to be sold.

If you don't have a career background in sales, either while working during college or in an earlier stage of your career, you may not adjust well to rejection. Far more prospects will turn you down than you will ever see as clients. For every no, you are just that much closer to another new client. If you have enough self-confidence to be marketing your own professional services, you should survive the rejections.

Personal Appearance

You make only one first impression. How do you look? There is no right and wrong about how to dress. But make sure that it is extremely tasteful and in keeping with the mode of dress of your prospective clients. Construction engineers probably won't get much use from three-piece suits during the business day if they are overseeing a road-building job, and the accountant probably won't impress too many corporate clients by showing up in jeans and boots at a downtown office. But that same accountant wearing that same outfit could do well establishing rapport with a construction or logging outfit, and probably be better received than when wearing a three-piece suit. Dress for your audience and your audience's expectations.

Companion Products and Give-aways

Selling such items as workbooks, outlines, and software can be a source of supplemental income, and the process of selling those items aggressively could also help publicize your practice as well. Giving items away, such as advertising specialty gifts, may work if the items convey your message in a clever manner. Orthopedic surgeons should be careful about the message of miniature crutches, and dentists using miniature false teeth may get a negative reaction. On the other hand accountants and engineers may consider using rulers, triangles, symbols.

Contributions

There is little direct market value in contributions to charity, arts, or athletic organizations. It may be expected in your community, but quite often if you did not contribute, that would have little effect. However, I have read of cases—and because they were featured may mean they're rare—where business and professional people were ostracized for not supporting the local high school or college team or band or the local performing arts festival. Weigh your own situation carefully. Consider whether the donation should be in your own name or the name of your practice. Of course, for many that's one and the same. I believe in financial support to the best of one's ability to local charitable, artistic, or athletic organizations, but I question the marketing necessity. Church donations should be private and done in your personal name if any recognition is to be received.

Clubs and Organizations

These are extremely valuable in terms of developing personal contacts but have slow results in terms of advertising. Local civic service and booster organizations can be beneficial if a significant percentage of your target audience participates. Trade groups are particularly helpful. Generally the real value is as a training ground for organizational leadership and as a positive contribution to the community or trade group. But for all my positive statements about organizations, do not expect any direct payback to your practice for the time spent and do not expect any substantial relationships to develop in less than a year. To put it another way, I'd encourage you to participate if you can serve on committees and become an officer, but be patient about seeing any direct benefits for your practice. Don't join and not participate. Understand the risks of becoming involved in political or cause organizations. Keep your target audience in mind.

Pricing

Pricing is as much a component of your marketing effort as it is with any other service or product. Whether you charge by the project or by time, determine the range of rates that your competitors charge. Know specifically which competitors charge what, and measure yourself against them. Are they more experienced, more established, or both? Do they have a specialized expertise that allows them to charge more than the general market? Also compare your rates as best you can with professionals in related fields. Make sure that your price reflects your position in relationship to the others. Being the lowest price will probably mean that you will have the least work, but being the highest price won't work if you are not established.

Whatever price level or strategy you choose, stick to it for at least six months. You may have different levels or a multi-tier pricing structure for different situations, charging both by project, by the hour, and by the day to fit the individual client and project situation. Health care professionals need to look carefully at prevailing rates if they plan to be involved with considerable insurance billings from clients who cannot afford much additional expense. How close your rates are to insurance schedules reflects how much of your billings are not directly supplemented by the client. In all cases your pricing strategy is a part of your "position" strategy.

Time Management

Among the most important keys to success is time management. I don't mean to stay out of the coffee shops or away from the golf club, but just make sure that it's the most important thing to be doing at that point in time.

Time budgeting is a concept that seems to escape so many people, not just professionals. But with professionals, your time is valuable to yourself or to your clients. Budget accordingly.

Assign a portion of your time to various portions of your personal and professional life. With your professional time break that down further into time allotted for marketing your services, billable work, nonbillable follow-up work with previous clients, reading and research on the latest methods in your field, etc. (see Figure 9–1). Spend all the time necessary, but it shouldn't be

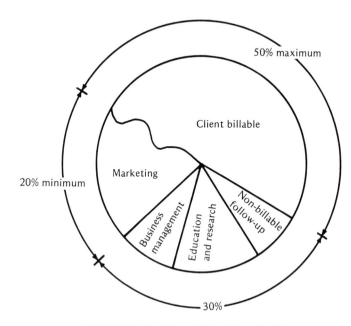

FIGURE 9–1. Time Allocation Limits

more than a small percentage of time to run the business aspects of the practice. Try to keep the clients' billable work time balanced. If you work too much, you are shortchanging your clients and that shows up in time. You might have substantial cash flow at the moment; but by not keeping up, you are not doing the clients the job for which they are paying. They expect you to be current with information and the best in your field available. If you get so greedy that the other areas of the practice slip, your cash flow will start slipping, too.

Use and live by a planning calendar. Plan your professional and personal activities. Don't overload certain portions of your calendar, either on a daily basis or a monthly basis. Many professionals fall into this trap, get very busy, then don't realize until too late that suddenly their being busy has nothing to do with client work. It just got to be such a habit that inefficiencies crept in. Eventually, and usually in not too long a period of time, cash flow plummeted; but the reputation for responsiveness and concern for clients was so damaged that it would be easier starting from scratch. Normally that isn't an option, so working out of the hole takes much time, but mostly considerable mental discipline.

In everything you do, keep your target audience in mind. How many of them will you reach with any tactic or combination of tactics? How does the tactic fit with your overall marketing strategy?

In developing your marketing, clearly define your objective. Commit it to paper. Leave it for a few days. Review. If it still makes sense, use the objective as the basis for your plan of action. Marketing and planning are nearly synonymous.

Study the marketplace. How large is the audience? Determine in specific quantitative terms the total potential number of clients. Is the audience changing in character or growing in a way that will affect your practice?

What are the professionals in your field doing? Devise your course of action to be a little different, not part of the crowd.

Inventory the marketplace in terms of competition, as well as prospective clients. Study all the competition to see how they are responding to the needs of the marketplace.

Develop a unique position. Find a niche or specialty or client group that doesn't receive adequate attention. Then assess whether that group could be developed to generate the amount of revenue you want. You may base this figure on supplying all your needs or as a supplementary area in which to expand.

Concentrate all your thoughts, efforts, and resources on the target audience. Do everything you can to reach the audience with your unique message. Carefully match the audience with the message. When you decide on either the professional specialty or area to concentrate, also develop the best methods you can use to tell the target audience of your proficiency in that specialty.

As time goes on, the distinction between marketing professional services and other products and services becomes less pronounced. That in turn produces one good and one bad reaction. It is good in the sense that more and more all the marketing tools developed for other goods and services can be applied for professional practices. It is bad because few professionals have given any thought to marketing; those few who have will soon dominate the markets, unless the rest of the professionals become more aggressive and take lessons from the other sectors of private economy.

In the development of your unique message that will distinguish you from all the other estate planners or orthopedic surgeons or financial consultants, get the theme so firmly implanted in your own mind that it becomes second nature. Your decision is of no value if no one else is aware. Concentrate on the unique message that you want to deliver, and carry it one step further. Think carefully before you take on any projects that do not underscore your statement of intention. No matter how tight cash may be at the moment, if you bastardize your own position, you will quickly lose the unique position and will survive on bits and pieces, rather than the type of practice that you had envisioned. You will have abandoned your unique identity with no substitute, so you become part of the crowd.

By the same token concentrate on your target audience. Every action, every deed, every communication should be done for their perception and their benefit. Live and act as if your target audience's appointed representative was one-half step behind you, watching closely but never commenting. The comment comes when your billings go out for services performed.

With your unique position and the target audience firmly in mind, select your clothes, personal grooming, residence, mode of transportation, organizations, stationery, and other printed material to deliver your position to the market. The manner in which you deliver your services is probably more important than the quality of the services themselves. Your office, secretary or secretarial service, receptionist or telephone-answering service, along with your personal appearance, have far more impact on the clients and prospects than anything that you can do. That's all part of the package.

Manage the business end of your practice well so that you can survive to deliver the services to clients. Maintain professional, ethical business relationships with suppliers as well as clients. A disgruntled supplier can do as much or more harm as a disgruntled client.

If you do nothing else, develop all your resources to focus on your objectives. Always do what you say in all ways. Don't make rash promises or statements that you can't support with performance. Few professionals actually do what they say they will, so that trick alone will help you survive quite handsomely.

10

Evaluation and Measurement

Marketing is the process of planning for and delivering what is needed. The earlier chapters are devoted to the planning and execution of the marketing program. That process includes the development and delivery of the advertising and sales messages, price strategy, and distribution system selection.

But delivering what the market needs requires you to be in the market. You can't be in the market if you go broke. Why then do so few managers of small businesses pay so little attention to the financial end of their business? For that matter few make much effort to learn about any field other than the one in which they are the strongest. Production people study production techniques. Personnel experts study labor relations and productivity. Technicians study the latest technological developments and people with sales and advertising background study marketing. To survive in business requires a knowledge and application in all phases of management.

This chapter takes a brief look at some evaluation and measurement techniques to apply to your marketing. At the same time, you may find some of the techniques applicable to other facets of your business. Testing, measuring, and evaluating can become almost a way of life.

At one point we talked about the relationship of art to business. The artist studies certain techniques and practices until proficiency is attained. But no matter how intuitive the process becomes to an artist, success is based on measuring and evaluating various elements making up the work.

In business, measuring and evaluating culminate in determining profit and loss. All efforts are designed to generate a profit; if everything works well, a profit is produced. Money is the medium used to keep score. You need to keep score as many different ways as possible to make sure that the final score is a profit.

In basketball we keep track of rebounds, turnovers, personal fouls, free-throw shooting, and on and on. But the purpose and end result isn't who won the rebound battle. The point is the final score. The other statistics are only quantitative measurements to understand relative strengths and weaknesses to determine why the score ended as it did. In football we study blocking techniques, pass patterns, and even punting, but those aren't the objectives. The score is what counts.

Financial management is a specialty even more complex than marketing. It involves highly sophisticated techniques for analyzing business situations in quantitative terms. It also includes the operational consideration of

balancing the checkbook and planning cash-flow projections. Financial management also includes developing and maintaining budgets, both operating
and capital. Above all, financial management is a series of systems, as is
marketing.

That single word, *systems,* probably does more to explain why small business managers do not do a good job of either financial management or marketing. Entrepreneurs by nature are not comfortable with systems. By
definition they are unstructured and creative. That's fine, but even if they
don't want to do it themselves, they had better understand marketing and financial management to survive and do what they like to do best.

In this book we can't begin to cover all the information you need to
manage your business finances successfully, but we can at least consider some
of the devices with which you should be familiar in order to evaluate your
marketing.

Goal Setting

Goal setting is the most logical starting point. For every task that you
undertake, for every project that you devise, for every advertising campaign
that you mount, set goals for yourself. The goals are nothing more than stating in quantitative terms exactly what you expect to achieve in a specific time
period. As you practice this device, your goals become both more realistic and
higher. And as those two things occur, you probably will find that your success ratio continues to improve.

By setting the goal you can determine whether in specific terms you attained your objective. Objectives tend to be a little vague and don't require
time frames. How can you tell if you reach your objectives if you don't set any
goals?

By measuring your performance against goals, you can also learn
whether your performance is bad, good, or excellent. If not excellent, then by
measuring you can tell what you need to improve. We talked about this as a
practical matter in Chapter 7. Large companies use the technique heavily. It's
called *test marketing.* If the test doesn't come up to some predetermined level of
results, then you save lots of time and money. The test shows where you've
fallen short, and you can revise your program before ruining your chances in
the primary market.

Use charts, graphs, and calendars. No one, no matter what one's education or inclination is, can relate as well to raw data as to graphics. Studying
sales reports, cash-flow projections, expenses, or any other measurement that
you may use in the business does not bring the level of understanding as
quickly as projecting those same pieces of information in graphic form. Many
firms lose sight of this fact, or they think that the graphs need to be works of
art. Both tendencies are wrong. Simple, easy-to-read graphs such as the one

shown Figure 10–1, done with a single color, are just as effective as the most elaborate six-color computer graphics. The more elaborate are more aesthetically pleasing but probably don't do any better job depicting the trends.

You can't pay your bills or meet your payroll with trends, but for management purposes and for planning strategic changes, trends are important. Even profits are a trend. The trend is to take in more money than you put out. Virtually everything in a business can be measured graphically, which shows trends, which are statements of relativity.

Display the charts and graphs so that all your employees can see the results of their efforts, good or bad. Post the production trends, sales trends, expense trends, or any set of information that helps people understand their role in the scheme of things in your business.

Probably the simplest and cheapest device is a large wall planning calendar posted where all relevant employees can see it. On the calendar make daily notations of significant events. Mark your advertising schedule. Show vacations, holidays, and business- or pleasure-related absences by key employees. Use the same calendar to mark when various projects will be in certain identifiable stages, including scheduled completion. Get your employees involved in the total process, and they will find it easier to be committed.

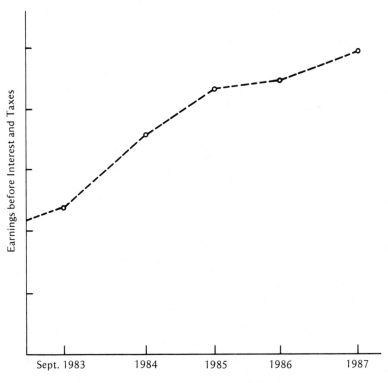

FIGURE 10–1. Five-Year Financial Goal/Actual

Cost Control

Cost control is another area that many small business managers do not seem to understand fully. Use a simple recap sheet, like the one shown in Figure 10–2. Most small business managers think that controlling costs is simply and arbitrarily to reduce spending. That certainly is cost control, but usually profits are cut as well. When expenses for advertising, including packaging and point-of-sale displays, are cut, an almost immediate effect is that sales decrease or decrease further. If your marketing expenditures are reasonable, intelligently conceived, and professionally executed, they are the last expenditures that should be reduced.

Another facet of cost control is to identify all costs when penciling out the profit feasibility of a project. Too often, significant but perhaps hidden costs are overlooked when doing the preliminary planning. Examples that come to mind instantly are the costs represented by the impact of the decision on other phases of the business.

	Month 1	Month 2	Month 3
Staff salary, taxes, benefits			
Rent			
Marketing/advertising			
Office supplies			
Telephone			
Utilities			
Insurance			
Taxes, including self-employment			
Maintenance			
Legal, accounting			
Equipment			
Travel, entertainment			
Transportation			
Improvements			
Education			
Personal draw			

FIGURE 10–2. Monthly Expense Recap

Should you decide to add a product to your line, will that detract from your other products? Will the new product take time, energy, and space from the original to such an extent that the loss will not be offset by business with the new product?

Hidden costs that usually aren't calculated until too late include such things as supervision time for the new project. Small business management almost invariably overlooks the additional management commitment of time to supervise adequately the new project, whether a new department, new product, or branch operation. There comes a point, and every individual eventually reaches that point, where you can no longer supervise and develop the people necessary to operate a number of separate operations, products, or whatever. When that point is exceeded, it is usually not recognized in time. Even with good accounting systems, the reduced profits or even losses don't show up until the trend is difficult to reverse. Personnel experts tell us that about six employees are the most that any supervisor can adequately and personally supervise.

Small business management must of necessity wear many hats. In fact, that's part of the appeal for many of us. That doesn't mean that we're good in all areas, nor are we infallible. Yet the tendency is to do too much ourselves without delegating and training people, not looking forward to slowing down, or conversely developing additional management help to allow for expansion. Management has the prime responsibility for developing personnel and improving management itself with more involvement by the people currently on staff.

In the area of costs this belief in our ability to absorb more and more responsibilities usually means that one area of the business that has been a strength will get inadequate attention while the new area is being developed. The great risk is that what started the success will be the first area to suffer when expanding. When considering new projects, services, branches, or even products, carefully measure how much management time is required to make the new area profitable, assign an hourly cost figure, and add that to the other costs, which may be more easily identifiable.

The other side of the management time cost is not only what the time spent on the new project will cost but also the monetary impact of paying less attention to the primary area of business. By adding a new service your management time in the new area may require two hours a day. At $30 an hour, the rate for skilled labor in most areas, that's $60 per day or $300 a week. If the project grows and is profitable, that investment may be excellent. But you are also losing the same $30 per hour from your primary business area, so the potential cost may be $60 per hour.

One time a client asked whether the firm should start a new service that on the surface looked like a good fit. In all respects it would complement the existing services, targeting the same customers and potentially generating a premium revenue rate. But the cost of lost time supervising the base business had not been considered. The work flow would in all likelihood be inter-

rupted. That potentially was more costly than the actual cash expense required to get the new service into operation.

Often a customer or even customers approach you with an idea for a service or a product that they say they would buy from you if you offered it. But even if all the people who said that they would buy, do buy—which they won't—what is the impact on your base business? Should all those "loyal" customers quit doing business with you altogether if you didn't offer the new product, would that dollar impact be worse than losing money in the process of initiating a new offering? Take a conservative approach when studying market potential.

New Products

When you are studying the possibilities of offering a product or service and have assigned a monetary figure to the offering, determine your profit point. How many units do you need to sell in order to recover all your costs, both direct and indirect overhead, the fixed and variable costs attributable to the offering? To be profitable, you need to recover your costs well before you sell all the product that you think the market will support.

If after careful consideration you feel that the new offering will be profitable in time, but some development will be necessary, or that the new offering will support your existing business, make sure that the existing profits are adequate. If you lose money on each transaction, you can't make it up in volume. The services that you offer and don't make money on must be paid for by the services or products that do make a profit. So what may seem like a large profit from the sale of Item B must carry its own weight and Item A. If Item A loses $10 for every unit sold, and Item B makes a $10 profit, you still aren't making money. Item B must make enough to return a profit on all the expense invested in it and Item A, or you won't be able to stay in business long.

A simple way to look at profit potential is to compare the new offering's cash requirement and payoff with other investments of the same amount of money for the same length of time, whether it be a $100,000 six-month commitment or a few thousand for two years. What would that same money do in the same length of time invested prudently in passbook savings accounts or stocks, bonds, treasury bills, or money market funds? Those investments require none of your labor, and most are low risk.

After comparing the relative return of your comparable investments, also add in how much the risk itself is worth. If it looks like a sure thing, you may not want to add much for the risk; but if you are going into uncharted territory, you must pay yourself something for the risk in addition to the cost of money and the rest of the expenses.

Your resources, whether time, money, or physical facilities, must be invested in such a way as to get a satisfactory return. Take the investment comparison one step further and compare additional investments for your

211

resources, adding in the relative risk factors. You should develop at least two possible alternative resource utilizations in addition to the "safe investment" on the open market. The "safe investment," of course, may not provide the personal satisfaction of developing your idea, and somehow you need to add that factor to the equation.

Discounted Dollars

When doing your own financial analysis of investment opportunities, keep the concept of discounted dollars in mind. That concept is nothing more than some devices to factor in the money over a period of time. The labels for these devices are *future value, present value,* and *annuity.* These concepts can measure money over the life of an investment, not just the rate of return. Usually your decision is made on whether a new product investment will pay a higher yield than the money market. But that may not address the time factor.

Future value expresses the value of a single payment received in the future of a monetary unit that was invested at a given rate for a certain length of time. One dollar to be invested for five years at the nominal rate of 10 percent per annum will be worth $1.6105. The simple formula to determine the future value can be used with a pocket calculator:

$$FV = P\,(1+i)N$$

where FV is future value, i is interest rate, and N is time in years.

Present value, as the name implies, measures the current value of a monetary unit invested at a given rate of return but collected totally at a point in the future. One dollar invested at the rate of 10 percent interest but not collected for five years is worth only $0.621 today. Using your pocket calculator, apply the following formula to your investment:

$$PV = \frac{FV}{(1+r)\,N}$$

where PV is present value, r is rate or interest rate, and N is time in years.

Annuity is nothing more than an expression of periodic payments, adding in a rate of return and arriving at the actual cash required to receive the benefit later. It can be arrived at by determining the periodic payment at a flat rate, adding in the interest to arrive at a preset amount at some point in the future. Or it can calculate the amount of money invested at a given rate to produce a flat income on a periodic basis.

Most of the time when we think of the term *annuity,* we think of an insurance term. But in the general sense dealing with financial management, the annuity represents the periodic payment over a period of time of the money invested at a preset rate of interest. Or the annuity can mean how much periodic principal to pay in, assuming a predetermined interest rate, to accumulate a given amount of money within the time frame.

All three concepts are often overlooked when working on financial analysis problems, and yet they are relatively simple devices used to measure the value of money and the amount that you need to accumulate to arrive at a predetermined point. Most books on financial analysis include tables for future value, present value, and annuities.

Such tools of financial analysis, together with an inexpensive computer with some variety of electronic spread sheet software, can greatly reduce the probability of assuming risks with inadequate return on investment. However, all the tools in the world do not alter the fact that the data input is still controlled by people, and your intuitive judgment as to market potential is still the key piece of data.

My only point in bringing up this subject is to help you consider all the costs and the rates of return that can be calculated to determine whether the new offering will truly be profitable. A book on marketing for small business is not the place to learn about financial analysis, even if you feel that you need additional strength in that area. Nor have many financial professionals, other than some financial consultants, worked enough with these concepts to be of much assistance. In the real world of daily business operations, financial institutions and accountants are more concerned with reporting the past than in analyzing the future. You must analyze your own future or hire someone to do it.

The Budget

One other concept that seems to be an anathema to many small business managers is the budget. The budget does not need to be a frightening document, chiseled in stone, allowing little latitude for unforeseen opportunities. Nor does it need to be highly complex and detailed. But a budget can be effective, even if it puts into writing only the anticipated expenses and revenues in broad categories. The purpose is to be a plan to follow to profit.

With the use of a budget you can systematize your expenses and revenues so that variances can be spotted quickly. The variances can be guideposts to improve profits and spot trends that may cause you to change tactics or even reconsider your overall strategy. A realistic budget also becomes another valuable tool in identifying costs as well.

A budget doesn't put money in the bank. We hear so much from public agencies, and even big business, about how this or that item "isn't in the budget" as if that were the determining factor by itself. It may be for public and private institutions that know exactly and precisely how much and when they will receive income. But in small business our revenue is not that assured. Our budget truly becomes a plan and not a document that describes in fact how much money is available for a certain project.

You are responsible for the resources at your disposal. The purpose of utilizing the resources properly is to be able to keep them in production. To keep them in production requires payment for their use, a profit. Without the resources we can do nothing in small business, the professions, or manufacturing. The whole point of the exercise is to make a profit.

In small business the fun is in getting immediate feedback as to whether we are successful in delivering what the market needs at a profit. Determining our success comes down to the process of reporting our business transactions and whether the results are profitable. The reporting function isn't the end in itself but is necessary to know how we are doing.

Unlike big business we can easily and quickly put the results of our efforts into a form that helps us improve and be responsive to the market quickly. We do not require large staffs of numbers crunchers to keep track of where we are going, and other staffs to tell us the implications of those numbers.

We can draw simple charts and graphs such as the one shown in Figure 10–3 so that we know at a glance how we are doing in every aspect of our business. If we know that we are profitable in every aspect, then the sum of the parts is a whole that is profitable.

Get control of your business. Monitor your progress, including revenue and expenses. But also watch carefully what is happening to your share of the market segment. If sales are up substantially, but your share is down, sales will turn down for you unless the trend is corrected.

By watching and monitoring your progress, measuring your results for as many aspects of each project as possible, and putting that information into a

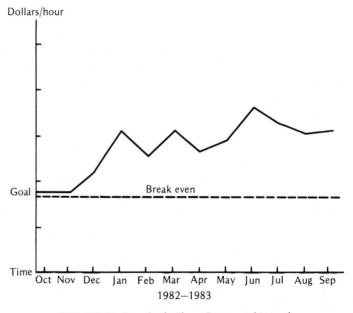

FIGURE 10-3.   Cash Flow Forecast/Actual

chart or graphic format, the decision-making process will be facilitated greatly. And by displaying the information in a form that more people can understand, you will be able to get more help in the analysis stages. The decision is yours. You don't need to consider the data alone. The synergistic effect of multiple resources being applied creatively to a challenge can produce phenomenal results. Get your employees involved and after the decision is made, explain why you chose the direction.

With these simple devices you should be able to relate your business not only to your employees but also the outside professionals on whom you rely to keep you profitable. The score card is not the objective of the game. To know whether you have won or lost, you need to understand what goes into the scoring process, whether football, basketball, or business.

The objective is to deliver what the market needs. And to fill those needs, you need resources to determine what the needs are and then the ability to fill them. The resources must be paid for in the process, whether physical or human resources. To pay for the resources requires profit. You must win, but that doesn't mean that someone else loses. There is no loser if you deliver what the market needs and will pay for, leaving you with a profit.

Summary

T hroughout the book we have talked about the special cases of small business, the small manufacturer, and professional firms and how to develop the marketing program. The small businessperson, manufacturer, or professional must understand and use all areas of management expertise to survive and make a profit. The fun and challenge of small business are the fact that you can practice such a wide variety of business skills. It's exciting to be able to read an article or book, attend a seminar or listen to a training tape on marketing, sales, advertising, distribution, and pricing strategy, and put the information to work in your business the same day. Those are just the elements of marketing. Even more fun is to add in skills from a knowledge of production, personnel management, business law, financial analysis, cash-flow management, credit and collections, in addition to the technical product expertise that probably started you in the first place.

Of all the disciplines required to manage a business successfully, marketing is the most pivotal. It is where all the preparation, production, and other management skills are put to the final test. If you can produce the product or deliver the service efficiently and profitably, and have excellent cost control, good relations with the financial institutions, and happy employees—all are the result of marketing efforts. No one or two areas of business can carry the others.

Finance, administration, production, and personnel, together with marketing, are required to work together for any business to succeed. Businesses are a reflection of the people who work there. Some have decided strengths in finance and administration, others in production and personnel, while some use their strengths in marketing areas to do well. Like people, businesses must build on their strengths but can't ignore their weaknesses and must constantly improve.

Summary   If your basketball team has Abdul-Jabbar, you still won't win automatically. You must also have two excellent forwards and two excellent guards. One star or strength by itself does not win ball games. Help is needed on both offense (production and marketing) and defense (finance and administration). We all must know and use our strengths, but they must be developed and refined along with filling in the gaps in our weaknesses.

Whether you are reading this book because you know little about any phase of marketing or because you know only one or two areas of marketing (such as sales or advertising), our purpose is to introduce you to all phases so that you can use the synergistic effect of all elements working together to your advantage.

Planning

The first concept to be introduced was planning, and planning is the thread that runs through the entire book. Planning is the process of starting by defining the objective, analyzing the situation, developing the strategy, setting the implementation schedule, and providing for periodic measurements and evaluation.

Marketing planning is no different. There is such a close relationship between the concept of marketing planning and strategic planning that the two ideas are quite often used interchangeably. The word *strategic* seems to imply longer-term analysis and development, whereas marketing seems to suggest the function of delivering what the market needs. But there are differences of nuances, and even though I have done considerable reading on the subject, my thinking has only been confirmed, rather than shaken.

Perhaps the reason for the two terms not being accepted as nearly synonymous is popular usage of both. Because *strategic* involves long-term conceptualizations, people tend to think that strategic planning can deal with only long-term developments. Most people in small business find that an impractical concept, although nice in theory. The thinking is that small business is subject to frequent and drastic change. People feel that this volatile economic environment essentially precludes long-term planning.

Nothing could be further from the truth. Planning involves nothing more than starting with the objective and developing the ability to attain the objective. From my observations of clients and acquaintances over 20 years, the problem seems to be that most small business people don't think in terms of objectives. They may realize the concept of management by objectives (MBO) exists, but that's the end of their concern with objectives. MBO is dismissed as a tool for big business.

Another reason for marketing planning not being uniformly accepted as synonymous with strategic planning is the popular use of the term *marketing planning*. Many people feel that marketing planning is the process of coordinating the advertising. Some even take the "liberal" interpretation and include the use of public relations or even the sales program in the coordination proc-

218

ess and call that whole package *marketing planning*. Occasionally people acknowledge all elements of marketing and call marketing planning the coordination of pricing and distribution along with sales and advertising.

All those interpretations are not wrong, but neither are they right. They don't include enough. Marketing planning is more than using the traditional elements of marketing to deliver the product to the marketplace. Marketing planning is also the process of determining what the need is in the first place and then analyzing the situation to see if the need can be filled profitably. It is this broader view of marketing planning that is used throughout this book, even in the sections dealing with each of the individual elements of the marketing program and the sections devoted to the special cases of small manufacturers and professional firms. The popular view of marketing planning is the implementation process alone.

Certain techniques and methodologies do not require exotic training or an MBA from one of the top five business schools. The tools can be used by anybody with enough intelligence to walk and chew gum at the same time. The basic skill required to use the tools effectively is *common sense*. Mix that with some rational thought and analysis, and you can succeed with these simple devices.

Even after going through the basic exercise in planning and coming to grips with the simple methodologies used to arrive at logical decisions, it is still necessary to understand the basic concepts used by professionals in marketing. These concepts need to be understood so that you can begin to develop a plan of action that will produce results. If you don't understand the concept of a pass-oriented offense in football, including the roles of the blockers, receivers, and decoys, it does little good to have a strong, accurate arm. You need to understand what is happening down field. If your resource is seven feet tall and mobile but prone to fouling, it's easier to understand alternative offensive patterns when substituting if the plays are labeled. A "wing screen right" is easier to understand than drawing diagrams. Understanding some of the basic concepts of marketing terminology speeds the process of your development.

Books are written about each concept, just as they are about passing the football. Our purpose, however, is to discuss how each of the concepts can work in a variety of situations. In other words, the intent is to serve as an overview or primer on marketing concepts due to the time constraints of small business managers.

Position

Probably the single most important concept on which you build your entire marketing program is the concept of position. To get to that stage, you must first divide the market that you are surveying into as many logical component parts as possible. That process may include division by geographic areas, customer age groups, probable use of the product, and on and on. None of this is as complicated as it may first appear. Marketing is the logical application of common sense. This process of division is called *segmenting*. It is nothing more than one technique to analyze the market in quantitative terms and leads to establishing a position.

Position is the term used to describe the posture or place in the market. When established, it is the point from which you reach out to serve the market. Is your position one of leadership? Or do you deliver the market needs primarily on the basis of price? Are you concentrating on a particular market segment that uses your product for a specific purpose at the exclusion of other possible uses? That describes your position or your targeting strategy.

There are several seemingly logical and easy-to-use techniques to solidify your market position further. They are nothing more than expressions of the message to the market about your intended position. These techniques take several forms, but the essential consideration is to make sure that the various techniques and devices used are all similar. If you send mixed signals with devices simultaneously communicating low price and high quality, you will likely miss both ends of the market, achieving such a low segment penetration rate that you would have been much better to concentrate on one or the other. The lack of coordinated signals will result in both sets not being as effective as possible.

Growth Strategies

The purpose of being in business and to learn about management skills is to expand and grow. Specific processes for the development of our market strategy are designed for growth. Some of these devices can be used by almost any business in any situation, so the matter is more a proper selection than whether growth itself is possible. Serving additional segments of the market that haven't been targeted is one strategy for growth. Filling the needs of the same customers with other products is an alternative. Changing our basic position to take advantage of a larger market is a possibility.

Basic strategy systems and concepts are explored in terms that can be understood by small business. There are cases well-chronicled in the business press about how large marketers have tried various strategies to expand. Mergers and acquisitions, additional products for the same customers, and other strategies have been tried. What we try to do is develop these thoughts in relation to the typical scenario in which business operates in the real world, and consider how to read and interpret the result of our efforts.

Sales Management

Sales force development seems the biggest mystery of all. Like the other areas of marketing, logic should prevail. The catch is trying to understand the perceived data. Much literature is available about the process of selling. The literature includes books, pamphlets, and magazines aimed at helping people achieve higher levels of performance. Systems have been developed to understand the selling process. Little has been developed to help the person responsible for the management and development of the sales force, however.

It is appropriate that so much is written about sales. The point of the marketing process is that the sale is made and is the reason and purpose for all the other steps. Sales is the process of pushing what's needed in exchange for something of value. Because that is the whole point and the pressure point of the operation of a business, it is all the more critical that the person responsible for sales force development have systems to use that simplify and make more effective the management of the sales force.

Sales force development includes recruiting, training, paying, and evaluating the salespeople. *Recruiting* involves projecting your company to potential recruits and selecting those that have the talents you need. In college athletics you don't recruit more linemen than your football team needs or attract 10 top quarterbacks, especially when the offense is geared to the running game. It is the same in basketball—you need five specific positions filled with five sets of talents that work together. In sales, if you sell a complicated product that carries a high price, the salesperson who wants to close many sales won't fill the role that you require.

Compensation is closely interrelated to the job to be done. It goes deeper than just determining how much to pay in order to attract the necessary talent away from other businesses. The method of payment or the calculation of the payment is the real issue. The salesperson who needs frequent feedback wants a pay plan that is more direct-commission oriented. The salesperson who enjoys dealing with complex product application and financing needs rewards for performance but is as much interested in the preliminary stages as the finalization itself. That person needs a subsidy between sales, so a good portion of his or her income is required in salary form. Perks, fringes, and bonuses are ways to augment sales income to reward for certain relatively unusual task performance.

Of all the issues facing salespeople the subject of *motivation* receives the most attention. The focus of the attention seems to center on achievement and emotional pumping. The basis of that line of thought is to convince yourself that you are capable of achieving certain specific things or attain objectives. That is true. However, given the fact that motivation comes from within, it is folly to think that sales managers can motivate salespeople. The label is wrong. The real task is to let the salespeople know what is needed and expected in terms that the salespeople understand. Then they can accept or reject your requirements. Acceptance leads to achievement. Specific, easy-to-use techniques are readily available to help the sales manager guide the salespeople to accomplish what is needed.

221

Advertising

Although advertising is just as highly specialized as sales force development and is probably the most visible of all the elements of a marketing program, information is available quickly and inexpensively to guide the small business into effective advertising.

Quite often small business tries to copy competitive advertising expenditures. Or different sets of competitors vie for attention through one advertising medium when the target audience doesn't even use that medium. By understanding the characteristics of the media, we can decide which to use. And this basic information is free and accurate for your market, whether it be a neighborhood or the state.

It is also necessary to understand the objective of the advertising. This objective may change from time to time in reaction to occurrences in the marketplace. Or the objective may be a statement of position in the advertising. In other words, what do you want to accomplish with advertising in specific terms? These objectives can be classed in three broad categories: to inform, persuade, and remind. Each is appropriate in particular situations but equally ineffective if not done correctly. Further, each of the objectives can be focused on either the direction of what or where. That determination is made in part as a result of the market position of the item being advertised, and in part according to where the advertiser is in the distribution chain. Market penetration has a bearing on all these decisions.

The Small Manufacturer

One of the special cases is that of the small manufacturer. This is classed as special because it represents a relatively small portion of the small business community, but its challenges and opportunities are distinctively unique to those of the more typical product or service firm toward the end of the distribution channel. Small manufacturing is a rapidly growing area and is the focus of a good deal of attention by the press.

In the case of the small manufacturer we use the word *marketing* but the popular interpretation is *strategy*. The reason for that perception is that most small manufacturers have identified a need and developed a product to fill that need. Usually the small manufacturer is expert either in the technical considerations and development of the product or in the production methodology. It is unusual for a small manufacturer to know what is necessary to get the product to market and ultimately into the hands of the customer.

One of the first considerations in developing the marketing strategy for the small manufacturer is to determine resources. Because presumably the need and the product to fill that need are already decided, the resource becomes critical. Among other things it is necessary to inventory the capabilities and capacity for production before the rest of the marketing program can be

developed. Tools to measure the market potential realistically are available.
Measuring product capacity becomes of utmost concern.

Production and market potential must be balanced. Market potential can be determined by ascertaining all the possible users of the product or segmenting the market into groupings and determining the potential within each grouping. Should the market be more than the production facilities can produce, it is necessary to focus on a segment. Trying to fill the need in a market that is larger than production capacity opens the door to competitors. By generating demand and leaving that demand unfilled, someone will see the opportunity that you have created. Your loss is in growth potential, which could be dramatic if the market gets saturated with alternatives.

Professional Practices

Professional practices are another special category. Small professional practices have available an even wider variety of devices than the traditional sales and service firm to let the market know how they can fill needs. And unlike other small businesses, they have opportunities to be paid to advertise—not just paid if the results of the advertising generate business but paid to produce the advertising. In many ways professional firm marketing is the easiest of any type but requires more thought and coordination to maximize effectiveness.

Professional firm marketing involves all the same techniques, planning, situation analyses, and implementation as for the other business situations. But the particular tools and tactics are markedly different. Also the opportunities are far greater in professional fields to the firm that does do a good job of marketing the product. The reason is simple. The public at large is frustrated and upset by the attitudes of unresponsiveness of most professionals.

To succeed in the professions probably means only that what is needed is delivered as promised. In that sense, because the needs are more clearly defined and because the abilities are determined in the planning process, there is less guesswork in marketing for professions than any other area. Professionals fall down badly in marketing because, like other technicians, they are more concerned with the work itself than communicating with the source of revenue. If professionals told their marketplace what they will do and then did it, they would succeed. There are some specific ways to communicate on several levels that will help the professional firm.

Professionals have the opportunity to change their basic marketing strategy more readily than other businesses. Because there are more opportunities to communicate with the marketplace on more levels, those same avenues are also avenues to change. The professional firms can change segments or establish new positions almost at will, but usually so many changes are attempted simultaneously that the market doesn't perceive what the professional wants to communicate and ends up ignoring the messages.

Measurement and Evaluation

Establishment of systems for measurement and evaluation is necessary to be successful in marketing. The primary measurement, of course, is the checkbook balance. But it goes deeper than that. Each part of the business must be measured. All measurements are relative. For any measurement to be meaningful to the management of small business, the objectives must be quantified and put into a specific time frame. For example, to be the leader in sales of widgets, your store must sell 6,000 the first month, growing in progressive increments to 12,000 by year end. If the period being measured starts July 1, then each monthly goal is increased by 1,000. Put that on a graph, such as a vertical bar graph or line graph. Then as each month is completed, mark the actual results in easily readable form adjacent to the goal for the period.

That process of graphically depicting goals with results adjacent also involves the employees in the goal-oriented activity more than any other device that I have seen. All the talking and counseling in the world won't bring attention to results as quickly and easily as graphics. What many firms do, though, is believe that the graphics need to be complicated or multicolored or professionally executed. Those are all nice ideas and may help when making a sales presentation to a customer, but for the internal operation of the business, simple, single-color graphs do just fine.

Setting goals and then measuring the results for all the variables may be impractical. Business is not conducted in a vacuum. In our school science courses we were taught not to draw conclusions until we had established a known result and then to conduct tests isolating different variables for each part of the test. In business there is no practical way to isolate all the factors. In evaluating various components of the marketing program the best that we can do is measure results with different variables in place. Then after we have some comparative results showing what seemed to happen with different elements changed, common sense becomes important. Examine the complete environment for other factors that may explain part of the differing results. In marketing, like art, we can control many of the elements but we can't control as finitely the total results.

A good part of the marketing process is not only planning and delivering but being able to continue to deliver. In other words it is the responsibility of management to make a profit so that the business can continue to deliver what the market needs. Resources are invested in the hopes of returning a profit at an acceptable rate. But what truly is an acceptable rate? How much is the money worth if invested at an established percentage but collected in the future? How much is the money worth if paid in at a given rate, with the principal accumulating and earning interest to be available at a future time? These are just two of the many tools that small business management can use to decide if the return on investment or the employment of resources will be profitable.

224

All these considerations are designed to quantify the known considerations in operating the business. Measuring results of advertising, revenue produced by salespeople, and determining what is an acceptable share of the market segment are still dependent on common sense or intuition.

Management judgment, intuition, common sense, creativity, or any other label falls short of reality. To make the determination requires considerable information. Convenient labels fall short of describing the process because the decision process based on intuition cannot be easily quantifiable. Entrepreneurs make intuitive decisions constantly without carefully examining all the relative data. But that is a risky course.

The purpose of understanding the decision-making factors and trying to quantify as much data as possible before making decisions is not as self-defeating as it might appear. Even though intuitive decisions frequently lead to successful marketing, the intuitive process cannot be practiced with much success by many people. When the firm is led by someone with a gift for correct intuition, business grows, but as more decisions are made more frequently, the chances of error magnify. Errors lead to failure. But by understanding why the decisions work as they do, other people with other gifts can still be effective managers through the practice of logic. Both skills are required to succeed for long.

But graphically measuring the results and understanding the quantification of the decision making process, opportunities expand to involve employees. Employee involvement cannot just be paid lip service but must become a manner of conducting operations. When employees are involved, their level of contribution rises substantially. Multiple resources can then be applied to meeting challenges.

Schedule carefully on an annual planning calendar. Each significant event in the course of the business year should be noted—not only holidays and vacations but scheduled completion of projects and phases of the projects. Cleaning out the storeroom of junk so that more space can be available for high-profit, high-turnover inventory stands a much better chance of happening if the due date is marked on the calendar. Chances of further increasing the success of a business are greater if one individual is responsible for seeing that the room is "dejunked." And the best way for that assignment to work is for the individual to understand fully the profit implication of the task and then to volunteer to see its completion. Those are examples of simple skills that can be practiced weekly in short staff meetings, no matter how small the staff.

Scheduling the coordination of all the elements of the marketing program, whether for the entire company or any given product or service, produces results that you probably wouldn't have predicted. On one level the employees gain respect if you have your act together. Their respect is translated into pride in their job and their employer, which adds another multiple to your success. On another more pragmatic level, by coordinating all elements of the marketing program the synergistic effect multiplies the results of each component by multiples that you won't believe unless you experience it. Besides, isn't it fun to have everything come out of the oven at one time? It's no fun having a well-done roast with undercooked potatoes, even if the nutritional value is the same.

Many small firms argue that it takes time, which is money, to be coordinated and to have all elements of a marketing program to work together. Nothing could be farther from the truth. If everything works together (interact is the definition of *synergistic*), the results are more sales. More sales should mean more profit, and isn't that more important than some temporary illusions of savings that may be realized by buying only a dish at a time rather than the whole meal? By using the synergistic effect to the fullest in the coordination between and within each element of the marketing program, less resources are required to reach a given objective.

Coordination within the elements includes consistency of all phases of each of the four elements. Pricing for products and services should reflect your market position. Distribution channels should be used in a consistent fashion to deliver the product. The salespeople should reflect the market position, the product, and the customers. Advertising elements should work together so that all media messages are the same. And not only should the strategies within each element be consistent, but they all should be delivering the same message at the same time.

Conclusion

We've gone full circle. The circle is planning. This is one circle that can be started or created with a single line or described in any manner that you choose. No matter how you describe the circle though, there is only one way to change its circumference. Pick a new starting point and at that point describe the circumference that you intend to draw.

The planning process is no different. The starting point is the objective. That holds true whether the planning is to reach an objective for the company as a whole, or the marketing program objective is to be met for any single product.

The concept of starting with a clearly defined objective is troublesome for many managers in small business. Nor is the affliction unique to small business. But without a clearly defined objective, it is impossible to achieve the kind of success of which we are inherently capable.

Once the objective is defined so that we understand where we want to go, the job of figuring out how to get there becomes relatively easy. In marketing, the situational analysis is a data-gathering process, pure and simple. Methodologies that help identify data relevant for our particular situation exist, but the principle is constant. We gather as much relevant information available about the environment in which we are trying to reach our objective.

Probably the single most important consideration in the analysis of our marketing program is the customer. We need to know and understand as much as possible about the customer. We need to know why a customer is our customer. What does the customer want (what is the customer's objective)? Who is the customer? Describe the customer in as many different ways as possible. Describe the customer in demographic, geographic, and socioeconomic terms. In many cases it is necessary to know the customer's special interests, avocations, occupation, personal life styles, and on and on. We can't know too much about the customer, although there eventually is the point where further data gathering is not warranted. The whole point is to fit the customer as best we can into a segment so that we can aim our message at that segment.

By understanding our objective, knowing the customer, we can then proceed to developing our unique market position. That market position and its uniqueness separate us from all the other possible ways that the customer will try to fill needs. The completion of the circle is being able to fill the needs in the marketplace.

Define your objective. Analyze all the resources and hindrances to meet the objective. Set goals; measure progress. Define market needs. Determine how to meet those needs. Inventory resources and capabilities. Develop all elements of the marketing process. Schedule events. Set goals. Measure results. Test, change, and continue to fill needs. That is marketing, no matter on what scale.

Small business offers the chance to watch all these occurrences at once and their interaction. Small business requires management to be involved in all phases. Small business lets you observe the whole process. That is the fun and challenge of small business.

Appendix: Sources of Information on Marketing

Following is a brief discussion of the most common sources of information about marketing available for managers. Each source has its advantages and disadvantages. No one source is best. Your selection is determined largely on the basis of time and money available. However, I can't encourage you enough to use more than one source to find answers to any question.

Multiple-source investigations of your questions are particularly important in small business. Otherwise there is the tendency to select methods to answer your problems that may not be appropriate for you, regardless of how successful they may have been for someone else. Additionally it seems that many sources are advocating a particular point of view and using examples to support that hypothesis.

This book has been written with the intent to present the tools for analyzing your own situation. Developing your own methods is the real purpose and value. When you have decided how you wish to proceed, these additional sources of information should be helpful.

With all these sources the large and important assumption is that the source itself is knowledgeable and experienced to fill gaps in your education or experience.

Seminars

Available primarily in medium and large cities, they are a stimulating source of fresh ideas. But only a relatively few concepts can be presented at any one seminar, whether in part-day or several-day formats. Seminars are a quick way to learn concentrated material on a subject. The usual handouts and workbooks plus material sold at the seminar are valuable. The primary disadvantage is the human tendency not to practice and regularly use the information presented. Costs are relatively high, plus travel and lodging, but low in terms of time effectiveness when compared with taking time away from your other duties to learn on your own. The interaction with other attendees is an important side benefit.

Cassette Tapes

These are particularly valuable if you spend considerable time traveling. Repeated listening is an important benefit available. The tapes are relatively inexpensive, bordering on cheap, but of little value if used only once. The cassettes' value would be enhanced if used in conjunction with a workbook or a note-taking, concentrated listening session. As a practical manner, cassettes are seldom used that way, so repeated listening while traveling becomes the most common and valuable usage. Available information tends to be generalized or of the self-improvement genre but can stimulate thinking, analysis, and evaluation.

Videotapes

Much as with cassettes, their chief value is the repeat-use potential. There are excellent videotapes covering a wide variety of management and marketing subjects, although their purchase price is relatively high. Rentals and loaner libraries are available in some cities, however. Many of the excellent training films originally done in movie version are becoming available on tape. Repeated use is necessary to be an effective investment for small business.

Consultants

Consultants bring an outsider's perspective to your business. Their experience and education can effectively supplement your own. Small business tends not to use consultants as effectively as possible, partially due to the relatively high costs and the few consultants specializing in small and medium business environments. Although the trend is changing rapidly, the reputation of consultants being extremely expensive and working with large public and corporate agencies unfairly prejudices their use. A consultant for a small business is particularly valuable if the objective is to learn, rather than rely on them to be trouble-shooters or fix-its. A consultant can focus on a particular challenge and help you determine how best to meet that challenge. The cost is considerably less than hiring a salaried employee with that expertise, and the consultant can be retained for a short time. The chief disadvantage of consultants for small business is that they may not be familiar with your particular industry, and you may not retain them long enough for them to learn. But for fresh insights, that may also be an advantage.

Although they are an informal source—unless they sponsor training programs—suppliers provide an opportunity to learn what other segments of your industry are doing. The supplier is sincerely interested in your success so that you continue as a customer. Often they do an excellent job of gathering, compiling, and disseminating information that could be helpful to you. The larger supplier firms also have expertise on their staff, which could be of assistance to you.

Peers

They probably are one of the most overused resources available, and the overuse is a result of the chief advantage: availability. Discussing with peers, even highly successful peers, potential ways to meet your particular challenges is of questionable value because their objectives may be significantly different from yours. Their perception of the marketplace and its challenges may be quite different. Even though their methods have worked for them, those same methods may not work for you. Before you rely too much on peer source information, analyze whether their market segment, operating methods, and apparent objectives are fairly similar to yours. Sharing information can be extremely valuable as a means of encouraging and developing creative thinking, but that is a different process from using others' methods to achieve your objectives.

Books

Books are the most effective, least expensive method to find answers to challenges in management and marketing. Books can reflect the latest academic thinking on a subject and report current practices in the marketplace. Using any one book as the sole source can be risky, but relying primarily on one book with additional reading in other sources greatly enhances your thinking and development and the reliability of the information used. However, the chief advantage can also be a disadvantage to the small business manager. Books require considerable time to be effective. If that time is used to step back and look at your own situation, then books can be extremely helpful. Far too often management merely purchases, thumbs though, and puts business books on the shelf without gaining sufficient value. In practice few people spend the time necessary to read books for them to be effective.

Libraries

Not only are libraries often a source of specific books, but they can be a reference source to study market potential, changes in market conditions, geography, and a wide variety of subjects with which you need to be familiar to do effective planning. Many libraries also have copies of specific reference books for media information, trade and industry data, and on and on. Your best friend could be the reference librarian. Ask that person almost any question, and you can be directed to the answer. I am always amazed at how seldom business people go to the library to study business challenges and opportunities, yet they have time for other activities that are not nearly as productive or creative for their business. It may take at least an hour per visit to be effective. The chief disadvantage of the library as a source of information for marketing is that current books are often not available.

Bibliography

These books should be particularly helpful. Reference books are listed for informational purposes only.

General

Appelbaum, Judith, and Nancy Evans. *How to Get Happily Published.* New York: Plume Books, New American Library, 1982.

Chase, Cochrane, and Kenneth L. Barasch. *Marketing Problem Solver.* Radnor, Pa.: Chilton Book Co., 1973.

Cohen, William A., and Marshall E. Reddick. *Successful Marketing for Small Business.* New York: Amacom, 1981.

Helfert, Erich A. *Techniques for Financial Analysis.* Homewood, Ill.: Richard D. Irwin, Inc., 1977.

Heskett, James L. *Marketing.* New York: Macmillan, 1976.

Hopkins, David S. *The Marketing Plan.* New York: The Conference Board, Inc., 1981.

Jolson, Marvin A., and Richard T. Hise. *Quantitative Techniques for Marketing Decisions.* New York: Macmillan, 1973.

Kelley, Robert E. *Consulting.* New York: Chas. Scribner Sons, 1981.

Likert, Rensis. *The Human Organization.* New York: McGraw-Hill, 1967.

Livingstone, James M. *A Management Guide to Market Research.* London: Macmillan, 1977.

Luther, William M. *The Marketing Plan—How to Prepare and Implement.* New York: Amacom, 1982.

McCarthy, E. Jerome. *Basic Marketing.* Homewood, Ill.: Richard D. Irwin, Inc., 1971.

Bibliography   Meyers, Paul J. *Goal Setting* (cassette). Waco, Tex.: Success Motivation Institute, 1980.

Ries, Al, and Jack Trout. *Positioning: The Battle for Your Mind.* New York: McGraw-Hill, 1981.

Shay, Philip W. *How to Get Best Results from Management Consultants.* New York: Association of Consulting Management Engineers, 1967.

Smith, Homer. *A Salesman's Guide to More Effective Selling.* New York: Sales Marketing Management Association, Sales Builders Division, 1977.

Reference Books

Commerce and Industry Directory.

Contacts Influential International Corporation, 20950 Center Ridge Road, Cleveland, Ohio 44116. Local and regional editions done annually for most of North America; lists entities by SIC code, by size with name, addresses, and contact person.

Standard Rate and Data Service. Skokie, Illinois.

Monthly editions covering many classifications of print and broadcast advertising media; the primary source for information about audience size and type along with advertising rates, mission statements.

Advertising

Cook, Harvey, R. *More Profits through Advertising.* New York: Drake Publications, Sterling Publishing Co., 1979.

Cook, Harvey R. *Profitable Advertising Techniques for Small Business.* Fairfield, Calif.: The Entrepreneur Press, 1980.

Dean, Sandra Linville. *How to Advertise: A Handbook for Small Business.* Wilmington, Del.: Enterprise Publishing Inc., 1980.

Engel, Jack. *Advertising: The Process and Practice.* New York: McGraw-Hill, 1980.

Wiegel, Connie McClurg. *How to Advertise and Promote Your Small Business.* New York: Hudson Group Book, John Wiley & Sons, Inc., 1978.

Simon, Julian L. *How to Start and Operate a Mail-Order Business.* New York: McGraw-Hill, 1981.

Index

235